REVOLUTIONARIES

Celebrating
30 Years of Publishing
in India

Advance Praise for *Revolutionaries*

'This landmark work by Sanjeev Sanyal is an important milestone in both revisiting and course-correcting the history of our freedom movement. Well-researched yet accessible, this thrilling book by Sanyal is a must-read for every Indian who wants to know the real truth behind our country's attainment of freedom and the heroes who contributed to this—many times with their own lives.'

—Vikram Sampath, historian, author and fellow at the Royal Historical Society

'There was another stream of our struggle for Independence: the revolutionary movement. This stream has been ignored completely in our official narrative. Sanjeev Sanyal's *Revolutionaries* is a superbly researched account of how our great ancestors sacrificed their all so that we may breathe free.'

—Amish Tripathi, India's highest-selling author and television documentary host

'It is said that until the lions have their historians, tales of the hunt shall always glorify the hunter. Thankfully, India's lions have Sanjeev Sanyal. Painstakingly researched and compellingly told, this book is a valiant effort at reviving the forgotten—and oft-suppressed—narrative of the struggle for India's Independence.'

—Ashwin Sanghi, bestselling author

REVOLUTIONARIES

THE OTHER STORY OF HOW INDIA WON ITS FREEDOM

Sanjeev Sanyal

HarperCollins *Publishers* India

First published in hardback in India by HarperCollins *Publishers* 2023
4th Floor, Tower A, Building No. 10, DLF Cyber City,
DLF Phase II, Gurugram, Haryana – 122002
www.harpercollins.co.in

2 4 6 8 10 9 7 5 3 1

Text copyright © Sanjeev Sanyal 2023

P-ISBN: 978-93-5629-594-0
E-ISBN: 978-93-5629-595-7

The views and opinions expressed in this book are the author's own and the facts are as reported by him and the publishers are not in any way liable for the same.

Sanjeev Sanyal asserts the moral right
to be identified as the author of this work.

All rights reserved. No part of this publication may be reproduced, stored in a retrieval system, or transmitted, in any form or by any means, electronic, mechanical, photocopying, recording or otherwise, without the prior permission of the publishers.

Typeset in 12/16 Dante MT Std at
Manipal Technologies Limited, Manipal

Printed and bound at
Thomson Press (India) Ltd.

This book is produced from independently certified FSC® paper to ensure responsible forest management.

When millions upon millions of voices roar out your name,
And millions upon millions of swords rise up to defend you,
Who says, Mother, that you are weak?

—*Extract from Bankim Chandra Chatterjee's* Vande Mataram,
as translated by the author

CONTENTS

	AUTHOR'S NOTE	ix
1.	THE AGE OF REVOLUTION	1
2.	BHAWANI MANDIR	25
3.	INDIA HOUSE	50
4.	THE GHADAR	74
5.	KALA PAANI	123
6.	THE HINDUSTAN REPUBLICAN ASSOCIATION	160
7.	CHITTAGONG	204
8.	'ONE MORE FIGHT. THE LAST AND THE BEST'	240
	EPILOGUE	291
	NOTES	313
	INDEX	331

AUTHOR'S NOTE

This book discusses many events and characters that I had wondered about since childhood. Somehow, the official narrative of India's freedom struggle never quite seemed to add up. Subhas Bose was much venerated in Kolkata, where I grew up in the 1980s, but there was always some unsaid hesitancy about discussing the events related to his life. I would often stumble upon pieces of history that looked like they were important but were never spoken about. For instance, I first learnt about the Naval Revolt of 1946 in my twenties, when I chanced upon a small memorial in Colaba, Mumbai. It seemed like a major incident, but I had never read about it in history class or seen it discussed in television documentaries. Almost no one in the city seemed to know much about it. Similarly, it came as a complete surprise to me to learn that the much-revered spiritual guru Sri Aurobindo was one of the founding fathers of the revolutionary movement.

In the course of researching my earlier books, I had picked up titbits of information about the revolutionaries that I had then kept aside. Enough pieces accumulated over time for a new picture of the freedom struggle to emerge. So many books have been written about the period and about individual freedom fighters that I had assumed that the history of the freedom struggle was a settled matter. However, another narrative seemed to suggest itself at every turn. At some point, perhaps in 2014, I decided that it was worth researching the matter more systematically. For the next few years, I collected books written by those who had participated in the revolutionary movement or witnessed it first-hand. I visited sites related to them across India and the world. Eventually it became an obsession—I had to write the book.

As readers will guess, some of the characters in this book are related to me. A handful had survived into the 1980s, and I knew them personally. However, I do not claim any special knowledge merely by virtue of this. The history of the revolutionaries only began to take shape in my head after I started to systematically study them. Even the significance of first-hand anecdotes that I had heard long ago fell into place only after I started to research this book. I began to look up old letters and dusty books scattered across the family. Some of my friends began to tell me that their family members, too, had been part of the movement. They, too, shared snippets of information or put me in touch with yet other people. In this way, I was able to steadily add colour to the story. And what a story it is—of unbelievable courage and ingenious plots, but also of treachery and heart-breaking failure. Moreover, it is bound up with the major global events of the twentieth century, including the World Wars, the Russian Revolution and Irish Independence.

AUTHOR'S NOTE

A book such as this is a team effort. I remember walking around London with Vikas Nanda in unusually heavy rain, looking for places related to Udham Singh, Madanlal Dhingra and Vinayak Savarkar, and then singing the full version of *Vande Mataram* in their honour at each location. The many long discussions with Jayanta Sengupta and the research team for the Biplobi Bharat Museum (Kolkata)—Arka, Poulomi, Meenal and Aryama. The research for this book discovered by chance a long-forgotten box of guns used by revolutionaries, including a Mauser C96 pistol, in the archives of the Nehru Memorial Museum and Library, Delhi. These are now displayed at the Biplobi Bharat Museum in Victoria Memorial, Kolkata.

Then there was the wonderful day I spent searching for Anushilan Samiti-related sites in north Kolkata with Yash Nathany and Iftekar Ahsan. I am grateful to my old partner-in-crime Odakkal Johnson who took me to see places related to the Naval Revolt in Mumbai; Partha Das who arranged for a tour of the Alipore Central Jail; Priya Kale who took me around Vadodara; Ashok Pal who accompanied me to see the homes of revolutionaries in Nadia; Asni Kumar, who showed me the various INA-related sites in Manipur; and Sameer Gautam, who took me to see Hedgewar's house in Nagpur. I would also like to thank Chandralekha Mukherjee and Shivendra Shukla, who arranged for a very emotional trip to Kakori station—that, too, on a guard van. Then there is the staff at the Delhi Gymkhana library, who dug out a treasure trove of out-of-print books. A special thanks to my friend Rudra Chatterjee for introducing me to the writings of his granduncle, Jogesh Chatterjee; Ranjit Savarkar and Savitri Sawhney for arranging photographs of their forebears; and Rashida Iqbal for old photographs of the Cellular Jail.

In addition, I would like to thank the entire Sanyal clan for all its active support—my parents, who refreshed my memory on family anecdotes; my cousin Saurabh, who dug up old letters and photographs; another cousin, Rishi, who discovered an interesting tape recording; and, of course, my wife Smita, who accompanied me to sites from Port Blair to Vadodara.

Finally, let me thank my editors at HarperCollins Publishers India—the ever-enthusiastic Udayan Mitra and Swati Chopra; the copy-editor Ujjaini Dasgupta and the designer Saurav Das. As I said, publishing a book is a team sport.

1

THE AGE OF REVOLUTION

THE DAY OF 26 AUGUST 1914 BEGAN AS JUST ANOTHER SULTRY monsoon morning in Calcutta (now Kolkata), the second most important city of the British Empire. The plan of shifting the capital of British India to Delhi had been announced three years earlier, but for all practical purposes, Calcutta still functioned as the capital. The city's inhabitants would have known about the gathering war in Europe. This had stoked the ambitions of a network of young revolutionaries, who saw it as an opportunity to throw off the colonial yoke through armed insurrection. However, they were also aware that their supply of guns was hopelessly inadequate.

A few days earlier, a group of revolutionaries had received information that a large consignment of arms was to be delivered to RB Rodda & Company, a well-known British-owned arms retailer with outlets in Birmingham, London, Calcutta and other large cities. The source of the information was Srish Mitra, a mole who worked in the company and was in charge of clearing consignments through customs.[1]

The young men met late in the evening on 24 August in a small park off Chatawala Gali. Srish told the others that the consignment included fifty Mauser C96 semi-automatic pistols and 46,000 cartridges. These German-made pistols were considered the best and most reliable in their category. It also had a distinctive wooden stock that was detachable and also functioned as its holster. The order had been shipped out just before the war began.

The group discussed various ideas about how to steal the guns, but not everyone agreed that it was a practical idea. Narendra Bhattacharya (later famous as M.N. Roy) left the meeting after warning the others that it was doomed to fail. The ringleaders, Haridas Dutta, Srish Pal, Khagen Das and Anukul Mukherjee, then retired to Srish's house to work out the details. The following day they reached out to some Marwari friends who lived in a working men's hostel, including Prabhu Dayal Himmatsinka and Hanuman Prasad Poddar. The plan was as ingenious as it was simple.

Around 11 a.m. on 26 August, Srish left his office at Rodda & Co. and headed for Customs House with the money and documents needed for the receipt of the arms consignment. After being cleared through customs, the consignment was to be loaded onto six bullock carts, which would carry the goods to the company warehouse. However, the revolutionaries had arranged for a seventh bullock cart, driven by Haridas Dutta disguised as a Hindi-speaking driver. Their friend, Himmatsinka, had helped dress him up in a shabby dhoti and a 'genji' vest, even a brass locket around the neck. He had also cropped his hair short. Srish then ordered the loading of the crates. Most of the consignment was loaded on the six official bullock carts, but the Mausers and their ammunition were loaded on the seventh.

The convoy of bullock carts next made their way through Dalhousie Square (now renamed Benoy Badal Dinesh Bag after a later generation of revolutionaries). Anukul and the others followed on foot at a safe distance. They were armed with revolvers in case of an emergency. One by one, the six carts turned into the lane leading to the warehouse, but the seventh went straight. Srish reported to his superiors with the six official bullock carts. He then calmly went to the railway station and left the city by *Darjeeling Mail* that evening.

Meanwhile, the others unloaded the stolen boxes at an iron stockyard before taking them by a hackney carriage through the monsoon drizzle to the home of Bhujang Bhushan Dhar at 3 Jellapara Lane. Here the Mausers and the ammunition were divided up into smaller steel trunks for easier transportation. The original packaging and papers were destroyed, and the evidence cleaned up. Some of the trunks were immediately distributed to different revolutionary cells while the rest were hidden in warehouses owned by Marwari merchants across the city.

It took Rodda & Co. two days to realize what had happened and alert the police. Many raids were done on the homes of suspected revolutionaries. The Marwari men's hostels were also searched. Eventually a number of Mausers were retrieved, including one box hidden in a warehouse owned by the well-known industrialist Ghanshyam Das Birla. He would always maintain that he knew nothing about it. Several of the conspirators were arrested over the next few years and imprisoned, but Srish, who had escaped by train, disappeared without a trace among the tribes of north Bengal.

Over the next few months, Mausers would find their way into the hands of revolutionaries across Bengal and beyond. Three of them would be used by Bagha Jatin and his companions at the famous gunbattle near Balasore, Odisha. One of them would be kept for personal protection by Rashbehari Bose, the chief planner of the unsuccessful Ghadar uprising. He would give it to his deputy, Sachindra Nath Sanyal, just before he escaped to Japan in 1915.[2]

Rodda & Co. closed down long ago, but its office building still exists. The only reminder of the dramatic events of 1914 is a pair of old cannons incongruously embedded into the doorway. However, enough of the buildings from the period have survived in the area and Srish would have little difficulty finding his way today from his office to Custom House.

CORRECTING THE NARRATIVE

The history of India's freedom movement, in what is now the mainstream narrative, is almost exclusively about non-violent opposition to the British colonial occupation led by the Indian National Congress (INC), and, more specifically, by Mahatma Gandhi. This narrative is not just taught in school textbooks and repeated in official documentaries, but also taken for granted by the rest of the world. However, India's struggle for Independence was a much more complicated process, which included generations of sustained armed resistance. Indeed, the non-violent stream of the freedom movement itself cannot be meaningfully understood without reference to the armed struggle.

Of course, most people are aware that the British colonial conquest between 1757 and 1857 faced military opposition from the nobility and traditional social groups of the time— the Marathas, the Sikhs, the Paikas, the Sanyasis and so on.

This culminated in the Great Revolt of 1857–58. After this was crushed, the defiance of traditional elites and social groups mostly broke down. A few embers occasionally sparked local rebellions, such as those by Birsa Munda in Jharkhand and Tikendrajit Singh in Manipur in the early 1890s, but these were never a serious threat to the colonial administration. A new cycle of armed resistance, however, emerged at the turn of the century.

This new cycle drew inspiration from India's long history of fighting back against foreign invaders. Figures such as Chhatrapati Shivaji, Guru Gobind Singh and Maharana Pratap were often invoked by the revolutionaries. As we shall see, the Revolt of 1857 was a special inspiration for their ultimate strategy of undermining the loyalty of Indian troops employed by the British. However, in addition to their pride in Indian history and civilization, the revolutionaries were also influenced by Western ideas and by contemporary world events—Italian and Irish nationalism, Pan-Asianism, socialism, Marxism and the two World Wars. It is worth noting, in this context, that the revolutionaries were not attempting to take India back to a precolonial past but to establish a modern republic. In this sense, it was an entirely modern movement and distinct from earlier rebellions against the British.

The names of many of the key leaders of this new movement, such as Vinayak Savarkar, Rashbehari Bose, Bagha Jatin, Bhagat Singh and Chandrashekhar Azad, are still widely remembered. The problem is that their story is almost always presented as acts of individual heroism and not as part of a wider movement. Thus, one is left with the impression that their activities neither had any overarching strategy nor any significant impact on the overall struggle for Independence. The reality is that they were part of a large network that sustained armed resistance against the British Empire for half a century. The revolutionaries would not only create a wide network inside India but also establish nodes in Britain, France, Thailand, Germany, Russia, Italy, Persia (now Iran), Ireland, the United States of America, Japan and Singapore. At various points, they would receive official support and recognition from the governments of some of these countries. In other words, this was no small-scale movement of naive individual heroism but one that involved a large number of extraordinary young men and women who were connected in multiple ways to each other and to the evolving events of their times. This is their story. It is a tale of swashbuckling adventure, espionage, incredible bravery, diabolical treachery and completely unpredictable twists of fate.

It should not be surprising that mainstream narratives have tended to ignore the revolutionary movement. Despite their enormous contribution, virtually none of their important leaders would live to see India gain Independence—many of them killed in gunfights, hanged from the gallows or dying in prison. Aurobindo Ghosh and Vinayak Savarkar, the only two surviving senior leaders, had drifted away from the movement decades earlier. The political leaders of post-Independence India, therefore, were almost entirely drawn from the INC, and it was inevitable that they would stress their own place in history.

Interestingly, Sachindra Nath Sanyal had had a premonition in the 1920s that the history of the revolutionary movement would be deliberately sidelined. In the preface of his famous book *Bandi Jeevan* ('A Life in Prison'), he clearly states that the reason for his writing the book was not merely to inspire contemporary revolutionaries but also to leave behind a personal testimony for future generations. 'I am writing this book so that in future a few chapters of Indian history can be correctly written.'[3]

This is not to suggest that books have not been written about the revolutionaries. Far from it—there are libraries of such books. Unfortunately, they tend to be hagiographic biographies of individuals that tend to overplay the role of the chosen hero. Almost none of them try to build a picture of how these individuals were connected and of their wider objectives. This book is an attempt to correct this gap. It also presents the revolutionaries with their human frailties. Most of them were idealistic young men in their twenties; some were in their late teens. They had their flaws, insecurities, doubts and internal rivalries. Hagiographic portrayals are not only inaccurate, but also underplay the courage it takes for ordinary people to do extraordinary things.

Every book of history is written from a perspective. While this book tells the story from the perspective of the revolutionaries, note that it does not try to make the case that the non-violent stream of the freedom struggle was irrelevant. The idea here is to balance the usual one-sided narrative. India achieved its freedom due to the complex interplay of both these movements, and it is not possible to meaningfully separate them. The revolutionaries always enjoyed strong support from a section of the INC, and many revolutionary leaders, from Aurobindo Ghosh to Netaji Subhas Bose, played an active role in the party. Even the thoughts and actions of the Gandhians need to be seen within the context of what the revolutionaries were saying and doing.

All history-writing is based on an underlying theory of cause and effect. It is the philosophical framework that explains why one event leads to another. Premodern writers would often explain the evolution of events in terms of Fate, the movement of planets, and the divine intervention of the gods or of the monotheistic God. Another popular approach was to base history on a particular heroic (or demonic) character, whose thoughts and actions disproportionately impacted the course of events. The Great Man Theory was formalized in the early nineteenth century by writers such as Thomas Carlyle. It played a role in most pre-modern histories and remains common to this day.

By the middle of the nineteenth century, we see the rise of intellectual frameworks that emphasize the importance of grand social and economic forces. In this approach, individual 'great men' do not matter but, rather, the workings of a socio-economic machine inexorably driving events in a particular direction. These frameworks usually suffer from Newtonian determinism. The Marxist interpretation of history is a product of this approach and was very influential for much of the twentieth century. However, the poor record of these approaches in predicting actual events, including the collapse of the USSR, led to the decline of this approach in the twenty-first century.

Those who have read some of my previous writings on history or economics will know that my approach uses the framework of a Complex Adaptive System, where the world is seen as a somewhat chaotic place in which the flow of events depends on the complex and often unpredictable interactions between a host of factors—grand socio-economic forces, geography, the actions of great individuals and of not-so-great individuals, culture, ideology, technology, sheer luck and perhaps the occasional divine intervention. Thus, history does not follow a predetermined path but can go down multiple ones. This does not mean that history is random, as some outcomes are more likely than others. But this is a world of unintended consequences, random shocks and 'butterfly effects'. There is no better way to characterize the twists and turns in the fortunes of India's revolutionary movement.

THE REVOLUTION OF IDEAS

The revolutionary movement did not emerge from a sociocultural vacuum but from a period of great intellectual ferment. The British had militarily pacified the country by 1857–58, and most Indians were forced to accept their political subjugation. However, the second half of the nineteenth century saw Indians respond in multiple ways, from religious revivalism to the absorption of new ideas from the West. The Japanese victory over the Russians in 1905, the Irish War of Independence and the Russian Revolution of 1917 all added to the heady mix. Printing presses, including those in Indian languages, were making books and newspapers common as well as enabling the mass production of subversive literature. The railways were making it easier to create networks within India, even as steamships and the Suez Canal were making it possible for middle-class Indians to routinely travel to Europe, North America and Japan. The revolutionaries were a product of all these influences.

The year 1857 also saw the establishment of three universities in Calcutta, Bombay and Madras (now Kolkata, Mumbai and Chennai, respectively). They were modelled on the University of London to provide Western-style education. The British had hoped that this would create an educated class that would not merely serve as useful clerks to administer their empire, but would, in time, imbibe enough of British tastes and ideas to be permanently loyal. While this project was partly successful in creating such a loyalist class, it also simultaneously exposed Indians to the European Enlightenment, the United States

Declaration of Independence and the French Revolution. Thus, the same middle class that provided the Loyalists also provided the bulk of the freedom fighters of various hues.

It is not often remembered today that the wars that led to Italian unification and independence had a big impact on Indians. The Italian thinker Giuseppe Mazzini and the rebel general Giuseppe Garibaldi made a deep impression on young educated Indians growing up in the last decades of the nineteenth century. The Mazzini–Garibaldi combination played well to the Indian idea of a philosopher and a soldier combining forces to save the country: Vashishtha and Sudasa; Chanakya and Chandragupta Maurya; Vidyaranya and the brothers Harihara–Bukka Raya; and so on. The first generation of revolutionaries, such as Aurobindo Ghosh and Vinayak Savarkar, would frequently refer to the two Italians in their writings and speeches.

When Savarkar first arrived at India House in London, he asked the manager if the library had a copy of Mazzini's autobiography. After finding just one volume of the six-volume set, he requested for the rest. The manager eventually managed to procure the rest of the volumes, and Savarkar devoured them as soon as they arrived. Mazzini's writings brought a lot of clarity to Savarkar on how Indian revolutionaries should proceed:

> It is essential to join forces with the enemies of Britain in Asia and Europe and sympathetic elements in America. Guerilla tactics must be used to attack British sources of power, its centres, its officers; individually and in groups, to induce Indians employed by the British to rise in revolt, to rise whenever there was a war between Britain and another foreign power, to carry out revolutionary activities one after the other—that was my plan of action.[4]

This was the broad Mazzini–Garibaldi-inspired strategy that the Indian revolutionaries would employ over the next four decades. The next generation of revolutionaries was just as impressed by the Irish. The Indian and Irish revolutionaries would often collaborate across the world. So it should not be surprising that when Sachindra Nath Sanyal formed an umbrella organization for the Indian revolutionaries in 1923, he named it Hindustan Republican Association, with a military wing named the Hindustan Republican Army—both names clearly inspired by the Irish Republican Army. The feeling was mutual. When the Provisional Government of Free India was formed by Netaji in Singapore in 1943, the Prime Minister of the Republic of Ireland was the only non-Axis premier to recognize it.

Another international phenomenon that strongly influenced Indians was the rise of Japan. Indians had watched with admiration as Japan modernized itself after the Meiji Restoration of 1868, but its victory over Russia in 1905 was a big inspiration for the revolutionaries. This was the first time in two centuries that an Asian country had defeated a major European power. The last Asian to have done this was Martanda Varma of Travancore, who had defeated the Dutch at the Battle of Colachel in 1741. Since then, Asians had occasionally won battles but had never managed to win a war. Given the backdrop of European colonial empires, the rise of a non-white power was no small thing. It led to a movement called Pan-Asianism, which called for the unity of all Asiatic people.

Several leading Japanese thinkers were proponents of Pan-Asianism. Kakuzo Okakura, once the curator of the Imperial Art Museum, travelled to Bodh Gaya and Varanasi with Swami Vivekananda in 1902. His writings kindled a lot of interest in

India. His book, *Ideals of the East* (published in London in 1903), began with the sentence 'Asia is one.', and was read with interest by Indian opinion makers such as the Tagores of Bengal and Lala Lajpat Rai in Punjab.[5] Mitsuru Toyama, the founder of the Black Dragon Society, was a big supporter of Pan-Asianism and provided backing for Indian revolutionaries, including political asylum for Rashbehari Bose when he escaped to Japan in 1915.

The idea of Pan-Asianism had many converts in other parts of Asia, including China, until the militarist misadventures of the late 1930s. These included Dr Sun Yat-sen, who spent a significant amount of time in exile in Japan. The Matsumotoro Café in Hibiya Park, central Tokyo, was a favourite haunt of foreign exiles to meet. Both Rashbehari Bose and Sun Yat-sen spent hours there in debate and discussion with fellow exiles and Japanese Pan-Asianists. There is still a piano in the café, believed to have been the first produced in Japan, that was played by Sun Yat-sen's wife. The piano somehow survived the Second World War bombings and is on display.

Of course, the ideas that impacted the revolutionaries did not all come from outside. Within India, there was a growing interest in religious reform and revival, as well as a renewed fascination with the country's long history of resistance to foreign invasion. Maharana Pratap, Guru Gobind Singh, Banda Bahadur and many other historical characters were extolled for leading the fight against tyrannical rulers. However, the figure of Chhatrapati Shivaji was particularly popular. His guerrilla tactics against overwhelmingly stronger enemies and his daring escape from Emperor Aurangzeb's clutches were an obvious inspiration for revolutionaries, who saw themselves in very similar circumstances. Popularized by Bal Gangadhar Tilak,

Shivaji Utsav (or the Festival of Shivaji) came to be celebrated not just in Maharashtra but also in other parts of the country. The great poet of Bengal, Rabindranath Tagore, wrote the following lines in Shivaji's honour:

> In what far away century, on what unmarked day
> We no longer know today
> Upon what mountain peak, in darkened forests,
> O King Shivaji,
> When did this thought light up your brow like a flash
> 'Under one dharma, the scattered lands of Bharat
> Shall I unite together into One.'[6]

The nationalist writings in both English and Indian languages in many parts of the country over the first two decades of the twentieth century reflect similar sentiments. Many of them would present contemporary freedom fighters as the torchbearers of a spark lit by Shivaji. Aurobindo Ghosh wrote an imaginary conversation between Shivaji and Aurangzeb's Hindu general, Jai Singh, after they were both dead. The two argue about what they had done during their lives. The conversation ends with these powerful lines from Shivaji: 'I undermined an empire, and it has not been rebuilt. I created a nation, and it has not yet perished.' It would have been clear to all readers that the empire to be undermined was no longer Mughal but British.

The Revolt of 1857–58 was also an important source of inspiration. Remember that the events had taken place within living memory and were imprinted in both Indian and British minds. While in London, Savarkar wrote a book, *The Indian War of Independence 1857*, that presented the characters and events in terms of a national revolution rather than as a mere 'mutiny', as the British preferred to present it. The book made two important points. First, it stressed the importance of Hindu–Muslim unity. Second, the book argued that the key to undermining British power was to trigger a revolt among the Indian soldiers who served them. The events of 1857 were therefore seen as a dry run for the real thing. The idea of triggering such a revolt was central to the revolutionary strategy and, as we shall see, would drive a lot of their activities. As Bhupendra Nath Sanyal, writing on the eve of Independence in the 1940s, would state,

> I had never believed even in my childish imagination that we could drive out the British—for that was my whole conception of Swaraj—by killing individual Englishman here and there. We believed in a second mutiny. The Mutiny of 1857 was our greatest inspiration: we gloated over the life of Tantia Tope.[7]

The colonial experience was not just about political and economic subjugation but also sociocultural subjugation. With their cultural practices mocked as backward and the activities of Christian missionaries growing, both Hindus and Muslims felt uneasy. The Revolt of 1857, therefore, was partly driven by religious concerns. Colonial-era narratives particularly targeted Hindus as idolatrous heathens steeped in superstition. This led to a variety of responses, and Bengal was its epicentre. One of the responses was led by Raja Ram Mohan Roy, who attempted a formulation based on Vedantic monism (although his formulation looks almost like monotheism). This led to the foundation of the Brahmo Samaj in Calcutta in 1829. Combined with a push for social reform, the Brahmo Samaj tried to create a version of Hinduism that was easier to defend against the criticism of contemporary Christian missionaries. Not surprisingly, this was opposed by the orthodox, who accused the Brahmos of bending too far to conform to Western sensibilities.

The debates between these two sides had important implications for Indian society. There was, however, a third group, which would prove to be even more influential in the long run. These were the revivalist modernizers. They agreed with the Brahmos on the urgent need for reform, especially on social issues, but saw no need to be apologetic about ancient rituals and idol worship. One of the key figures of this movement was Rani Rashmoni (1793–1861), a wealthy landowner and canny businesswoman, who pushed back against the colonial government's undue intrusions into religious life and generously funded temples, bathing ghats and scholarship. One of the temples she built was the Dakshineshwar Kali temple, north of Kolkata, where she invited the remarkable, if unorthodox, saint Ramakrishna Paramahamsa. His disciple, Swami Vivekananda (1863–1902), articulated a more confident Hinduism to the world, which was comfortable with both modernity and its ancient roots. Although Swami Vivekananda was not a political figure, his rekindling of civilizational confidence had a huge impact across India and the political spectrum. Virtually all branches of the revolutionary movement would come to regard him as an inspirational figure.

Other parts of India also experienced important religious developments. Punjab saw the rise of the Arya Samaj and of the Sikh reform movement. The Muslim community, similarly, experienced the modernizing Aligarh Movement as well as the rise of pan-Islamic ideologies. In Maharashtra, Tilak popularized the Ganapati festival and turned it into a community event, open to all sects and castes. It was not a new festival and was known to have been celebrated enthusiastically during the Maratha period. However, by the late nineteenth century, it had gradually become a more modest affair, celebrated privately at home. It was Tilak who popularized the large-scale public celebration that we see today, and it was consciously meant to mobilize political momentum against the British.

All these religio-cultural changes had an impact on the revolutionaries, many of whom were deeply religious. Most of the revolutionary groups developed elaborate initiation rites infused with Hindu symbolism. When Aurobindo Ghosh initiated his brother Barin into the movement, it was done in a solemn ceremony, where Barin swore with a sword in one hand and a Bhagawad Gita in the other, that he would fight to the death for India's freedom.[8] It was common for these initiation rites to involve a vow made in front of a form of Adi-Shakti (Mother Goddess) such as Durga, Kali or Bhawani. This should not be surprising, as the Shakta strand of Hinduism was particularly strong among revolutionary groups. Indeed, many nationalists, including non-revolutionaries, would come to view India itself as Goddess Bharat Mata (or Mother India). The song *Vande Mataram* (also spelt 'Bande Mataram') by Bankim Chandra Chattopadhyay explicitly extolls the motherland in the form of a Goddess. Infused with Shakta imagery, the song became the anthem of the freedom movement, but anyone hearing the full version sung even today will quickly realize why it would have been especially evocative for Goddess-worshipping revolutionaries:

> *You are ten-armed Durga, ready to strike*
> *You are Kamala, on a lotus throne [Lakshmi]*
> *You are the Goddess of Speech and Wisdom [Saraswati].*[9]

Many post-Independence historians, in an act of misplaced secularism, downplay the importance of Hindu revivalism in the freedom movement in general and on the revolutionaries in particular. However, it is a historical fact that the majority of revolutionary leaders were deeply religious—in many cases, this flowed into their political worldview. Aurobindo Ghosh would end his famous Uttarpara speech of 1909 with the following words:

> This Hindu nation was born with the Sanatana Dharma, with it it moves and with it it grows. When the Sanatana Dharma declines, and if Sanatana Dharma were capable of perishing, with the Sanatana Dharma it will perish. The Sanatana Dharma, that is nationalism. This is the message that I have to speak to you.[10]

The strong influence of the Hindu–Sikh imagination on the revolutionary movement does not mean that non-Hindu/Sikh members were not welcome. Far from it—the revolutionaries welcomed several nationalists from other religions. Many of the views held by the likes of Tilak, Savarkar and Bismil mark them out as Hindu nationalists, but readers should remember that their most trusted lieutenants were non-Hindus—Joseph Baptista, Madame Bhikaji Cama and Ashfaqullah Khan, respectively. In other words, their unapologetic Hindu identity does not make them bigots. As we shall see, the revolutionaries were essentially pragmatists and would work with groups with varied ideologies, including Pan-Islamists and Japanese imperialists, as long as it served their goal of undermining the British Empire.

The last two decades of the freedom struggle saw the rise of a new set of ideas derived from communism. Until the Bolshevik

Revolution in Russia (1917–23), virtually no one in India knew much about communism and Marxism. The term 'socialism' was more commonly used, but it had a general anti-imperialist connotation and did not denote a defined political or economic ideology. It was only in the 1920s that a handful of educated youth began to take an interest in Marxist ideas. For instance, Bhagat Singh was influenced by Marxism in the last couple of years of his life. However, he was not the founder of the communist movement in India. In his essay 'Why I Am an Atheist', written on death row in Lahore Jail in 1930, Bhagat Singh himself points out that he was virtually the only member of the revolutionary movement in India who was a Marxist. Senior leaders of the movement such as Sachindra Nath Sanyal were well known for being vehemently opposed to Marxism.

The real founder of Indian communism was Manabendra Nath Roy. After many adventures in Southeast Asia and Mexico, the former nationalist revolutionary turned up in post-revolution Russia. He set up the Communist Party of India (CPI) in Tashkent in 1920. His efforts to gain recruits within India, however, lost momentum and Roy himself drifted away from the mainstream communist movement.

The growth of communism in the 1930s happened due to a surprising factor: the systematic indoctrination of nationalist revolutionaries in jail by the British authorities. There is more than enough evidence of how Marxist literature was supplied to political prisoners and how jailors would personally encourage the conversion. British intelligence was deliberately trying to create a rift in the revolutionary movement, but it was a risky strategy. Despite the hold of British communists over the Indian movement, there was always the danger of creating a pathway for

Russian influence. In the end, however, it paid back handsomely during the Second World War as the communists collaborated with the British against Gandhi's Quit India Movement of 1942 as well as their former revolutionary colleagues.

THE SAFETY VALVE

The Revolt of 1857 had a profound impact on the British as well, even if the official line downplayed it as a mere mutiny. Hence the colonial administration took all intelligence about widespread dissatisfaction seriously. The death of between 5 million and 9 million Indians in the famine of 1876–78 led to growing murmurings of dissatisfaction in the early 1880s. British officials such as Allan Octavian Hume of the Indian Civil Service grew increasingly concerned about how this could lead to a new uprising. Hume evidently went through seven volumes of ground reports that suggested there was an 'imminent danger of a terrible outbreak'.[11] Much of the population, especially the poor, was 'convinced that they would starve and die' and was consequently ready to 'do something, and that something was violence'. He took it upon himself to convince his colleagues in the administration that a safety valve was needed. Hume retired in 1882 and dedicated the next few years to creating such a safety valve. He had the direct blessings of Lord Dufferin, the new governor general of India.

Hume reached out to several of the leading educated Indians of the time, and began to build a common platform. After a few iterations, this led to the formation of the Indian National Congress in December 1885. The first conference was held in Bombay, as the venue in Pune was affected by a cholera outbreak. It included seventy-two carefully chosen delegates from different parts of India. It was a strictly controlled affair and the general public was not admitted, even as spectators. Hume made sure that Surendranath Bannerjea, then considered the leading voice of educated Indians, was not made the president of the Congress. Surendranath was hardly a radical, but Hume was not taking any chances. Instead, barrister Womesh Chander Bonnerjee was elected as the first president. As historian R.C. Majumdar puts it, 'The selection of W.C. Bonnerjee as the president of the first Congress gives a fair idea of the political outlook of the founders of the Congress. Mr Bonnerjee lived the life of an Englishman and not only kept himself aloof from, but almost ridiculed, all sorts of political agitation.'[12]

The speeches and statements of the early Congress leaders were embarrassingly servile. They appear to be falling over themselves to declare loyalty to the British Crown. Even Dadabhai Naoroji, perhaps the most assertive of his generation of leaders, stated in his presidential address of 1893:

> I have never faltered in my faith in the British character and have always believed that the time will come when the sentiments of the British Nation and our Gracious Sovereign proclaimed to us in the Great Charter of the Proclamation of 1858 will be realized.[13]

The writer Bankim Chandra Chattopadhyay mocked the Congress as a group of 'beggars' that had no connect with the wider population.[14] It is a good illustration of the law of unintended consequences that such an organization, created deliberately to subvert Indian aspirations, would later become an important part of the freedom struggle.

The INC began to grow beyond its debating society origins in the late 1890s due to the emergence of new leaders, in particular Bal Gangadhar Tilak, who were capable of putting forward Indian demands with new aggression. Using the Ganapati festival, Tilak began to mobilize people in Maharashtra. Along similar lines, he inaugurated the Shivaji festival in Raigad, Pune, in 1896. It saw an outpouring of songs, plays and lectures celebrating the Maratha empire. Tilak would soon find allies in Lala Lajpat Rai from Punjab and Bipin Chandra Pal from Bengal. The Lal–Bal–Pal trio would articulate a more clearly nationalist line in the first decade of the twentieth century.

Economic deprivation was an important driver of this new nationalism. This book will not delve into the colonial policies that impoverished the subcontinent in the nineteenth century, ranging from the forced cultivation of opium and indigo to the unfair tariffs that led to de-industrialization. There are several writers who have documented the economic decline of nineteenth-century India and the sharp increase in famines and epidemics. For our purposes, it would suffice to note that the 1890s was a time of great economic hardship. *The Lancet*, a well-known medical journal, estimates that around 19 million Indians died in famines during the decade.[15] The famine of 1897 alone killed 4.5 million, according to official estimates, and perhaps as many as 16 million, according to independent observers. The imperial authorities and the general public in Britain were aware of these events, as they were routinely reported in London newspapers. However, the debate was usually about the need for ramping up 'charity' but not the reversal of economic policies or providing Indians more say in the government.

Less appreciated is the impact of epidemics in nineteenth-century India. These were partly caused by a famine-weakened population exposed to the large-scale movement of people made possible by steam-driven railways and ships. However, it was also caused by the breakdown of the traditional medical system. For instance, Indians had long practised a form of mass inoculation for smallpox, done by a network of travelling 'tikadars (vaccinators)'. A detailed description of the Indian system of mass inoculation was made to the Royal College of Physicians in London by Dr Holwell in 1767.[16] After Edward Jenner published his seminal paper on smallpox vaccination in 1798, the British quickly spread the technology. The first modern vaccination in Bombay was carried out just four years later. To spread the imported vaccine, the East India Company banned the traditional system in 1804, even though these vaccines would continue to be dependent on imports from England for several decades. Although the new system steadily improved and eventually became more effective than the traditional one, the breakdown of the old system meant that a large part of the population was now left out. With epidemics becoming more common, it is not surprising that Indians were suspicious of what the colonial administration was doing.

THE FIRST SHOT

The famines, epidemics and the political mobilization by Tilak provide the broader political context for an incident in June 1897 that is often said to be the first act in a new cycle of armed resistance. A plague was raging through Poona (now Pune) and the colonial authorities had just given themselves new powers under the Epidemic Diseases Act, 1897. Firm administration is needed during an epidemic, but Poona's chief plague commissioner, Walter Rand, by all accounts, exercised his powers in a most draconian manner. Soldiers raided homes and burnt down property, molested women and desecrated shrines. Plague victims were forced to vacate homes and move to quarantine centres with no food or facilities. Epidemics were not new, and Punekars would have normally accepted stern measures, but Rand's tyrannical behaviour managed to alienate the average citizen. Tilak bitterly criticized the government in his column in *Kesari*.

Two brothers, Damodar Hari Chapekar and Balakrishna Hari Chapekar, decided to assassinate Rand. It was 22 June 1897, the Diamond Jubilee of Queen Victoria. Rand and other officials had gone to attend an official event at the Government House. Armed with pistols, Damodar and Balakrishna hid at a spot on Ganeshkhind Road and waited for Rand to return home. It was completely dark when they saw an official carriage coming down the road. Balakrishna leapt at the horse-drawn carriage and shot the occupant point-blank. It was only then that he realized it was not Rand but his lieutenant Charles Ayerst. Meanwhile, another carriage came out of the darkness—the one in which Rand was travelling. Damodar attacked the second carriage and shot Rand. He was rushed to hospital but died a few days later.

The incident shook British officials across India, and a large bounty of Rs 20,000 was offered for information. The Dravid brothers, former associates of the Chapekars, came forward and provided leads. Damodar and Balakrishna were arrested and hanged. But their third brother, Vasudev Chapekar, and a friend hunted down the informants and killed them. Vasudev, too, was arrested and hanged. As one can imagine, the sequence of events caused quite a sensation at that time. Tilak was arrested too. Although no direct link could be established, he was sent to prison for incitement of violence. It made him a national figure.

Ganeshkhind Road still exists, although it is no longer the lonely tree-lined avenue of the late nineteenth century. The spot where Rand was killed is marked by a small memorial to the Chapekars (it is across the road from a popular shopping mall, but most Punekars do not seem to be aware of it).

According to some writers, the Chapekar brothers marked the beginning of the revolutionary movement in India. The Chapekars were certainly influenced by the political forces unleashed by Tilak, but they were neither members of a significant network, nor did they have any long-term political objectives. They merely wanted to punish Rand and cannot be said to be part of a major 'movement'. However, they did inspire a new generation of Indians to take up arms. It is said that when a teenage Vinayak Savarkar learnt of the execution of Damodar Chapekar, he went to his family temple and swore in front of Goddess Bhawani that he would commit his life to freeing India of foreign rule through armed struggle. Together with Aurobindo Ghosh, Savarkar would build the intellectual basis of the revolutionary movement. We now turn to their story.

2

BHAWANI MANDIR

Aurobindo Ghosh is today remembered mostly as the philosopher and yogi Sri Aurobindo. Many of his millions of ardent followers may not be aware that he is also one of the founders of India's freedom movement. He was born in Calcutta on 15 August 1872 to a civil surgeon, Dr Krishna Dhun Ghosh, and his wife, Swarnalotta. He was their third child.

The Ghosh family were members of the Brahmo Samaj, a community that had been started in Bengal half a century earlier as a Hindu reform movement. However, at the time of Aurobindo's birth, the community was going through a bitter split. On one side were mainstream Brahmos, who continued to think of themselves as Hindu reformers—Swarnalotta's family belonged to this camp. On the other side was a group led by Keshub Chander Sen, who wanted to break away and Westernize themselves to be able to ingratiate themselves with the British rulers. Krishna Dhun belonged to this group. The tension between the two strands would have a profound impact on Aurobindo.

The doctor was so keen to imitate the British that he gave Aurobindo an English-style middle name—Akroyd. He even forbade the use of Bengali at home so that his children would grow up speaking only English. The only Indian language Aurobindo learnt as a child was a smattering of Hindi from the household servants.[1] In 1877, when he was barely five years old, Aurobindo was packed off with his older siblings to a missionary school in Darjeeling called Loretto House, run by Irish nuns. By this time, Swarnalotta seems to have become alienated from her obsessively Anglophile husband, and the forced separation from her young children led to her developing clinical depression. Nonetheless, Krishna Dhun took his family to England in 1879. The couple had another son there, who was named Emmanuel Mathew. He would grow up to be known as Barindra (Barin) Ghosh.

The couple then sailed back to India, along with their newborn son and a toddler daughter, leaving behind Manmohan, Benoy and a seven-year-old Aurobindo. The boys were left behind in Manchester with Reverend William Drewett and his wife, so that they could be brought up as proper Englishmen. Being educated by Irish nuns in Darjeeling was clearly not good enough—one needed to live in England with an English family as well. The Drewetts were strictly instructed that the boys 'should not be allowed to make acquaintance with any Indian or undergo any Indian influence'. Thus, Aurobindo grew up with almost no contact with his native language, culture or religion.

One of the reasons for Krishna Dhun's obsessive behaviour was his ambition that his sons would join the Indian Civil Service (ICS) and return to India as part of the ruling class. However, by the time the boys were in their late teens, it was obvious that

Manmohan and Benoy did not have the academic ability to pass the rigorous examinations, but Aurobindo was intellectually gifted. In December 1889, Aurobindo went to Cambridge to sit for the King's College scholarship examinations. All day he did translations to and from Latin and Greek, answered questions on classical history and grammar, and wrote essays in English. He stood first.

Aurobindo arrived in Cambridge to start his education in October 1890. His scholarship at King's entitled him to free tuition, certain privileges and a modest £80 a year. He was there to earn a degree in the classics, but his real objective was to prepare for the ICS examinations. This is why he began to study Hindu and Muslim customs, the civil and criminal procedures of British India, Sanskrit and Bengali. It was the first time that he had learnt anything related to his country of origin. Although he initially struggled, the sudden exposure to his own culture made a deep impression on the young man.

The two years in Cambridge were happy ones for Aurobindo, despite the dual workload and occasion financial problems—his father, for some reason, had stopped sending him money once he had received the scholarship. He had full intellectual freedom and read widely, beyond what was needed for his degree or the ICS entrance exams. He left King's with a first in the Tripos, but before he could get a degree. He had passed the preliminary ICS examinations and needed to move to London in May 1892 for the final examinations. It was during this summer that Aurobindo was exposed to the emerging political trends in India. Unlike Cambridge, London had a significant Indian community of all classes, including students, and they talked to the young ICS aspirant about what was happening back home. There is evidence that he and his brothers attended a meeting of a secret society dedicated to liberating India, called the Lotus and Dagger. Nothing else is known about this society.

In October, ICS examiners wrote to inform him about the final formality of a riding test. The test was compulsory, and the date was set for 26 October. Aurobindo shocked everyone by refusing to take it. Given that riding was a common skill at that time, rather like being able to drive a car today, no one could understand why someone would refuse to do it. The matter reached the Secretary of State John Wodehouse, who, understandably, allowed no exemption. Aurobindo was removed from the list. Something had snapped inside the talented young man who had been driven all his life by his father to join the ICS. Krishna Dhun did not survive this disappointment, and died suddenly in December—some say due to heartbreak.

At this stage, it is unlikely that Aurobindo knew what he would do next. It so happened that Sayajirao Gaekwad III, the maharaja of Baroda (now Vadodara), was visiting London. After a brief meeting at the Savoy, Gaekwad hired him for the civil service of his own princely state. In January 1893, Aurobindo sailed back to India. He had been away for fourteen years.

THE PRINCE WHO WOULD NOT BOW

The Gaekwad family rose to power in the eighteenth century as generals and governors of the Maratha empire. After the Marathas were defeated by the East India Company in the early nineteenth century, several Maratha chieftains continued as rulers of princely states, albeit subordinate to British suzerainty. The Gaekwads thus became the maharajas of the princely state of Baroda. In 1870, the dynasty faced a succession crisis. Maharaja

Khanderao II passed away without leaving a male heir. His queen, Jumnabai, was then pregnant but the child turned out to be a girl. The throne passed to his brother Malharrao, but this proved to be a disaster. Malharrao was erratic and arbitrary, and within a few years he had emptied the treasury and turned the population against him. It is said that he ordered cannons made of solid gold and even attempted to poison the British resident. Eventually, everyone tired of him and he was removed.

The task of finding a successor was given to Maharani Jumnabai, the dowager queen. She decided to interview all suitable boys of the extended Gaekwad clan. This included a young twelve-year-old boy named Gopalrao from a distant branch of the family. He was just a village boy, who would never have been in the line of succession if not for the turn of events.

The story goes that Jumnabai asked each candidate why they had come to Baroda. When Gopalrao's turn came, he unhesitatingly said, 'I have come here to become the king.' The queen seems to have liked the spark and opted for him. Gopalrao was crowned the ruler of Baroda and assumed the name Maharaja Sayajirao III. His reign would last until 1939.

Sayaji turned out to be an inspired choice. Under his rule, Baroda witnessed major social reforms, huge investments in industry and the founding of the Bank of Baroda. He also spent liberally on building schools, colleges and libraries. Baroda's ruler would go on to provide generous financial support to many talented Indians of that era, including Dr B.R. Ambedkar and, of course, Aurobindo Ghosh. At a time when most Indian princes were wary of displeasing the British, Sayaji sailed close to the wind. One incident in 1911 illustrates this trait in his personality.

The Delhi Durbar of 1911 was a grand affair, the first time a ruling British monarch was visiting India. All the Indian princes were expected to pay homage to King-Emperor George V. The princes were explicitly told of the proper etiquette of greeting him. They had to walk up to the throne in full regalia and pay obeisance by bowing three times. Then they were expected to back away without turning. In other words, no one was to be left in any doubt about who was the boss. As the third most senior prince after Hyderabad and Mysore, Sayaji got his turn early—but he broke all the etiquette rules. First, he refused to wear the full regalia. Then he walked up to the dais and made a single perfunctory bow, before turning around and walking off, showing his back to the emperor. Sayaji was later forced to write a letter of apology, but his was a brave act of defiance in front of tens of thousands of people. No one who had witnessed the event was left in any doubt about what he had done. A witness recorded that Sayaji was laughing mockingly as he walked away from the throne.[2] Motilal Nehru was also one of the witnesses and wrote disapprovingly to his son Jawaharlal, 'I am sorry to say that the Gaekwad has fallen from the high pedestal he once occupied in public estimation.'[3]

Anyone visiting Baroda should visit the Lakshmi Vilas Palace built by Sayaji. This extraordinary piece of late-nineteenth-century architecture would have been brand new when Aurobindo Ghosh arrived in the city in early 1893.

AUROBINDO'S DISCOVERY OF INDIA

As a civil servant, Aurobindo would spend the next several years doing what bureaucrats do: dealing with land records, revenue stamps and so on. He appears to have been a competent officer, but he did not find the work intellectually stimulating. So he spent his free time reading everything from ancient Hindu epics to contemporary politics. He was acquainting himself with India. He also made his way east to meet his family. When he arrived in Deoghar, where his maternal family lived, his mother could not recognize him, and he had to prove his identity by showing her an old scar on his finger. He was warmly embraced by uncles, aunts, cousins and nephews. He soon developed an especially close relationship with his sister Sarojini and younger brother Barin.

Meanwhile, he was persuaded by the journalist K.G. Deshpande, his best friend from Cambridge, to write for the English section of a weekly journal called *Indu Prakash*, which was published from Bombay. This is the first time Aurobindo began to express his views on national issues. Writing a series called 'New Lamps for Old', he derided the tiny elite that ran the Congress for celebrating minor concessions made to them by the British. 'Our actual enemy is not some force exterior to ourselves, but our crying weakness, our cowardice, our selfishness, our hypocrisy, our moribund sentimentalism.'[4]

One should be in no doubt that the young Baroda civil servant would not have been able to write like this unless he had the tacit backing of Sayaji Gaekwad. In fact, the maharaja seems to have noticed his flair for language and begun to use him to draft his speeches and letters. Aurobindo, however, did not find his work as a civil servant stimulating, and requested permission to spend a few hours every week teaching French at Baroda College (now known as Maharaja Sayajirao University). It was granted. Some time later, when the English professor went on furlough, he became the acting professor of English.

With his professional life now settled by 1901, Aurobindo decided to get married. At twenty-nine, he was old for a first-time groom by existing standards. His bride, Mrinalini Bose, was half his age and was thought to be pretty. He insisted on a full Hindu wedding, complete with all ancient rituals. Although both sides of his family were Brahmos of different hues, Aurobindo wanted to make a point. He had come to the conclusion that despite its contributions in social reform, Brahmoism was a cultural and intellectual dead end—'a rehash of that pale and consumptive shadow, English Theism'.[5] When the newly married couple returned to Baroda after a honeymoon in Nainital, the maharaja decided to use Aurobindo more actively. He gave him a lot of new responsibilities, including that of writing his biography. The two became quite close and together began to develop a more radical anticolonial worldview.

ANUSHILAN SAMITI

Since ancient times, India has had a tradition of local gymnasiums across the country, known as *akhada*s, which functioned as a system of imparting both military and spiritual training. Although women were allowed in some akhadas, they were usually places where young men were taught wrestling, the use of the sword, archery and so on. It should also be noted that most of them were affiliated to a Hindu religious order or a temple. In the middle ages, the akhadas played an important role in mobilizing local resistance against the Turkic conquest. They were sometimes more effective than the armies of the Hindu nobility. Of course, they were not beyond getting into fights with each other.

When the East India Company was attempting to conquer India, they occasionally faced resistance from this network of akhadas. Once in power, the British systematically defanged them. This was not difficult, as changes in military technology and training had made them obsolete. The larger networks were encouraged to become purely religious institutions. Many of the akhadas that today gather for the Kumbh Mela are the remnants of these quasi-military orders. Meanwhile, the local akhadas gradually became more like sports clubs, which continued to teach wrestling and other traditional forms of martial arts. They have survived in many parts of the country today, although many do not know of their original purpose.

In the late nineteenth century, the military purpose of the akhada network was still fresh in everyone's memory. This is why Bankim Chandra Chattopadhyay's *Ananda Math* was so successful. It was not just based on the Sanyasi rebellion of the late eighteenth century, but on an evocative shared memory of soldier monks. As a more aggressive nationalism began to take root, some Indians began to wonder if akhadas could be used to build a network of secret societies that would work towards armed insurrection against the British.

Aurobindo was exploring this idea around the time that the Chapekar brothers killed Walter Rand. It was also at this time that a certain Jatindranath Banerji visited him in Baroda. Aurobindo arranged for Jatindranath to join the Baroda army so that he could gain some military training. In 1901, Jatindranath returned to Calcutta to set up an akhada. He also began to link up with other akhadas that harboured nationalist ideas. One of these was a wrestling club called Anushilan Samiti, set up recently by Satish Chandra Bose, a follower of Swami Vivekananda and his Irish disciple Sister Nivedita.

In 1902, Aurobindo made a trip to Bengal to meet the people involved in the growing network. Within a year, new nodes had started popping up across Bengal, and the name 'Anushilan Samiti' came to denote a wider network. Incredibly, the original club still exists in north Kolkata but seems to specialize in badminton these days. There are no obvious signs of its link to India's freedom movement, except a large map of undivided India painted in blue and white behind the badminton court.

Sister Nivedita visited Baroda in October of that year, and Aurobindo received her at the station. Her spiritual guru, Swami Vivekananda, had died a few months earlier and she had decided to take a more political path from here. Developments back in her native Ireland must have influenced her thinking. Aurobindo thanked her for helping set up the Anushilan Samiti. The two then met the maharaja. Sayaji encouraged them but stopped short of funding their plans. He correctly realized that British intelligence would eventually find out about it and would not take kindly to his providing direct financial support to a group that it considered terrorists.

Sayaji, however, kept pushing the boundaries. In a speech written by Aurobindo and delivered in December 1902 at an industrial exhibition, Sayaji contrasted the poverty in India with the energy and prosperity in Europe. He then blamed it on the lack of a risk-taking culture and scientific knowledge, but most of all on 'the result of acquisition of political power by the East India Company and the absorption of India in the growing British Empire'. He then stated that India needed a 'great national movement', although carefully couching it as a social rather than a political programme.

To understand why this was so bold, one needs to see the contrast between Sayaji's speech and the cringeworthy statements made a week later at the annual conference of the INC. One of the first speakers proclaimed 'that it is for our benefit that British power should continue to be supreme in our land'. Surendranath Bannerjea, in his presidential address, stated, 'We plead for the permanence of British rule in India.'[6] Aurobindo attended the conference, and it was here that he met Bal Gangadhar Tilak. Given their shared antipathy for the servile behaviour of the mainstream Congressmen, there was an instant bond between the two.

It was also around this time that Barin Ghosh came to spend some time with his brother in Baroda. He was soon deeply inspired by the idea of creating a network of revolutionary akhadas. In early 1903, in a solemn secret ceremony, Aurobindo initiated him into the Anushilan Samiti. Holding a sword in one hand and a Bhagawad Gita in the other, Barin swore that he would dedicate his life to freeing India from foreign occupation. Such initiation rites would become common among all revolutionary groups across India, and usually involved a vow to a form of the Goddess Adi-Shakti—Durga, Kali or Bhawani.

Barin now returned to Bengal and, over the next two years, travelled across the province, setting up branches of the Anushilan Samiti. On his part, Aurobindo wrote a tract, 'Bhawani Mandir', where he explicitly laid out the idea of building a Bhawani temple-school at a secluded location in the hills, where a generation of warrior monks could be trained. The idea was that they would spread across India and trigger the coming insurrection.

The tract lays out explicitly the idea of the motherland as Goddess Bhawani:

> For what is a nation? What is our mother-country? It is not a piece of earth, nor a figure of speech, nor a fiction of the mind. It is a mighty Shakti, composed of the Shaktis of all the millions

of units that make up the nation, just as Bhawani Mahisha-Mardini sprang into being from the Shaktis of all the millions of gods assembled in one mass of force and welded into unity. The Shakti we call India, Bhawani Bharati, is the living unity of the Shaktis of three hundred millions of people; but she is inactive, imprisoned in the magic circle of *tamas*, the self-indulgent inertia and ignorance of her sons. To get rid of *tamas* we have but to wake the Brahma within.[7]

The tract expressed the need to build a temple dedicated to Bhawani Bharati and provides details of how an order of warrior monks was to be established. Aurobindo then began to scout for a suitable location. After some searching, he decided on the temple town of Karnali, near Chandod, on the banks of the Narmada. Appropriately, the town already had an ancient temple to Goddess Kali and was within striking distance of Baroda. His journalist friend Deshpande, then assistant collector of the district, even started a pilot project in the area called Ganganath Bharatiya Vidyalaya, a school where the students could be taught both Sanskrit and modern nationalist ideas. Sayaji Gaekwad was almost certainly aware of what was happening, but was careful not to establish any direct links.

Meanwhile, Aurobindo became the vice principal of Baroda College and, with the principal away on leave, was the person in charge. His pay went up sharply and he was in a responsible position. His office has been preserved by the university. It is a relatively small room at the end of the first-floor gallery of the grand convocation hall. It has his table and chair, and some bookshelves. The vice principal also moved into a beautiful bungalow. This, too, has been preserved perfectly by the Sri Aurobindo Ashram and is now run as a meditation centre.

I spent a wonderful afternoon wandering through its airy rooms and browsing through anthologies of his early writings while imagining the idealistic academic and his dreams of revolution.

In 1905, there was a new twist to the story of India's freedom movement. Lord Curzon announced in October that Bengal would be partitioned in two. The idea had been debated for a few years and justified on the grounds of administrative efficiency—the province was indeed a large one. However, it was clear from the way the division was done that it was at least partly driven by political considerations. East Bengal would now have a Muslim majority while the Bengali Hindus of the western half would be diluted by the inclusion of a large number of Biharis and Odiyas. Thus, the politically assertive Bengali Hindus would be weakened by religious and linguistic counterweights.

Such an obvious attempt at divide-and-rule was immediately met with strong protests. In Calcutta, all business was suspended, shops were shuttered and vehicular traffic stopped. Large crowds marched down the streets, singing *Vande Mataram*. On 16 October, mass rakhi-bandhan ceremonies were conducted, and many people across Bengal tied rakhis on each other's wrists as a symbol of their unbreakable bond. At least initially, the movement had the support of most prominent Muslim leaders, and many of them participated in the protests enthusiastically. In a public meeting that attracted fifty thousand people, the great poet Rabindranath Tagore and veteran politician Ananda Mohan Bose made a passionate proclamation:

> Whereas the Government has thought it fit to effectuate the partition of Bengal in spite of the universal protest of the Bengali nation, we hereby pledge and proclaim that we, as a people, shall do everything in our power to counteract the evil effects of the

dismemberment of our province and to maintain the integrity of our race. So God help us.'[8]

An important innovation of the 1905 protests was the idea of Swadeshi—the boycott of British-made goods in favour of locally made ones. It was an idea that spread quickly across Bengal and then across the rest of the country as many Indians came out in support of the Bengal agitation. British-made clothes and other goods were thrown into bonfires. The cobblers of Mymensingh vowed that they would not mend British-made shoes, the washer men of Kalighat promised that they would no longer wash foreign-made clothes and Brahmin priests refused to officiate in marriage ceremonies where foreign-made clothes were worn.

The key Bengali leader who emerged from this was Bipin Chandra Pal, who soon received strong backing from Tilak in Maharashtra and Lala Lajpat Rai in Punjab. This was the genesis of the Lal–Bal–Pal trio.

It should be noted that the original idea of Swadeshi was not about a return to pre-modern manufacturing. We have this mental association today because of the popularization of the charkha, the hand-turned spinning wheel, by Mahatma Gandhi at a later date. The original idea was a more general expression of economic nationalism that included rapid modernization—Japan was an important inspiration, after all, in 1905. The mood of the times led to a flurry of Indian entrepreneurs entering new fields hitherto dominated by foreign businesses. Bengal, for example, witnessed the setting up of Calcutta Chemicals (producers of the Margo soap), Mohini Mills (cotton textiles) and Indian Tea & Provisions (survives today as Luxmi Tea).

Barin Ghosh, meanwhile, had been setting up branches of the Anushilan Samiti across Bengal. The protests led to a sudden increase in young recruits. Branches were independently sprouting even outside Bengal, and some, such as the unit in Dacca (now Dhaka), had a mind of their own. The experiment had not just worked, it now threatened to grow out of control. Aurobindo realized that he had to shift to Bengal to be in the thick of things. So, in early 1906, he resigned from Baroda College and moved to Calcutta. There, he and Barin set up a newspaper called *Jugantar* (The New Era) to spread nationalist ideas. It soon had a dedicated following, and Bhupendra Nath Dutta, Swami Vivekananda's younger brother, became one of its editors. Leaving Barin and his associates to run the paper, Aurobindo busied himself with the setting up of the National College in Calcutta as an alternative to the British- and missionary-controlled institutions. The college would evolve into today's Jadavpur University. It opened in July 1906 with Aurobindo as its first principal.

Around the same time, Bipin Pal also started a newspaper provocatively named *Bande Mataram*. He invited Aurobindo to write regularly for it. The paper quickly became popular and Aurobindo's hard-hitting editorials generated a lot of debate. Gandhi, in faraway South Africa, and Jawaharlal Nehru, in England, would comment on them. British intelligence in India read them carefully, and tracts were quoted in *The Times* in London. An obscure civil servant from Baroda had become one of the most influential thinkers in the capital of British India. He had triggered a rapidly expanding revolutionary network, created a nationalist institution and was now driving the political conversation. There was also no doubt from his writings that he supported the Lal–Bal–Pal trio, which had started to challenge the old, cosy club that ran the INC.

The friction between the two factions is usually referred to as the rivalry between 'extremists' and 'moderates'. The very use of the terms tells you who would later write the official history of that period. One is left with the impression that the demands for full independence articulated by the former were unreasonable, while the insipid petitions of the latter were sensible. However, since this book is written from the perspective of the revolutionaries, they will hereby be referred to as the Nationalists and the Loyalists, respectively. This is how Aurobindo referred to them.[9]

The INC conference of 1907 was originally meant to be held in Nagpur, but Loyalist leaders Pherozeshah Mehta and Gopal Krishna Gokhale decided to shift it to Surat to deny Tilak the advantage of home turf. The cultural divide between the two camps would have been obvious to Aurobindo and Barin when they arrived in Surat on 24 December. The Loyalists were housed in luxury tents near the podium while the Nationalists were crammed into *dharamshalas* in the city's bazaar.

The Nationalists wanted that their candidate, Lala Lajpat Rai, be elected president and for the conference to pass a resolution endorsing the continuation of the Swadeshi agitations. Lajpat Rai had just returned from prison in Mandalay. Late at night, a compromise was reached between the two sides that Rashbehari Ghosh (not to be confused with Rashbehari Bose) of the Loyalist faction would be made president, but that many of the demands of the Nationalists would be included in the resolution. Nonetheless, despite many assurances, Tilak had still not received a draft of the resolution when the session started the next afternoon. When he did receive it, it was obvious that none of his demands had been included. A murmur went through the Nationalist camp and led to sloganeering. Surendranath Bannerjea's speech had to be stopped and the session suspended.

The session could only be resumed the next day. As Surendranath resumed his speech, Tilak sent a note to the organizers that he would second the nomination of the president but would also like to move an amendment to the proposed resolution. This was accepted. However, when Surendranath ended his speech, Tribhuvan Das Malvi proposed Rashbehari Ghosh's name, and Motilal Nehru hurriedly seconded it before Tilak could even walk up to the podium. Rashbehari Ghosh then started his presidential address. Tilak lodged a protest but was shouted down. A gang of hired goons then attacked him and dragged him off. A group of young Nationalists from Maharashtra rushed to protect him. There was pandemonium as shoes and chairs were thrown at each other. Aurobindo and his entourage walked out even as Loyalist supporters spat at them. The split was complete. That evening the two camps held separate meetings. Aurobindo presided over the Nationalist session, with Tilak as the principal speaker.

THE GARDEN HOUSE

The Swadeshi movement had brought in new recruits and created many branches, but Barin realized that the Anushilan Samiti had neither the know-how nor the organizational capability to do anything that would meaningfully challenge British hegemony. Some of the early attempts to carry out assassinations or disrupt the colonial administration were laughably amateurish, and almost all of them ended in failure. So Barin decided to make the risky move of creating a physical headquarters. It is not known if Aurobindo approved of this. Although he did not rein in Barin, he does seem to have been apprehensive of the things his brother was doing that could be too premature in the revolutionary cycle.

Barin decided to establish his headquarters in a *baganbari*, or a garden house, in Maniktola, just north of the city. The property belonged to a supporter and consisted of two acres of land with a dilapidated house, a couple of ponds and a small family temple. It was not as romantic as the warrior monastery originally envisaged in 'Bhawani Mandir', but it was at a practical distance from the city. The Maniktola area is today within the urban sprawl of Kolkata, although some parts of it still have a semi-developed rural feel. The exact location of the garden house, however, is difficult to discern now, as the original buildings have not survived and have been built over by later structures. Note that Aurobindo, at this time, was living at 23 Scott Lane in north Calcutta. This building has survived in good condition.

At the garden house, Barin gathered a group of around twenty young recruits. They were all drawn from the educated Hindu middle class, the *'bhadralok'*. Despite their enthusiasm, and the acquisition of a few small arms, they knew they did not have the know-how to carry out any serious revolutionary act. Thus, Hemchandra Das was sent to Paris in late 1906 to acquire bomb-making skills. At that time, Paris was home to anarchists and revolutionaries of every description from across Europe. Hemchandra enrolled himself to study chemistry but spent his free time meeting activists of all kinds. He also made friends with Pandurang Bapat, who had been sent from London by Savarkar for the same purpose. The duo eventually got hold of an excellent bomb-making manual from a Russian anarchist, who gifted it to them in a fit of drunken large-heartedness. It was in Russian and they had to get it translated before making copies. Hemchandra then sailed back to Calcutta with a suitcase full of information on how to run an armed rebellion, including the seventy-page translation of the Russian manual. It appears that the Indian love for Russian military technology predates the Cold War!

The revolutionaries back in Calcutta had also been hard at work. Barin had found an explosives expert in Ullaskar Dutt, who had independently developed bomb-making skills. A few weeks before the Congress session of 1907, the revolutionaries had managed to blow up the train carrying the lieutenant governor Sir Andrew Fraser. Although the lieutenant governor was not hurt, it had proved Ullaskar's capabilities. The acquisition of Hemchandra's manual added to their skills. The problem was that Barin was becoming reckless. Aurobindo noticed this, but was either unable or unwilling to restrain him, despite the fact that he was aware that both the office of *Bande Mataram* and the Scott Lane house were under police surveillance.

The colonial administration knew that Aurobindo's writings were evoking an upsurge of nationalist feelings across India, but the editorials in *Bande Mataram* were too carefully worded to be taken to court. So they decided to go after *Jugantar*. Its staff was questioned and some were imprisoned. This was done by a district judge named Douglas Kingsford, who had a reputation for passing harsh judgments against Swadeshi protesters. The revolutionaries decided to teach him a lesson. The authorities got wind of this and transferred him to Muzaffarpur in Bihar. Barin decided to hunt him down in Bihar.

The job was given to Prafulla Chaki and an eighteen-year-old Khudiram Bose. Armed with revolvers and a small bomb, they made their way to Muzaffarpur and spent a few days observing Kingsford. On 29 April 1908, Kingsford went to the local British club with his wife and spent an evening playing bridge with the wife and daughter of Pringle Kennedy, a barrister. Meanwhile,

Khudiram and Prafulla were waiting behind some trees on the road leading to the judge's house. Around 8.30 p.m., the foursome finished their last rubber, and the Kennedy women got into a horse-drawn carriage to head home. The Kingsfords, in an almost identical carriage, were not far behind. As the first carriage passed the trees, Khudiram jumped out of the darkness and threw the bomb in through the carriage window. Both women were fatally wounded. The two attackers then escaped in the confusion, before splitting up to make their way back separately.[10]

Khudiram walked all night to reach the railway station in Wani. Two local police constables noticed something suspicious about him and grabbed him before the tired boy even had a chance to take out his revolver. He was later sentenced to death by hanging. Prafulla, meanwhile, had caught a train directly from Muzaffarpur to Calcutta. It was bad luck that an off-duty sub-inspector was sitting next to him. The previous day's attack was fresh in everyone's mind, and the policeman guessed that his co-passenger might have had something to do with it. So, at one of the stops, he wired ahead that he was tracking a suspect. At the next station, the police tried to arrest Prafulla, who ran down the platform. He pulled out his revolver and fired wildly at the pursuers, but realizing that he was trapped, he turned the gun around and killed himself with the last bullet.

News of the events in Muzaffarpur reached Calcutta a day later, and the authorities had a hunch that the attacks on Fraser and Kingsford had been carried out by the same group. They zeroed in on Barin's network. In the early morning of 2 May 1908, the police launched simultaneous raids in several locations across the city. Barin and many of his associates were arrested from the garden house and a lot of incriminating evidence was found, including a copy of the bomb manual. They also raided Aurobindo's new home in Grey Street. He had moved in just three days earlier with his wife and sister. Both Mrinalini and Sarojini were at home when Aurobindo was rudely woken up and arrested. He was handcuffed and a thick rope was tied around his waist to make sure he did not attempt to escape. All his possessions were then searched, and boxes full of papers were carted off to the police headquarters. All the prisoners were housed in Alipore Jail. Aurobindo was taken to a block of solitary cells and put in Cell No. 6. These arrests and subsequent investigations led to *Emperor versus Aurobindo Ghosh & Others*, popularly known as the Alipore Bomb Trials. The case attracted a lot of attention in India as well as in Britain.

Even as the trial progressed into August, the revolutionaries managed to smuggle in two revolvers. Barin arranged for these to be delivered to Kanailal Dutt and Satyen Bose. The original idea was to gradually smuggle in several of these and then fight their way out before making their way south to the Sunderbans. However, around this time, one of the prisoners, Narendranath Goswami, decided to turn approver and agreed to reveal everything he knew about the Anushilan Samiti network. Kanailal and Satyen decided that they would rather kill Narendranath before the wider network was further compromised. They confronted the approver in the jail yard and shot him. When he tried to escape up the stairs, they chased him and emptied their revolvers into his dying body. The two were then captured and later hanged.

On some level, one also feels sorry for Narendranath. He had indeed betrayed his comrades, but he was not a willing collaborator or informer of the kind that we will shortly meet. He was a young man who probably genuinely believed in the cause, but simply broke down under aggressive police questioning. The revolvers used to kill him are today on display at the Kolkata Police Museum. It is a lovely little museum housed in a heritage building and contains guns used in several of the events mentioned in this book, sometimes even the used cartridges.

As one can imagine, the incident inside the jail further intensified press coverage. The remaining Anushilan Samiti units across Bengal stepped up their attacks on British officials. The sub-inspector who had identified Prafulla Chaki was tracked down and killed. The administration responded by increasing raids and arrests. Away from the prying eyes of the Calcutta press, police methods were far more brutal in the hinterland.

The Alipore trials resumed after a few days. Unable to afford his initial lawyer, Aurobindo switched to a junior lawyer, Chittaranjan Das. It turned out to be a good choice. The police saw Aurobindo as the kingpin behind the attacks, but could not prove a direct link between him and any act of violence. They had not found any guns or incriminating documents in his house. His writings in *Bande Mataram*, while bold, were carefully worded and could not be connected to any specific revolutionary deed. Witnesses say that Aurobindo sat almost detached through the entire trial. He would later write:

> Watching, day after day, the endless stream of witnesses and exhibits, the counsel's unvaried dramatic performance, the boyish frivolity and light heartedness of youthful magistrate, looking at the amazing spectacle I often thought that instead of sitting in a British court of justice we were inside a stage in some world of fiction.[11]

The judgment was delivered in May 1909. Barin Ghosh and Ullaskar Dutt were sentenced to death by hanging (later reduced to life imprisonment at the dreaded Cellular Jail in Port Blair). Many of the others were given life sentences. Incredibly, Aurobindo was acquitted.

THE SAINT OF PONDICHERRY

Aurobindo emerged from prison a national hero. Sister Nivedita proclaimed him India's Mazzini. With Tilak imprisoned in Mandalay, he was the most important leader of the Nationalists. As *Bande Mataram* and *Jugantar* had been shut down by the authorities, he started a new paper called *Karmayogin* in June 1909. It was an instant hit across India and soon had Tamil, Hindi and Bengali editions. Many influential foreign visitors, such as Ramsay MacDonald, a British member of Parliament and future Prime Minister, came to meet him.

Celebrity also meant that Aurobindo was a much-sought-after speaker. Over the next few months, he delivered speeches in many locations across Bengal—Khulna, Howrah, Jhalakati, Bhawanipur and so on.[12] Large crowds attended his talks. This is also the period in which he delivered his famous Uttarpara speech. He declared, 'I say that it is the Sanatana Dharma which for us is nationalism. This Hindu nation was born with the Sanatana Dharma, with it it moves, and with it it grows.'

His statement on Sanatana Dharma does not mean that Aurobindo was a religious fanatic. He had, on many occasions, stated that non-Hindu Indians, such as Muslims, were an integral part of Indic civilization. However, at the same time, he was unapologetic about the fact that he drew his inspiration from

Hinduism—defined broadly—that was at the core of Indian nationhood and civilization. Moreover, he had begun to articulate the view that Hindu ideas were not just meant for India but were universal ideas meant for the world.

It was in February 1910 that Aurobindo received information that the British authorities were about to issue a new warrant against him. He was in his office when he got the information, and without a moment of hesitation, he and a couple of associates made their way through the back alleys to River Hugli. They hired a small wooden boat to take them to the French enclave of Chandernagore (now Chandannagar). Here Aurobindo was kept hidden by the local Anushilan Samiti unit, the same group that had smuggled the revolvers into Alipore Jail. They also kept changing his location. Although the British did not have legal jurisdiction in the tiny French enclave, there were British agents and informers everywhere. Nonetheless, he was able to keep in touch with Sister Nivedita, who temporarily took over the editing of *Karmayogin*.

After six weeks, Aurobindo realized that his position was untenable and decided to move to the larger French enclave of Pondicherry (now the Union Territory of Puducherry). He slipped back into British-controlled Calcutta under an assumed name and got himself a cabin on the *Dupleix*.

When Aurobindo first arrived in Pondicherry, he had only expected to stay there for a few months, perhaps a year, before heading back into British India once things had cooled off. However, as the months passed, he steadily drifted towards the exploration of spiritual, religious and civilizational themes. With one exception, he would never again participate actively in India's political life, although he would follow events with interest.

Some of his followers felt let down and many kept hoping that he would return, but Aurobindo Ghosh was well on his way to becoming Sri Aurobindo.

Aurobindo's change of direction may seem inexplicable, but his writings explain his reasons. He seems to have come to the conclusion that he had already accomplished his role as India's Mazzini by triggering the flame of nationalism. It was now a matter of time before the British were forced to leave. However, he also felt that there was a more important civilizational battle that India would have to fight, which would prove much harder than just gaining political freedom. After centuries under foreign rule, Indians had come to see their own culture from the perspective of those who had conquered them. Many members of the Indian elite had imbibed the idea that sacred texts such as the Vedas and the Upanishads were just superstition—like Aurobindo's father, they had come to believe modernization meant Westernization. One could argue that this shows incredible foresight, as more than a century later, seven and a half decades after gaining political freedom, this remains a matter of hot debate in contemporary India. He felt that it was his duty to rediscover the true core of Indian civilization and present it to Indians and the wider world. With this in mind, Sri Aurobindo dived deep into the Rig Veda, the most ancient and revered of Hindu texts.

3

INDIA HOUSE

Vinayak was born on 28 May 1883 to Damodar and Radhabai Savarkar in the village of Bhagur, near Nashik in Maharashtra. He was the second of four surviving children. Ganesh (more commonly known as Babarao) was four years older than Vinayak. His sister, Maina, was born in 1886 and younger brother, Narayan, in 1888. Political resentments against the British were always simmering just beneath the surface in Maharashtra. This was the heartland of the Maratha empire that the British had pushed aside to conquer India. The ancestors of the Savarkars had been mid-level officials in the Maratha administration, and the memories were still fresh.[1]

The Great Famine of 1877 triggered a new phase of discontent across India. Taking inspiration from Chhatrapati Shivaji, a charismatic speaker Vasudev Balwant Phadke (1845–1883) decided to organize a rebel group in Maharashtra. Within a couple of years, he had built a sizeable network among the Ramoshee, Koli, Mahar and Dhangar communities. He then carried out a series of daring robberies along the Konkan coast to collect money and guns. Not surprisingly, the authorities put a bounty on his head. Vasudev responded by announcing double the bounty on the governor of Bombay, Sir Richard Temple! A declaration of revolt was posted across Poona.

Phadke next reached out to the Lingayat community in the south, and to Muslim and Sikh soldiers working for the nizam of Hyderabad. The British took this seriously and the matter was discussed in the British Parliament. Phadke's luck eventually ran out. He was betrayed and captured after a fierce gunfight in 1879. He was sentenced to life imprisonment and sent away to Aden, where he made a dramatic escape from prison. Recaptured and permanently kept chained in his solitary cell, he starved himself to death in 1883. His rebellion, like that of Birsa Munda in Jharkhand and that of the Manipuri nobility in 1891, was never a serious threat to the British occupation of India, but it kept the spark alive. Some of his followers ended up in the penal colony of the Andaman Islands.

Since Phadke was a Brahmin and his followers were mostly from other communities, the colonial administration began to invest systematically in creating a schism between Brahmins and non-Brahmins in Maharashtra. All this provides the political backdrop for Tilak's attempt to unite and mobilize the populace using the Ganapati and the Shivaji festivals, along with his writings in *Kesari*. Vinayak Savarkar grew up in this milieu.

ABHINAV BHARAT

The killing of Walter Rand by the Chapekar brothers and their subsequent hanging had a big impact on Vinayak. He did not sleep for several nights, and then went to the idol of Bhawani at the family shrine in Bhagur and swore, 'I will wage war against the enemy and slay them till my last breath.' When his family moved to Nashik in 1899, Vinayak organized a small group of friends called 'Mitra Mela'. They met regularly to discuss political ideas in a small room, with portraits of their heroes lining the walls—Chhatrapati Shivaji, Nana Saheb, Rani Laxmibai of Jhansi, Tatya Tope, Vasudev Balwant Phadke and so on.

These were difficult times for the Savarkars. Damodar had passed away and the twenty-year-old Babarao had not been able to arrange a regular source of income. The family were forced to sell off all their property and even jewellery to somehow keep going. It was under these strained circumstances that Vinayak received a proposal to marry the eldest daughter of a wealthy aristocrat, Bhaurao Chiplunkar. The two families had known each other for several generations. Vinayak was frank with Bhaurao about his family's financial situation as well as his interest in pursuing further studies. Bhaurao heard out the young lad and seems to have taken an instant liking to him. He promised to provide money to support both his family and his education. Thus, Vinayak married Yamuna in 1901, when they were both still teenagers.

With support from his in-laws, Vinayak joined Fergusson College, Poona, in January 1902 to pursue an undergraduate degree in arts. He also set up a branch of the Mitra Mela in the college, which soon attracted a large number of students. Many of them would go on to become prominent Indians of their generation. A year later, Vinayak also began to attend classes at Deccan College for an LLB (Bachelor of Law). The rules of that time permitted students to pursue simultaneous degrees. Thus, he also set up a Mitra Mela in Deccan College. The Mitra Melas organized talks by prominent speakers of that time on a variety of subjects. They also published plays, poetry and essays, often with a nationalist tilt. The success of the Mitra Melas led to the establishment of branches in even more colleges across Maharashtra, and Vinayak began to develop a reputation as a rising student leader.

In 1904, the Mitra Melas held a convention in Nashik that was attended by more than 200 delegates. At the event, Vinayak renamed the network Abhinav Bharat (New India or Young India). The choice of name was not a coincidence and was inspired directly by Mazzini's Young Italy. Then, in front of a portrait of Chhatrapati Shivaji, a solemn oath was taken that began with: 'Vande Mataram, in the name of God, in the name of Bharat Mata, in the name of all the martyrs who have shed their blood for Bharat Mata ...'[2]

The Japanese victory over Russia in 1905 was closely watched in India—it was the first time in centuries that an Asiatic power had defeated a European power. Maharashtra would have felt this keenly—it was something that it had once come close to doing. Then the Swadeshi movement erupted over the Partition of Bengal. Vinayak met Tilak and offered him the Abhinav Bharat cadre to collect foreign-made clothes in large quantities.

On the day of Dussehra, 8 October, a large procession with cartloads of foreign-made clothes made its way through the streets of Poona. Vinayak led the procession and was joined midway by Tilak. Many well-known personalities joined the crowds. A student named Vishnu Ganesh Pingle, who would later play a role in the Ghadar movement, was also there. When they reached Lakdi Pul, speeches were delivered, and at 9 p.m. a huge bonfire was lit, with all the clothes and other goods in it.

The principal of Fergusson College, Sir Raghunath Purushottam Paranjpe, was not pleased when he heard that one of his brightest students was leading the Swadeshi boycotts. He expelled Savarkar from the college hostel and fined him ten rupees. This backfired, as the students of Poona did a collection drive and easily raised the money. Tilak and several prominent Punekars spoke up for the student leader. Vinayak Savarkar was now a celebrity.

Savarkar managed to finish his BA degree in December 1905. He then moved to Bombay's Wilson College to finish the final year of his LLB. Through all of this, Vinayak somehow found the time to visit Yamuna in Nashik and spend time with their first child, Prabhakar, born earlier in the year.[3]

In the next few years, the Abhinav Bharat network spread quickly and was soon in touch with like-minded organizations across India. Babarao Savarkar and a hundred Abhinav Bharat members attended the troubled INC conference in Surat in 1907. Even as the two factions of the INC fought each other, Babarao and his team held a secret meeting with Aurobindo Ghosh and the Anushilan Samiti members from Bengal. They also scouted for young talent that could spread their network to other states. This is how Babarao met V.O. Chidambaram Pillai, who would go on to become a prominent political figure in the deep south of the country.

THE INDIAN SOCIOLOGIST

Shyamji Krishna Varma was born in Kachchh, Gujarat, in 1857. He lost his parents by the time he was ten, but generous relatives helped him pursue his education in Bombay. Around 1874, he met the religious and social reformer Dayanand Saraswati, and, a year later, became one of the first to be formally initiated into the Arya Samaj—a Hindu reform movement that advocated a return to simpler Vedic rites. That same year, he also married Bhanumati, the daughter of a wealthy businessman.

Shyamji was academically gifted and his lectures on Sanskrit and Hinduism attracted a lot of early attention. The Boden Professor of Sanskrit at Oxford, Monier Williams, invited Shyamji to Oxford, where he soon became a well-known academic. He was given a membership of the prestigious Royal Asiatic Society in 1881. Not satisfied with being a star academic, Shyamji also studied law and became a barrister by 1885. He then returned to India, where, in addition to practising law, he served as the dewan of three princely states. He was quite a favourite with the colonial administration at this time, although it appears he secretly harboured nationalist views. When he began to express some of these views, the ruling class immediately started to treat him with suspicion. Thus, Shyamji and Bhanumati decided to move to Europe in 1897.

Living between London and Paris, Shyamji discovered yet another talent—financial market investment. He would acquire a large fortune from stocks, which allowed him to pursue his ideas independently. In January 1905, he started an English monthly called *Indian Sociologist*, which expressed his own views and carried articles by others advocating 'home rule'(i.e., independence), albeit being careful not to be seen as supporting violence. He also established contacts with other revolutionary publications, including the *Gaelic American*, published by John Devoy of the Irish Republican Party from New York.

That same year, Shyamji decided to establish a hostel for Indian students, called India House, in London. Britain had the world's best universities at the time, and he felt that talented nationalist Indians should be exposed to them. The hostel was inaugurated in July 1905 in the presence of Lala Lajpat Rai, Dadabhai Naoroji, Madame Bhikaji Cama and a handful of sympathetic British politicians. The three-storey building in Highgate, north London, still exists and is marked by a blue plaque, although it seems to be a private residence now.

To complement the hostel, Shyamji and his friend Sardar Sinh Ravaji Rana (a successful jeweller in Paris, popularly known as S.R. Rana) instituted three scholarships named after Maharana Pratap of Mewar, Mughal Emperor Akbar and Chhatrapati Shivaji. Interestingly, the students who received the scholarships had to pledge in writing that they would not join the British government service in India or elsewhere. The call for applications was published in the *Indian Sociologist* in December 1905, and Vinayak Savarkar applied for it a few weeks later. His application included a letter of recommendation from Tilak himself and, interestingly, the Fergusson College principal R.P. Paranjpe, who had earlier rusticated him. He got the scholarship.

Savarkar left Bombay for England aboard SS *Persia* in June 1906. He was given a tearful farewell by Yamuna and Babarao. This would be the last time he would see his firstborn son, Prabhakar, then eighteen months old. The route was through the Red Sea and the Suez Canal to Marseilles in France. From there, passengers would usually take a train to Paris and then Calais, before crossing the English Channel by ferry. The town of Marseilles had a special attraction for Savarkar, as his hero Mazzini had spent time there as an exile and had also established the first branch of Young Italy there in 1831. He could not have guessed then the circumstances under which he would return a few years later to this port town. He would not have been surprised, however, to learn that a letter from the Special Crime Branch, Poona, was also making its way at the same time to the India Office Crime Branch in London. The letter made it clear that Scotland Yard needed to keep an eye on a certain Vinayak Savarkar.

DUELS WITH SCOTLAND YARD

Savarkar was admitted to Gray's Inn in late July 1906, and began his legal studies. He also took up lodging at India House. Almost immediately he set up a branch of Abhinav Bharat and began to look for members. India House became a hive of revolutionary activity, with regular meetings and lectures held there. Savarkar would himself deliver some of the lectures, on topics ranging from contemporary international events to Sikh history. In the next few months, he recruited an extraordinary group of young men (there were very few female Indian students in London), who would leave a mark on India's struggle for Independence—Lala Hardayal, Madanlal Dhingra, V.V.S. Aiyar, Virendranath Chattopadhyay (nicknamed 'Chatto'), Pandurang Bapat and Bhai Parmanand, to name a few. Using Shyamji's contacts, he connected with a group in Paris, which included Madame Bhikaji Cama and S.R. Rana. It is not possible to write here about all the individuals inspired by Savarkar, but the reader does need to be introduced to a few of the key personalities.

Varahaneri Venkatesa Subramaniam Aiyar (V.V.S. Aiyar) was born in 1881 in a village in Madras Presidency. His father ran a small finance and audit business. VVS had been very concerned since childhood about the aggressive proselytization by Christian missionaries and their abusive invectives against Hinduism. He initially sought help from the Shankaracharya of Kanchi to bring recent converts back to the Hindu fold, but received no help. So he decided to deliver lectures to children and take them on temple tours. Having passed the pleaders' examination in Madras in 1902, he left for Rangoon (now Yangon), where he practised for a few years. In 1907, he moved to London to become a barrister and ended up in India House in search of a place that served tolerable vegetarian food. Aiyar was initially suspicious of Savarkar, but they soon became close friends as they were both studying law. He would become Savarkar's effective second-in-command.

Madanlal Dhingra was born in 1883 in Amritsar, where his father was a well-known eye specialist and civil surgeon. He was the sixth of seven children; two of his elder brothers were doctors and two were barristers. So this was a solidly upper-middle-class Punjabi family that had no obvious reason to oppose British rule. In 1906, Dhingra travelled to London to study civil engineering at University College. A lively and well-built man who liked singing, he easily attracted boisterous friends, both male and female. He was not known to have had any strong political views until he met Savarkar at India House.

Madame Bhikaji Cama was born in a wealthy Parsee family in Bombay in 1861; she was a lot older than her other siblings. Even as a student in Alexandra Parsi Girls' School, she seemed to take an inordinate interest in tales of heroic resistance to foreign invaders. Her father certainly did not approve of her support for the nascent freedom movement. In 1885, she was married to Rustom Cama, a lawyer from a well-established family. Unfortunately, Bhikaji continued to hold strong political views, much to the discomfort of her family. She even got infected by the plague in 1896, when she insisted on going out and doing relief work. Eventually, the marriage broke down and the couple was divorced in 1901.

Bhikaji moved to London between 1902 and 1907, and worked as Dadabhai Naoroji's private secretary. However, she then came under the influence of Shyamji and began to contribute to the *Indian Sociologist*. Her views became even more radical after she met Savarkar. She moved to Paris in 1907, where she set up a revolutionary group with S.R. Rana. Together they attended the International Socialist Congress in Stuttgart, where she not only gave a speech on the devastation caused by the British rule in India but unfurled a flag of free India. The flag had three horizontal bands in green, yellow and red, with 'Vande Mataram' embroidered in Devanagari in the middle band, a sun and moon on the lower band, and a string of lotuses on the top band. The overall design would be considered a bit too busy for today's taste. The speech and the flag so incensed delegates from the British Labour Party that Ramsay MacDonald staged a protest walkout.

The date 1 May 1907 marked the golden jubilee of the Revolt of 1857. It was observed in Britain through major events commemorating the heroism and sacrifices of British officers and soldiers. In plays, articles and editorials, the Indian rebels were presented as marauders and bandits. *The Daily Telegraph* ran a headline a few days later: 'Fifty Years Ago, This Week, an Empire Saved by Deeds of Heroism.'

Almost no Indian dared to openly challenge this narrative, except the Abhinav Bharat group in India House. As historian Vikram Sampath puts it, 'It is noteworthy that no political party or groups back in India organized any commemoration of such an important milestone of the nation's past and the task was left to a few young students in distant London.'[4] More than 200 people attended the event at India House. In a moving speech, Savarkar argued that 1857 was not a mere 'mutiny' but the 'First War of Indian Independence'—a rehearsal for a revolution that would overthrow the empire.

Given such open calls for rebellion, it should not be surprising that Scotland Yard kept a close watch on India House by sending detectives in plain clothes. The students were aware of this, as they could see random men loitering outside. Anyone who visits the place today will understand that it was always a quiet residential lane, and that there is no way of hanging around without looking suspicious. The detectives would sometimes follow an individual around the city. The students, therefore, took to mocking them by asking them for directions or speaking to them in familiar terms. This immensely annoyed the policemen. Savarkar also mastered the art of giving them the slip. He would walk along the road until he saw a single free taxi coming down it, and he would suddenly jump in. The detectives would have to wait until another taxi came along, by which time Savarkar had already made his getaway.

Scotland Yard next decided to place a couple of moles inside India House. One of them was Kiritkar, who claimed to have come to London to study dentistry. By virtue of being fluent in Marathi, he befriended Savarkar. However, it was soon clear that he had very little interest in dentistry but a lot of interest in the English maid who worked in India House. They had an open affair until she was eventually asked to leave, but Kiritkar found her accommodation nearby and carried on visiting her. Eventually, Savarkar and Aiyar decided to find out a bit more about the dentistry student. They first found out that he had not attended any classes after his first week. So when Kiritkar was away one evening, Aiyar entered his room using a master key and discovered a copy of his report to Scotland Yard. When Kiritkar returned, Aiyar held a revolver to his head and made him confess. After some discussion with the others, Savarkar decided to let Kiritkar stay in India House on the condition that the students would first read and edit his reports. One can imagine them sitting around the dinner table late at night, amusing themselves by inserting deliberately inaccurate information into the reports.

THE 1857 BOOK

One of the things Savarkar realized while in London was that the British were systematically rewriting Indian history in a way that bolstered their rule in India and reinforced the myth of white supremacy. A prime example of this manipulation was the narrative around the events of 1857, which tarred Indians as the villains. Savarkar decided to rectify this. In the author's note in his book *The Indian War of Independence 1857*, he stated, 'A nation that has no consciousness of its past has no future.'[5] He not only read all the available books written by British authors but also managed to sweet-talk his way into getting access to the library of the India Office. It contained many private papers, correspondence and files. He humoured the librarian by constantly berating the treachery of Indian sepoys and received full access to restricted papers. Scotland Yard did not realize what he was doing there until he had nearly finished his book.

The Indian War of Independence 1857 was originally written in Marathi. Savarkar wrote passionately about how Hindus and Muslims had risen up together against oppression by a foreign invader. Importantly, he again mentioned clearly that 1857 was just the 'great rehearsal' and that 'there slumbers a volcano under that surface'.[6] In other words, another revolt in India, and specifically in the British Indian Army, was only a matter of time. As we shall see, this was a powerful idea that would play an important role in shaping the long-term strategy of the revolutionaries.

As the book neared completion, Scotland Yard received one of its chapters from a mole in India House. Savarkar also noticed the missing chapter and quickly completed the manuscript. Then a copy was sent secretly to Babarao for printing in India. By this time, Scotland Yard had realized what was going on and the full network of British intelligence was alerted. The viceroy, Lord Minto, heard about the book and issued strict orders for it to not be allowed into India. Of course, the book was already in India, but Babarao was simply unable to find a printer willing to publish it. He was forced to send the manuscript to France and then to Germany, where a growing interest in Sanskrit learning meant that a couple of printers were at least familiar with the Devanagari script. However, they were not familiar with the Marathi language and did a shoddy job of printing it.

Back in London, Aiyar decided that it would be worthwhile to translate the book into English. With the help of Marathi-speaking members of Abhinav Bharat, Aiyar quickly translated the book. Again, the manuscript was sent to France and Germany for printing, but no one wanted to take it for fear of offending the British. Eventually, a small printer in Holland agreed. The revolutionaries spread rumours that the book was being published in France to keep the moles misinformed. Copies were then smuggled into India wrapped in the innocuous covers of books such as *Don Quixote* and *The Posthumous Papers of the Pickwick Club*. One box of such books was smuggled in by Sikandar Hayat Khan. Simultaneously, copies were sold to the Indian diaspora across the world—in Paris, London and all over the United States. Note that the book was not banned in Britain and was circulated widely in the Indian student community.

The book was an instant hit and would become almost required reading for those espousing a revolutionary path to Indian Independence. Bhikaji would get a second edition printed in France as well as translate it into French. A few years later, a third edition was printed in the United States by Lala Hardayal and sold openly. In the late 1920s, Bhagat Singh would secretly print another edition in India. Yet another edition was later printed by Rashbehari Bose in Japan. Thus, the book would have a big influence on generations of revolutionaries and, as we shall see, explains their strategy during the two World Wars.

AN EVENING AT THE IMPERIAL INSTITUTE

It was not just Scotland Yard that knew about the revolutionaries in India House. Revolutionaries of every shade in Europe were aware of it, and many well-known activists visited the hostel and met Savarkar and other Abhinav Bharat members. This included Irish nationalists and Russian communists. In mid-March 1909, an important Russian activist came to India House to meet Savarkar—Vladimir Ilich Lenin. What transpired between them, however, is not known.

Another well-known personality who visited India House was Mohandas Karamchand Gandhi (the moniker 'Mahatma' had not yet been used for him). There is an eyewitness account that the first meeting between the stalwarts did not go well. Savarkar was cooking prawns and had invited Gandhi to join his group for a meal. Given that several members of Abhinav Bharat were vegetarian, it is unlikely that he expected Gandhi to actually eat prawns. Nonetheless, Gandhi refused on grounds that he was a strict vegetarian and Savarkar is said to have retorted, 'Well, if you cannot eat with us, how on earth are you going to work with us?'[7]

The friction between the two was more than just a personality clash, or even a difference of opinion about the use of violence. The revolutionaries were very suspicious of Gandhi from the beginning. *Indian Sociologist* had been severely critical of Gandhi's open support of the British against the Zulus during the Bambatha Rebellion of 1906 in South Africa. Thousands of Zulus would be massacred. These suspicions were reinforced by Gandhi's active recruitment of Indian soldiers for the British cause during the First World War. It is important to recognize these real tensions within India's freedom struggle, as they are often presented as mere personality clashes. The independence movement was made up of a large number of disparate world views, and the sequence of events was impacted by their divergence and convergence at different points of time. This was true even within camps. In turn, these were driven by a variety of factors, ranging from ideology to the social dynamics of the followers of each group. As with any large movement, the freedom movement is not a story of linear progression but peppered with mistakes, U-turns, the vagaries of fortune and leaders working at cross-purposes.

In early 1909, the revolutionary network began to ramp up its activities. Sikandar Hayat Khan and Mirza Abbas procured twenty Browning pistols and a large cache of ammunition from Paris. These were packed into a false-bottomed box and taken to Bombay by Chaturbhuj Amin, the chef at India House. Amin successfully delivered the pistols to the Abhinav Bharat group in Maharashtra. Unfortunately, the police found out about this and raided Babarao's house in Nashik. Although they did not find the pistols, they found a copy of the Russian bomb manual that Hemchandra Das and Pandurang Bapat had acquired in Paris. The police were already aware of the manual, as it had been found in Barin Ghosh's Maniktola garden house.

Vinayak heard of Babarao's arrest around the same time that he heard that his son Prabhakar had died of smallpox. Babarao was convicted and eventually sent away to the Cellular Jail in the Andamans. It was a difficult time for the Savarkar family. The London press was full of stories about the activities in India House and Vinayak's admission to the Bar at Gray's Inn was indefinitely postponed for obviously political reasons. The key person who had blocked his admission to the Bar was Sir William Curzon Wyllie, a former officer of the British Indian Army, who now served as aide-de-camp to Lord George Hamilton, the secretary of state for India. Part of his role was keeping an eye on Indians in London, whether visiting princes or students. He would occasionally invite members of the community, including those from India House, for a friendly meal and pump them for information. It was he who had created a file on Vinayak Savarkar and passed it on to Gray's Inn.

The National Indian Association held one of its regular evening parties on 1 July 1909. The idea was to encourage interaction between Indians and the British elite. The event was held at the Imperial Institute in South Kensington. Madanlal Dhingra arrived punctually and chatted with many guests. It was quite late in the evening when William Curzon Wyllie turned up. As he walked around exchanging pleasantries with various students, he stopped for a conversation with Dhingra. All of a sudden, Dhingra pulled out a small Colt and shot him point-blank four times. There was pandemonium in the room even as Dhingra turned the gun on himself, but was overpowered. His glasses had fallen off in the scuffle, and, unfazed, he told his captors, 'Wait, let me just put my spectacles on!'

Investigations would later find that Dhingra had been preparing for several months and practising shooting at a range on Tottenham Court Road. His original target was Lord Curzon, the viceroy who had spearheaded the Partition of Bengal in 1905. Having narrowly missed killing him at a similar event, he decided to target Curzon Wyllie at the Imperial Institute. The buildings of the Imperial Institute no longer exist but for a tower (Queen's Tower) that stands today within the campus of Imperial College.

The assassination drew a lot of condemnation from the British as well as prominent Indians. Dhingra's family publicly disowned him and Gopal Krishna Gokhale stated that his act had 'blackened the Indian name'. Gandhi wrote a stinging article criticizing Dhingra. On 5 July, the Indian community of London congregated at Caxton Hall under the chairmanship of the Aga Khan to discuss how they could 'rehabilitate themselves among their fellow-subjects of the Empire'.[8] A resolution expressing 'horror and indignation' was put to the vote. It was expected to be unanimously adopted, when a young man jumped up and screamed, 'No! Not Unanimously!' It was Savarkar, who had turned up to defend his friend. He was immediately attacked and punched. Even with his spectacles broken and blood streaming down his face, Savarkar stood up on a chair and announced that he would oppose the resolution until the last drop of his blood. He and Aiyar were then thrown out of the hall. Three decades later, the same venue would witness another major incident.

The trial began a few days later. The prosecution put forward a heap of evidence and a large number of witnesses. Dhingra stood silently through it all. When the judge finally asked him if he wished to defend himself, Dhingra said that he merely wanted to read out a statement:

> I do not wish to say anything in defence of myself, but simply to prove the justice of my deed. As for myself, no English court of

law has any authority to arrest and detain me in prison, or pass sentence of death on me. That is the reason I do not have any counsel to defend me. And I maintain that if it is patriotic in an Englishman to fight against the Germans if they were to occupy this country, it is much more justifiable in my case to fight against the English. I hold the English people responsible for the murder of 80 millions of the Indian people ... Just as the Germans have no right to occupy this country, the English people have no right to occupy India...[9]

The courtroom heard this in a hushed silence before the judge pronounced him guilty and sentenced him to death by hanging. With Dhingra's family having disowned him, Savarkar was virtually the only one who went to meet him in prison. It was an emotional meeting, where Dhingra revealed that his final wish was to be cremated in strict accordance with Hindu rites. He also passed on a final statement that the revolutionaries managed to publish, with some difficulty, in the *Daily News:*

> I admit, the other day, I attempted to shed English blood as a humble revenge for the inhuman hangings and deportations of patriotic Indian youths. In this attempt I have consulted none but my own conscience; I have conspired with none but my own duty.
>
> I believe that a nation held in bondage with the help of foreign bayonets is in a perpetual state of war. Since open battle is impossible for a disarmed race, I attacked by surprise; since guns were denied to me, I drew forth my pistol and fired.
>
> As a Hindu, I feel that a wrong done to my country is an insult to God. Poor in health and intellect, a son like myself has nothing to offer to the Mother but his own blood, and so I have sacrificed

the same on her altar. Her cause is the cause of Shri Rama. Her service is the service of Sri Krishna. This War of Independence will continue between India and England so long as the Hindu and the English races last (if this present unnatural relation does not cease) ... Vande Mataram.[10]

On the morning of 17 August 1909, a group of Indian students gathered outside Pentonville Jail. At the stroke of nine, Dhingra was hanged. He was twenty-five, and is said to have embraced martyrdom with a smile. There is evidence that leading British politicians such as Winston Churchill and Lloyd George privately expressed their admiration for him. His body was not handed over for a Hindu cremation as per his last wish, but was buried inside the jail. His family had already disowned him. Nonetheless, Gyanchand Verma performed all the Vedic rituals for him. Madanlal Dhingra's remains were brought back to India in December 1976. A statue in his memory today stands in his hometown, Amritsar, at one end of a recently pedestrianized road that leads to Jallianwala Bagh.

SS MOREA

One of the predictable outcomes of the Wyllie assassination was that India House was closed down. In the last meeting of Abhinav Bharat at the venue, Savarkar made an impassioned speech in Dhingra's memory. However, he and his associates were now homeless, and it was difficult to find anyone who would rent out their premises to them in London. With Scotland Yard now keeping a close watch on all their movements, Savarkar was forced to share a dingy room in a London slum. Meanwhile, his health deteriorated.

Back in India, however, the Abhinav Bharat network had ramped up attacks on colonial officials. Two bombs were thrown at the viceroy Lord Minto in November 1909 when he was visiting Gujarat. The bombs were thrown as the procession with Lord and Lady Minto was making its way from Ahmedabad station towards Raipur Gate.[11] The bombs failed to explode, but the message was clear that even the senior-most British officials were no longer safe. It was one thing to attack the plague commissioner and quite another to target the viceroy so publicly. Intelligence agencies were also discovering that the Bengal and Maharashtra revolutionaries were closely working together. The accused, Mohanlal Pandya, was linked to both Barin Ghosh's Anushilan Samiti and to Abhinav Bharat.

Just a few weeks later, another young member of Abhinav Bharat—Anantrao Laxman Kanhere—assassinated Arthur Jackson, the district collector of Nashik. Jackson had not only arrested Babarao, but had paraded him handcuffed through the streets of Nashik to intimidate the population. Importantly, the assassination was carried out with a Browning pistol from the cache that had been smuggled in from Europe. Unsurprisingly, the police saw the Savarkar family at the heart of these developments. Vinayak's younger brother Narayanrao was soon arrested as part of the investigations and subjected to severe torture in prison to extract information.

With both his brothers in police custody, it was obvious to Vinayak that he was next. In early January 1910, he moved to Paris, where he was welcomed by S.R. Rana and Bhikaji Cama. It was a relief to be among friends in an environment that was not actively hostile. Over the next few months, Savarkar published several fiery articles and wrote a new book titled *History of the Sikhs*. Three copies of the manuscript were made, but with surveillance heightened, the book was never printed. The manuscript has been lost and we only know about it from references in Savarkar's memoirs.

Compared to the student activists of London, members of the Paris group were mostly older and well off. S.R. Rana, for instance, was a successful businessman and lived in a comfortable apartment at 46 Rue Blanche, where he would host the likes of Lala Lajpat Rai, Rabindranath Tagore, Bhai Parmanand and Vithalbhai Patel.[12] The apartment block still exists, although neither the current occupants nor anyone in the local Indian community seems to be aware of its significance. When I requested one of its current inhabitants to take a photo of me on the doorstep, the young man looked at me very suspiciously.

Living with this group, and in relative safety and comfort, Savarkar's health got better. However, the colonial government in India wanted him extradited and made out a prima facie case against him. A warrant was issued against him in London and he was declared a fugitive. Note that the British wanted to try Savarkar in India, where they could use draconian laws and stacked courts, whereas in England he would have got away with a light sentence.

Despite being fully aware of the situation, Savarkar decided to return to London in March 1910. Shyamji and the others warned him against it, but he was insistent. It is not clear why he made this decision, given the obvious dangers, but it is likely that he felt guilty about living in relative comfort in Paris while many of his followers were facing arrest in London. Whatever his reasoning, it turned out to be an unfortunate decision. As soon as he got off the train at Victoria station, he found a large contingent of policemen waiting for him. He was immediately arrested and taken to the Bow Street police station. There is a photograph of

Savarkar in a striped suit taken soon after his arrest. His obviously hopeless situation does not seem to have diminished the fiery defiance in his eyes.

Vinayak was sent to Brixton prison while the formalities of his extradition to India were worked out. Even as the court hearings were taking place, Irish revolutionaries of Sinn Fein decided to rescue him. They had noticed that Savarkar was taken to court in a certain cab and decided to waylay it before making a getaway by car. On the appointed day, the Irish team did stop the cab but discovered that it only contained the detectives, but not Savarkar. Evidently, British intelligence had received a tip-off and had sent Savarkar by a different vehicle. Thus, what may have been a very dramatic escape was prevented. Winston Churchill, then secretary of state for home affairs, signed the extradition order in June 1910.

Under heavy security, Vinayak was put on board the Peninsular and Oriental liner SS *Morea* on 1 July. Two British police officers, an Indian police officer and two Indian head constables were on the ship to keep an eye on the revolutionary. Indeed, they never let him out of sight and he even had to use the lavatory with the door slightly ajar.

SS *Morea* made a scheduled two-day stop at Marseilles on 7 and 8 July. The police officers were aware of the Indian revolutionary groups operating in France and were edgy. They kept him in their line of sight for all of the first day and even ensured that he had his evening bath in a bathroom that did not have a porthole. Next morning, however, Savarkar made an unusual request—to use the lavatory at 6.15 a.m. One of the British officers sleepily took him to the nearest toilet and left him with the two constables. They did not pay attention to the fact that it had a porthole. They also did not stop him from locking the door from the inside.

Savarkar lost no time and immediately opened the porthole. He was a small, thin man and began to squeeze himself out. By the time he was halfway out, one of the constables looked into the toilet through a crack and realized what was happening. The two tried to break down the door but it was locked solid. So they raised an alarm. By now Vinayak had managed to jump off and swim to the quay. He then began to run towards the town to look for the getaway car that was supposed to be waiting for him. Sadly it was not there. An exhausted Savarkar could run no further, and his pursuers were closing in. Meanwhile, Brigadier Pesque of the French Gendarmerie Maritime arrived and arrested him. Savarkar desperately tried to explain to him that he was a political prisoner seeking asylum in France, but the Frenchman did not understand English and promptly handed him back to the party from SS *Morea*.

The getaway car with Bhikaji Cama, Aiyar and Chatto arrived just moments after Savarkar had been handed back. It is unclear why they had been delayed—perhaps a closed railway level crossing or stopping for tea on the way. They had come within inches of pulling off a spectacular escape and must have felt terrible when they realized what had happened. Madame Cama now raised the issue of allowing foreign officials to drag away a political refugee from French soil as an insult to French sovereignty. It immediately became a cause célèbre in the French press, and the French ambassador to Britain demanded that Savarkar be handed back to France. The issue was hotly debated in the French Chamber of Deputies. With diplomatic temperatures rising, the matter was sent for arbitration to the international tribunal at The Hague. Savarkar was now an internationally recognized figure and his case attracted a lot of attention not just in India and Britain, but all over Europe.

The colonial administration in India, meanwhile, had fast-tracked Savarkar's trial by a special tribunal in Bombay. His fiery speeches and articles were presented against him, and he was also accused of sending the cache of Browning pistols used in the Nashik assassination. His lawyers first tried to delay the proceedings by arguing that the international arbitration should be settled first, but were overruled. Several witnesses turned hostile and accused the police of extracting testimonies under coercion. Nonetheless, on 30 January 1911, the special tribunal ruled that Vinayak Savarkar was guilty of abetment to murder and sentenced him to double transportation for life—i.e., fifty years of incarceration at the dreaded Cellular Jail in the Andamans.

Everything now depended on the outcome at The Hague. The French argued their case strongly, but on 24 February, the case was decided in Britain's favour. There was no escape left. To rub it in, the jailors forced Vinayak to wear an iron plaque around his neck at all times, with '1960' written on it. It was meant to remind him of the year he would be released. When the superintendent saw Vinayak's sad expression, he mocked him, 'Don't worry, His Majesty's benign government will release you in 1960 for sure.' Vinayak replied, 'Death is kinder; it may release me earlier!' Then they both laughed.[13]

While he waited to be shipped to the Andamans, he had a visitor in Dongri Jail. It was his young wife Yamuna. Tearfully, Vinayak consoled her. For all they knew, it would be the last time they would see each other. A few days later, he was sent by train to Madras and then by ship to the Andamans. He was handcuffed, his legs were chained and he was roped to a policeman. After what had happened in Marseilles, the authorities were taking no chances.

4

THE GHADAR

The constant attacks and the visible spread of revolutionary ideas among the youth finally convinced the colonial authorities that some concessions had to be made to the Indians. These came in the form of the Indian Councils Act introduced in November 1909 (commonly known as the Morley-Minto Reforms). It provided for somewhat greater representation of Indians through elected members in legislative councils, although it also insidiously introduced a separate electorate for Muslims. The reins were still firmly in the hands of the British, but Indians would get more of a say on many issues.

It was widely recognized at that time that the changes had been forced by the revolutionaries, rather than by pressure from a badly divided Congress. Even Gandhi acknowledged this in an interview at the time: 'England is, I believe, easily influenced by the use of gunpowder.'[1] Thus, it is fair to say that the first generation of revolutionary leaders had achieved quite a lot within a decade—they had provided the movement with intellectual underpinnings, established a large and growing network, and extracted concrete concessions from the British. Nonetheless, they had still not threatened the foundations of the colonial edifice. That changed with the arrival of the second generation of revolutionary leaders. Enter Rashbehari Bose.

CHANDNI CHOWK, 1912

Rashbehari was born in a remote village in Bengal in 1886 but grew up in his maternal uncle's house in the French enclave of Chandernagore. As we have seen, the enclave was a hotbed of revolutionary activity and it should not be surprising that a teenage Rashbehari was exposed to the activities of the Anushilan Samiti. He was particularly influenced by the ideas of Swami Vivekananda and Aurobindo Ghosh. His father, Binod Behari Bose, was a government clerk working at a government press in Simla (now Shimla). Realizing that his son was not interested in pursuing academic studies, Binod Behari arranged for a job for his son as a copyeditor at the press. Rashbehari did not like the job, but used the opportunity to hone his English-language skills. Some time later, he worked briefly at the Pasteur Institute in the nearby town of Kasauli.

In 1906, Rashbehari got himself a job as a laboratory assistant at the Forest Research Institute (FRI) in Dehradun. At that time, FRI did not have the grand campus that one sees today, but was a more modest facility in town (near what is now Tibet Bazaar). FRI still has an office at the location and there is a two-storey red-brick building at the back. The building is now semi-abandoned, but it is most likely the place where Rashbehari worked.

While in Dehradun, Rashbehari made friends with Jitendra Mohan Chatterjee from Saharanpur.[2] Chatterjee was part of a network of revolutionaries in Punjab and the United Provinces (now roughly Uttar Pradesh). The Punjab group was led by Sardar Ajit Singh, and included his brother Kissen Singh (Bhagat Singh's father) and Sufi Amba Prasad. They were in touch with Savarkar's group in London through Hardayal, who was then studying at Oxford. Similarly, there was a group in Delhi led by Amir Chand, a schoolmaster. Rashbehari came to know some of these individuals.

Although remembered today as Bhagat Singh's uncle, Ajit Singh is an important historical character in his own right. He was involved in organizing peasant farmer movements in the first decade of the twentieth century and later led a life of adventure that took him across the world. Although practising Sikhs, Ajit Singh's family members were ardent followers of the Arya Samaj. It may come as a surprise to today's readers, but the Arya Samaj and the Sikhs had close links at that time. When they drifted apart in the later decades, it was over linguistic rather than theological disagreements (the Arya Samaj wanted to promote Hindi written in the Devanagari script while the Sikhs preferred Punjabi in the Gurmukhi script).

In 1907, the colonial administration decided to crack down on nationalists in Punjab, and sent both Lala Lajpat Rai and Ajit Singh to prison in Mandalay, Burma (now Myanmar). British intelligence continued to gather more information on the clandestine web and arrested several others over the next two years. At some point, Jitendra Mohan Chatterjee realized that he had been compromised and decided to leave the country immediately. However, just before leaving, he summoned Rashbehari and hurriedly gave him a detailed overview of the existing revolutionary network. With senior leaders suddenly unavailable, Rashbehari was now the only one who understood the linkages between various groups in north-western India. Rashbehari had, meanwhile, forged links with the Anushilan Samiti unit in his hometown, Chandernagore. Thus, a Bengali laboratory assistant in Dehradun became the nerve centre of revolutionary activity. Interestingly, the British had no idea about his nocturnal activities and his superiors at FRI thought of him as a loyal and diligent worker. Over time, he was even promoted to the position of head clerk.

Rashbehari made a couple of trips to Chandernagore in 1911. During this time, he became closely acquainted with Moti Lal Roy, a close associate of Aurobindo Ghosh, and was deeply influenced by the latter's religious views.[3] He also began to study the Bhagawad Gita. Sitting in the room where Aurobindo Ghosh had spent time in hiding, Rashbehari mooted the idea of carrying out a major strike against the British. The plan was to assassinate Viceroy Hardinge—it was decided that the attack would be carried out when he entered Delhi in a grand viceregal procession in December 1912 to mark the shift of the capital from Calcutta to Delhi. Bose asked for an accomplice to help him, and the Anushilan Samiti chose Basanta Kumar Biswas. His ancestor, Digambar Biswas, had been one of the leaders of the Indigo Rebellion of 1859 against the forced cultivation of the cash crop.

Rashbehari took Biswas to Dehradun disguised as his cook and gave him several months of mental and physical training. He then arranged for him to work in Lahore as a compounder in a dispensary owned by a member of the network. The date of the viceregal procession was 23 December 1912, and the revolutionary team assembled in Amir Chand's house in Delhi two days earlier.

The ceremonial entry into Delhi (what we now know as Old Delhi) was a pompous affair, with horses and elephants, intended to impress the Indians. It was to make its way through Chandni Chowk to the Red Fort, reminiscent of Mughal-era cavalcades. On the morning of the procession, Rashbehari and Biswas (dressed as a woman) positioned themselves at Chandni Chowk's Katra Dhulia wholesale cloth market. The traditional market still exists and it is just across from the famous Parathewali Gali. We know Rashbehari loved food and it is quite possible that he treated himself and Biswas to a couple of parathas while they waited. Some of today's traders at Katra Dhulia are descendants of those who witnessed the incident—they recalled being told about it by elders in their family.

Around 11.45 a.m., the procession reached Katra Dhulia. Lord Hardinge and his wife were on the third elephant, and Biswas accurately threw the bomb. The explosion killed an attendant and severely injured the viceroy. In the ensuing commotion, Rashbehari and Biswas left the area and quietly made their way to the railway station. The latter had removed his disguise along the way. There were policemen looking for suspects everywhere but no one knew who they were looking for. So Biswas took a train to Lahore and Rashbehari to Dehradun.

On reaching Dehradun, Rashbehari organized a meeting at FRI to condemn the attack in the harshest terms! He was so convincing that when Hardinge visited Dehradun a few months later, he was put in charge of the welcome committee of local Indians. One cannot fault Rashbehari's sense of humour.

The incident shook the empire: The revolutionaries had nearly killed the viceroy himself at an event meant as a display of British power. What made it worse was that the authorities had no idea who carried it out.

Rashbehari, meanwhile, carried on with his duties at FRI as if nothing had happened. This changed after Biswas carried out a second attack in May 1913 on a British official in Lahore. This time Biswas lost his nerve and the bomb ended up on a road, and a passer-by was killed. Although Biswas escaped from the venue, the police quickly realized that the picric acid bomb was exactly the same design as the one thrown in Chandni Chowk. A huge operation was launched to hunt down the suspects. The net began to close around the group, and eventually several members were arrested. Biswas was arrested when, against Rashbehari's advice, he went back to Bengal to attend his father's funeral. It was his uncle who informed the police. Biswas, Amir Chand, Avadh Behari and Bal Mukund were hanged for their involvement in the attacks.

Biswas's ancestral home is in a picturesque rural area, half an hour's drive from Kishnanagar town in Nadia district. Part of the large house built by Digambar Biswas, the leader of Indigo Revolt, still stands at the site—although it was in a dilapidated condition when I visited it in August 2021. The section of the house where Biswas was born collapsed many decades ago, but there is a small memorial at the spot. The area did not have proper roads until well into the twentieth century, and access was originally through a rivulet behind the house. Some from the Biswas family still live there. They are not well off, but one can see a dignified pride in their family's role in resisting colonial occupation. Ironically, the uncle's family not only prospered under British rule but remains politically powerful to this day.

The colonial government now gave itself draconian powers under the Indian Criminal Law Amendment Act and the Defence of India Act. There was a public outcry, but the Loyalists who dominated the new legislative assembly put up little resistance. When Hardinge asked Gokhale what he would do if all the British officials one day just decided to go home, the latter replied that he would telegraph them before they reached Aden to come back![4]

Rashbehari soon realized that it was a matter of time before the police closed in on him, so in August 1913 he shifted to Chandernagore. It was around this time that he reconnected with Sachindra Nath Sanyal of Varanasi as well as Jyotindra Nath Mukherjee (popularly known as Bagha Jatin). A few days later, Rashbehari, Bagha Jatin and another prominent revolutionary, Amarendra Nath Chatterjee, met secretly under the trees of the Panchavati garden in Dakshineshwar. The location is significant, as it is in the grounds of the famous Kali temple and marks the place where the saint Ramakrishna Paramahamsa, guru of Swami Vivekananda, used to meditate. Here the revolutionaries decided that the time had come to organize a mass rebellion modelled on the Revolt of 1857. They also reached out to Aurobindo Ghosh in Pondicherry and received his blessings.[5]

Sachindra Nath Sanyal (henceforth shortened to Sachin Sanyal) was born in 1893 into a Bengali family that had settled generations earlier in Varanasi (also called Benares or Kashi). His grandfather and great-grandfather were renowned Vedic scholars, who were considered among the leading authorities of their time on the Rig Veda and on the Nyaya school of Hindu philosophy (i.e., the rationalist school). The Sanyals were originally from Belur in Bengal and had been close to Rani Rashmoni, the wealthy merchant who not only built the Dakshineshwar Kali temple but also invested in religious and scholarly institutions in Varanasi. Having settled in Varanasi's Madanpura area, they intermarried with other Bengali families such as the Lahiris, who had settled in the neighbourhood. Thus, in three generations, the Sanyal–Lahiri clan came to have a web of family and friends in the narrow lanes of this part of Varanasi. The revolutionaries would soon exploit this labyrinth.

Like many educated Bengalis of their time, Sachin Sanyal's ancestors had watched with concern the political, economic and cultural domination of India by the British. As discussed earlier, this had elicited many responses, ranging from that of the Westernizing Brahmos to that of the orthodox. The Sanyal–Lahiri clan was part of a third response—that of modernizing revivalists, who agreed with the Brahmos on the need for social and educational modernization but did not wish to compromise on cultural traditions. Thus, they were quick to embrace the English language and, in 1853, built the city's first 'modern' school called Bengali Tola Intercollege (it still exists). At the same time, the family was also invested in promoting and spreading Indic ideas. Sachin Sanyal's granduncle Shyama Charan Lahiri, popularly known as Lahiri Mahashaya, is still revered for giving kriya yoga its modern form and spreading its practice widely; it was earlier an esoteric practice known only to a few.[6]

Sachin Sanyal founded a branch of the Anushilan Samiti in Varanasi in 1908. The akhada had a small open area with a few trees, a platform and a room.[7] Young men gathered there to practise wrestling, boxing, the use of daggers and so on. The room had a small library that contained religious and revolutionary literature, and there were regular lectures on the Bhagawad Gita, Indian history and international revolutionaries such as Garibaldi. Following the arrest of Anushilan Samiti members in Bengal, Sanyal changed the name of the group to Young Men's Association to stay under the radar. Members would later recall that the group would sit together on some evenings to chant the last hymn of the Rig Veda, which ends with the following lines:

> *Common your resolve, common your hearts;*
> *Let your thoughts be common, and together may you succeed.*

Sanyal and Rashbehari had first met in 1911 or 1912, and Sanyal probably had some small involvement in the Chandni Chowk bombing. However, it was really in 1913 that he became Rashbehari's chief lieutenant and co-conspirator. When they met in Chandernagore in August of that year, Rashbehari had already realized that the police would eventually locate him in the French enclave. So he decided to shift his base to Varanasi, where the Sanyal clan could hide him. Anyone who has visited the Madanpura area of Varanasi will know that it is a warren of medieval lanes and by-lanes; old buildings connected in myriad ways through internal doors, interconnected roofs and hidden courtyards. It is not easy for anyone, including police informers, to operate here without being noticed by the locals and allowing for time to escape. Rashbehari, nonetheless, took the precaution of moving houses from time to time.

It was in the winding lanes of Bengali Tola, Madanpura, that Rashbehari and Sanyal began to put together a plan for instigating a large-scale revolt in the British Indian Army. A steady stream of trusted revolutionaries visited the effective headquarters in Sanyal's ancestral home, including Vishnu Ganesh Pingle from Poona, Pratul Chandra Ganguli from Dacca and Bagha Jatin. Although they had no way of predicting the sheer scale of the First World War, they must have sensed that the gathering clouds in Europe would provide them an opportunity.

THE SIKHS IN NORTH AMERICA

Following the death of Maharaja Ranjit Singh in 1839, his kingdom quickly descended into turmoil as members of the Punjabi nobility fought among themselves. Eventually, a five-year-old Duleep Singh was placed on the throne. Defeats in the First Anglo-Sikh War of 1845–46 and in the Second Anglo-Sikh War of 1848–49 resulted in the East India Company occupying Punjab. Despite fresh memories of a bitter war, the Sikhs remained loyal to the British cause during the Revolt of 1857. Therefore, the colonial administration decided that the Sikh elite, and more generally the Punjabi elite, could be useful native allies.

As part of this strategy, the British invested systematically in a Sikh identity, which was distinct from its Hindu roots. The initial effort was to spread Christianity among the Sikhs. Duleep Singh was converted to Christianity and sent away to England, where he was given the comfortable life of a country gentleman. However, he was not allowed to return to India and connect with his former subjects. Although the British continued to support missionaries in Punjab, they soon recognized that a softer approach was needed. Just like a section of the Bengali elite was won over through favourable access to Western education and government jobs, the Punjabi elite was given favourable enrolment in the army, titles, government contracts and land grants in canal-irrigated areas. The revolutionary writer Lala Hardayal would dub this as 'social conquest'.

Meanwhile, the wider population rapidly became pauperized. Six famines ravaged Punjab in the first fifty years of British rule. The simmering resentments led to the Kuka Rebellion of 1872 by Namdhari Sikhs. It was quickly crushed but socio-economic conditions worsened. Government records show that 3 million people perished in the province from epidemics between 1897 and 1918.[8] In the first decade of the twentieth century, inspired by Bal Gangadhar Tilak's efforts in Maharashtra, Sardar Ajit Singh formed the Bharat Mata Society and began to mobilize the peasantry. Recognizing the threat, the colonial authorities deported Lala Lajpat Rai and Ajit Singh to Mandalay in 1907. This only added to the feeling of discontent, which spread to a growing diaspora in North America.

The building of railway lines and the extension of farming on the west coast of North America sucked in a significant number of Indian workers in the 1900s. It is estimated that there were about 10,000 Indians along the Pacific coast of Canada and the United States in 1910. This included a small number of Indian students who had come to study in Californian universities, but most were Punjabi Sikhs drawn from modest farming backgrounds. They lived eight to ten in a log cabin and developed a reputation for hard work. Some of these Indians became quite successful as farmers and contractors. Jwala Singh, for instance, came to be known as the 'Potato King' of California and amassed a significant fortune.

Not surprisingly, the immigrants began to grow roots in the new country and started to invite their families to join them. The Canadian government suddenly woke up to the possibility that a growing Indian population could permanently settle in British Columbia. Blatantly racist laws were introduced to stem the inflow. Although other Asians also faced racism, things were worse for Indians. For instance, an order-in-council in 1908 laid down that an immigrant from India was required to possess at least $200 on arrival, whereas the requirement was only $40 for a Japanese immigrant.[9] The Indian migrants knew exactly what was being done, as they had faced the same thing earlier in Australia. Former soldiers of the British Indian Army felt particularly insulted by an empire for which they had risked their lives in various colonial wars. They began to organize themselves through a network of gurudwaras. Since many of them came from villages in Punjab that had been part of Ajit Singh's movement, they were already familiar with the ideas of the revolutionaries.

Their efforts at mobilization were given a boost in 1907 by the arrival of Harnam Singh Sahri and Taraknath Das. Both of them were educated and, therefore, capable of articulating the aspirations of the migrants. Taraknath Das was an active member of the Dacca Anushilan Samiti and had escaped to the United States ostensibly to study, before making his way to Vancouver. Taraknath was soon involved in organizing protests against racist laws targeting Indians. He also began to publish a periodical named *Free Hindustan* on the same lines as Shyamji's *Indian Sociologist*. Harnam Singh was an ex-soldier from the village of Sahri in Hoshiarpur district of Punjab. Like Ajit Singh, he was a Sikh involved in the Arya Samaj movement. He began to publish a Punjabi monthly in Gurmukhi script named *Swadesh Sewak* (Servant of the Motherland).

The British intelligence network in both India and Canada was aware of what was happening and decided that something had to be done to contain it. The job was given to William Hopkinson, who had previously worked for the police in Calcutta before moving to Canada. Born in India, he was proficient in both Hindi and Punjabi. His brief was to infiltrate the Indian community, particularly the gurudwaras, to gather information and subvert any anti-British movement from the inside. He soon recruited a number of informants, such as Bela Singh and Arjan Singh.

Their first target was Taraknath, who had been publishing articles exhorting Sikh troops to rise up against the British. He was expelled from Canada. He moved back to the United States, where he continued to publish *Free Hindustan* with the support of Irish nationalists based in Seattle and New York. Meanwhile, the Punjabi community in British Columbia formed two organizations—the United India League and the Khalsa Diwan Society. They were both headquartered in the same gurudwara in Vancouver and had several common members. But the former was more concerned with socio-political issues of the wider Indian community while the latter was more concerned with specifically Sikh religious issues.

Hopkinson saw the establishment of these organizations as a major threat and informed his superiors. He was soon provided significant resources to penetrate the gurudwaras to provide support for pro-British groups within the Sikhs as well as cause internal divisions by instigating puritanical Sikhs against more eclectic members of the community. At the same time, the Canadian authorities continued to make immigration ever more difficult for Indians. By 1911, it became virtually impossible to bring one's wife and children over from India. Given the increasingly hostile treatment, many Indians decided to leave Canada and move down the coast to the United States. Thus, California became a hub of anti-British sentiment. This was the backdrop when Hardayal arrived in San Francisco.

YUGANTAR ASHRAM

Lala Hardayal was born in 1884 in Delhi, the youngest of four brothers. He earned a bachelor's degree in Sanskrit from St Stephen's College, Delhi, before doing a master's from Punjab

University, Lahore. He was academically gifted and topped both the courses. Even as an undergraduate, he became a critic of Christian missionaries, who used their control over academic institutions for proselytization. During his time in Lahore, he came in contact with Lala Lajpat Rai and Bhai Parmanand, who drew him into the Arya Samaj fold.

In 1905, Hardayal won a scholarship to study history in London and, in 1907, became a Boden scholar at St John's College, Oxford. (As an aside, I was part of the same institution more than eight decades later.) Like many contemporary Indian students in Britain, Hardayal was deeply influenced by Vinayak Savarkar's lectures at India House. He soon became an active member of Abhinav Bharat. When he returned briefly to India in 1908, he already had a reputation as a revolutionary thinker. He met several of the nationalist leaders of north India, including Lala Lajpat Rai, who had just returned from Mandalay. A few months later, Lajpat Rai received a tip-off that the government was planning to arrest Hardayal. The latter was reluctant to leave, as his wife was pregnant with their first child. However, with the police cracking down heavily on anyone suspected of having revolutionary links, Hardayal was forced to leave the country. He would never again meet his wife or ever see his child, a daughter.

Hardayal now moved to Paris, where he and Madame Cama published a revolutionary paper, *Bande Mataram*, named after the periodical edited by Aurobindo Ghosh. However, after the failure to rescue Savarkar in Marseilles, Hardayal began to feel restless. He travelled to Algiers and then Martinique in the Caribbean. In 1911, he arrived in San Francisco and started to live close to the University of California, Berkeley. Fame of his scholarship soon spread and he was invited to deliver lectures at Stanford on philosophy, Sanskrit and Indian history. He also became the focus of the Indian student community on the West Coast. An informal group called Nalanda Club was set up in a rented apartment in Berkeley and members would meet regularly to discuss India-related issues.

Hardayal's growing activities were made possible by the generous financial support of the newly rich Punjabi community in California, particularly the 'Potato King' Jwala Singh. Sadly, almost no one in India or North America today remembers this remarkable pioneer, but Jwala Singh played the same role of benefactor in North America as Shyamji did in Europe. He and his friends also funded six Guru Gobind scholarships to help bring talented Indians to study in West Coast universities. Most of the recipients became part of the revolutionary network forming around Hardayal.

By 1912, Hardayal's network started to spread beyond students into the migrant worker community. This expansion was made possible by the efforts of Sohan Singh Bhakna, a forty-one-year-old who had built a network among Punjabi migrants in the Portland area of Oregon. Bhakna was a Namdhari Sikh and had links to Ajit Singh's farmer movement, so he was already primed for the ideas of the revolutionary movement. A large number would gather to hear Hardayal when he visited Portland in March 1913. Monarch Mills alone, where Bhakna worked, employed 200 Indians. There was widespread enthusiasm in the audience for actively supporting the revolutionary movement in India to oust the British.

With Jwala Singh's support, a formal association headed by Bhakna and Hardayal was established. It was headquartered at a rented house in 436 Hill Street, San Francisco. The house served as a gathering place, printing house and accommodation for a small group of volunteers. The house was named Yugantar Ashram after Barin Ghosh's revolutionary paper *Jugantar*. Swami Vivekananda's younger brother, Bhupendra Nath Dutta, one of the editors of the original paper, would soon visit the ashram.

By now readers will have begun to realize the scale of the intellectual, personal and organizational linkages between the various revolutionary groups operating inside and outside India. This was not a set of isolated individuals but a well-knit web of people connected in multiple ways to each other.

The ashram hosted events and acted as a meeting place, but its most important function was the publication of a weekly called *The Ghadar* (The Uprising). Published in Urdu, and in Punjabi in the Gurmukhi script, the paper was announced on 1 November 1913 as: 'Today there begins in foreign lands, but in the language of the country, a war against English rule.' In case anyone was still in doubt about its aims and objectives, the top of the front page was inscribed with 'Vande Mataram' and '*Angrezi Raj ka Dushman* (Enemy of the British Rule)'.

The paper contained news and opinion pieces that would be of interest to the Indian diaspora not just in North America but also in places such as Singapore and Hong Kong. It also contained patriotic verses, bits of history and updates on armed revolts in other colonized countries such as Ireland. The consistent line was an exhortation to all Indians to rise up against the British. Hardayal seems to have worked like a man possessed to keep the publication going. He was supported by a handful of volunteers, including a seventeen-year-old Kartar Singh Saraba, who had come to study at Berkeley but opted to work full-time at Yugantar Ashram.

The Ghadar rapidly became popular and was soon circulated by post and by hand in faraway places such as Trinidad, Singapore, Manila and Malaya (now Malaysia). The network of Sikh gurudwaras played an important role in disseminating the paper. In fact, the public singing of some of the verses became a regular feature in many gurudwaras. One of the most popular songs urged the Sikhs to wipe away the sin of helping the foreign invaders in 1857 by rising up in revolt:

> We fought many a battle for the Whites,
> That was a grave unwitting mistake, brothers ...
>
> The whole world taunts us,
> Liberate the country soon, O'Singhs,
> Get up! Let's wash away the stigma of treachery,
> If you remember the Guru's words, O'Singhs.[10]

The British authorities across the empire were aware of the new paper and its dangerous contents, thanks to Hopkinson's intelligence reports. The entry of the weekly was banned under the Sea Customs Act, and on 30 January 1914, 215 bundles of *The Ghadar* were intercepted at the Bombay port. The British also began to put pressure on the United States to somehow curb the activities of Hardayal. On 24 March, Hardayal was served a warrant of arrest. Since he was guaranteed freedom of expression under the US Constitution, he was accused of spreading anarchism through one of his speeches. Although he was soon released on bail, his supporters were concerned that he would be handed over to the British on some pretext. Thus, a few weeks later, Hardayal slipped out of the United States for Berlin.

Ram Chandra Peshawari now became the chief editor of *The Ghadar*. He was an old associate of Amir Chand, who had been involved in the Chandni Chowk bombing of 1912. He had edited some publications before he escaped to the United States, and he was able to keep the paper going. If anything, the attempt to arrest Hardayal had increased popular interest in the weekly and its associated movement, now identified as the Ghadar Party and the Ghadarites. As Europe began to lurch towards a war in mid-1914, Bhakna decided that the time had come for the Ghadarites to move back to India to participate in the coming revolution.

THE *KOMAGATA MARU* INCIDENT

As already mentioned, the Canadian authorities had been systematically sealing off immigration from India to British Columbia. This resulted in a significant number of Punjabis being stranded in East Asia, many of them relatives of those already in Canada. A somewhat favourable verdict by the Supreme Court of British Columbia gave them renewed hope, and, in 1914, a businessman, Gurdit Singh, decided to take a group from Hong Kong to Vancouver. He chartered a Japanese coaling ship named *Komagata Maru* and made some basic fittings for passengers. The ship set off with 165 passengers from Hong Kong on 4 April, picking up more in Shanghai and Yokohama. By the time it was crossing the Pacific, it had 376 passengers on board, 340 of whom were Punjabi Sikhs. Although many of them were readers of *The Ghadar*, they had no real link with the movement at that stage.

When they arrived in Vancouver on 23 May, however, the authorities refused to let them disembark. The local Indian community took up their cause and approached the courts, but was rebuffed. Meanwhile, the ship was running out of provisions, and the ship's owners needed to be paid for the delays. A frantic fundraising was done, even as conditions on board deteriorated. In a joint meeting of the Khalsa Diwan and the United India League, 500 Indians and over a hundred Canadian well-wishers raised some money and debated the next steps. They argued that as subjects of the British Empire, Indians had a right to travel to other parts of the empire. The arguments fell on deaf ears, as the Canadian government was in no mood to allow more non-whites into British Columbia.

Finally, on 21 July, the *Komagata Maru* was forced to leave Vancouver under the gaze of a Royal Navy cruiser. The Canadian government did pay for additional provisions for the crossing, but conditions onboard were appalling. The ship now made its way back to Yokohama, where Bhakna had earlier arrived to make arrangements for returning Ghadarite groups. He briefly boarded the ship and discussed Ghadarite ideas with the passengers. By now, he had a very willing audience. He also smuggled in some pistols and ammunition to be carried back to India.

Hopkinson's network in the Sikh community kept him abreast of these developments, and he advised the authorities against letting anyone disembark before the ship reached Calcutta. So, when the ship docked in Shanghai, Hong Kong and Singapore, no one was allowed to get off. This incensed the Indian community in each of these ports.

On 29 September, the *Komagata Maru* finally anchored at Budge Budge near Calcutta. The passengers had been stuck on an improvised coaling ship for six months and were exhausted. The authorities, however, were firm that they would be directly transferred to trains going to Punjab. Some agreed, but Gurdit Singh wanted to carry out one last act of defiance. He placed the

Guru Granth Sahib, the Sikh holy book, on his head and said that he would first visit the local gurudwara. Many passengers now walked behind him as he made his way on foot. There was heavy police deployment all along. By this time it was dark, and tempers were frayed on both sides. An argument arose, a riot broke out and gunshots were fired. Eighteen passengers and two Bengali passers-by were killed. So were two British officials and an Indian police constable. Over 200 of the passengers were arrested and jailed, but Gurdit Singh and several others escaped in the melee.

The whole episode sent shockwaves across India and the diaspora. In Canada, a group of Ghadarites decided to kill those they suspected of working for British intelligence. One by one their bodies were found. This included Arjan Singh, one of Hopkinson's most valuable informants. Another of Hopkinson's agents, Bela Singh, panicked as he realized that he could be next, and decided to hit back pre-emptively. He turned up with a gun at the funeral prayers for Arjan Singh at the gurudwara and opened fire; two were killed and seven injured.[11]

Bela Singh was arrested but British intelligence was determined to protect its men—it was a necessary show of strength if they wanted continued loyalty. It was arranged that Bela would be acquitted after a show trial by claiming that he had fired in self-defence. Hopkinson was present in the court for the trial, when suddenly Mewa Singh, a Ghadarite, pulled out a gun and shot him dead. Mewa was immediately arrested and condemned to death. Bela would survive a couple more assassination attempts in Canada before being killed in Punjab years later.

With the recruitment of a large number of Sikhs into the British Indian Army with the outbreak of the First World War, British intelligence became even more paranoid about the activities within gurudwaras across the empire. Even more resources were devoted to building a pro-British lobby among the Sikhs of Canada and Britain. This would cause a major fissure in the community.

THE FEBRUARY PLAN

Even as groups of Ghadarite Sikhs were moving back to India, Sachindra Nath Sanyal and Rashbehari Bose were hard at work at their headquarters in Varanasi. A constant flow of trusted revolutionaries reported the latest developments and went out with instructions. Rashbehari's old network in Punjab meant that he was in touch with sympathizers in the province, including the returning Ghadarites. Since the police were looking for him in connection with the Chandni Chowk bombing, Rashbehari sent Sanyal to Punjab so he could speak to various groups and also sound out some of the army regiments. The declaration of war in July 1914 appeared as a godsend. Here was an opportunity to rake up trouble while the British diverted their European troops to the battlefields of Europe and the Middle East, and at the same time recruit and arm new Indian regiments.

In his famous book *Bandi Jeevan* (A Life in Captivity), Sanyal would later describe how he crisscrossed north-western India, secretly meeting revolutionary groups and sympathetic soldiers from different army regiments.[12] The meetings were sometimes in the barracks and sometimes in a secluded grove near the railway station—always nervous gatherings, despite the patriotic zeal. He tells us that many Hindu and Sikh soldiers were inspired by the events of 1857. Similarly, there was discontent among Muslim soldiers due to the fact that the Ottoman Turks had sided with Germany against Britain and France. Whatever their motivations for wanting to rise in revolt, the soldiers knew that British intelligence was keeping a close eye, and any misstep would have grave consequences.

Secrecy was critical, but concealing a plan involving so many people was no easy task. Many of the Ghadarites, especially those returning from North America, were pumped up and would get into unnecessary fights with the authorities. In one incident, a group travelling by horse carriage got into an argument at a police picket outside a village near Ludhiana. The argument eventually led to a gunfight, which resulted in several casualties on both sides. The remaining members of the group were subsequently arrested, and their leader, Pundit Kashi Ram, was hanged. Such incidents meant that Sanyal and Rashbehari had to be very careful about whom they involved in their planning. They needed a trusted point person operating in the Lahore–Amritsar area, and decided on Kartar Singh Saraba, who had been Hardayal's assistant at Yugantar Ashram. He was barely eighteen and had only recently returned from California, but he proved to be an energetic organizer.

Similar networks were also being activated in the United Provinces. Vishnu Ganesh Pingle was sent to work on the barracks in Meerut. Sanyal was already in touch with regiments in and around Varanasi. However, Bengal was more complicated. The movement had widespread support in the province, but with the arrest of Aurobindo and Barin Ghosh, it had split into several autonomous groups. Even when Barin was running the show, he did not have full control over all the branches of the Anushilan Samiti, but now it was even more splintered.

It is quite interesting to read Sanyal's frank assessment of the various groups in Bengal. The Dacca Anushilan Samiti was the largest. It had a reasonably well-organized network in many parts of east Bengal, including rural areas. In contrast, there were a large number of factions in the western districts of Bengal, each with an independent mind. Their leaders were generally better educated than those in the east, so they tended to look down on the leadership in Dacca. This made the Dacca Anushilan Samiti reluctant to collaborate with their cousins in western Bengal and gave it a reputation of being difficult.

Sanyal and Rashbehari eventually opted to work with a group led by Bagha Jatin. He had brought together surviving fragments of Barin's original team. It would, therefore, come to be known as the Jugantar group, after Barin's paper. It was disciplined and, unlike the others, invested in capacity-building for large-scale operations rather than just isolated attacks. Initially, the group was strong only around Calcutta, but it developed a strong network in districts such as Nadia and Medinipur (also spelt Midnapur). Importantly, Bagha Jatin had built up a working relationship with the Anushilan Samiti branches in Dacca and Chandernagore. The Rodda arms heist in August 1914 was a joint operation of this alliance. Therefore, the Jugantar group was given the task of coordinating the revolution in eastern India.

Global events were moving quickly. In July 1914, war broke out in Europe. Although no one could have imagined then that it would become the 'Great War', it was clear from the beginning that the British would not only have to divert military resources from India but also be forced to make fresh recruitments. This was the opportunity that the revolutionaries had been waiting for. A flurry of revolutionaries from across India visited Rashbehari and Sanyal in Varanasi and went back to organize local units in preparation of the coming revolt. None of them would have noticed a teenager named Subhas Chandra Bose, who was also in the city at that time on a spiritual quest. The paths of the two Boses would meet many years later during the Second World War.

The British intelligence services were aware by now that something was afoot. They began to arrest and question Sikhs returning from North America. Ships plying the Pacific route between India and North America were not allowed to let pass-through passengers disembark in Singapore, Hong Kong or Penang, out of fear that Ghadarites would instigate Indian regiments based there. Bhakna had met the passengers of *Komagata Maru* in Yokohama, but was promptly arrested when he came to India by another ship. Similarly, when 'Potato King' Jwala Singh arrived in India, the authorities confiscated $50,000 that he was carrying with him—a very substantial sum in those days.

Rashbehari and Sanyal realized that they could not delay things too much in the face of such pressure on the Punjabis. They also received information that some of the primed regiments in north-west India would leave for the Middle East or Europe in March 1915. In contrast, the Bengali revolutionaries were in touch with the Germans and wanted to wait until they received some promised support. Eventually, while holding a clandestine meeting after dusk on a boat in the middle of the Ganga, Rashbehari told the representative from Bengal that he could no longer wait and that the Jugantar group should get ready to coordinate attacks on the police and treasury establishments across Bengal. A few weeks later, he left for Punjab, where he took charge of arrangements with Mula Singh as his right-hand man. Sanyal stayed back in Varanasi to coordinate operations in the United Provinces. The date for the revolt was fixed for 21 February 1915.

The plan was that the first uprising would take place at Mian Mir cantonment, Lahore. This would be the signal for simultaneous revolts in Rawalpindi and Ferozepore. In turn, this would be followed by the regiments in Jubbalpore, Varanasi and so on. The Bengal revolutionaries would then start their attacks and try to take over Dacca. Unfortunately, the whole plan collapsed!

On 13 February, the conspirators had a setback when Mula Singh was arrested. At the same time, a British intelligence mole, Kirpal Singh, managed to get into the inner circle. Suspicions were aroused when he was seen on 15 February speaking to a police officer in Lahore station. Rashbehari responded by bringing the date of the revolt forward to 19 February, but was unable to neutralize Kirpal Singh, who found out about the new date and again informed the authorities. Just hours before the revolt was supposed to be triggered, the police carried out several raids in Lahore on suspected hideouts, including the house where Rashbehari was staying (although he was not there). The army was put on high alert across the province and all Indian guards were replaced by Europeans at arms depots and key installations.

Once it became obvious that the British officers were fully aware of the plan, the Indian soldiers in the regiments in Punjab decided it was foolhardy to revolt. Kartar Singh Saraba arrived in the evening at the Ferozepore military camp with seventy lightly armed revolutionaries but found that the British officers had already been alerted and taken pre-emptive action. Without any uprising in the north-west, the rolling wave of rebellion simply did not take off.

The only place where an uprising occurred in mid-February 1915 was in faraway Singapore. The predominantly Muslim regiments in Singapore were unhappy that they could be sent to fight against the Ottoman Turks. Although Rashbehari and Sanyal were not directly in touch with them, they were in contact with the wider Ghadarite network and would have been aware of the murmurings. The mutineers shot dead several British officers and took control of the city. It took three days of fighting before naval marines were able to recapture Singapore. Given what would take place here three decades later, it is ironic the British would be helped by marines from Japanese navy ships that happened to be in the vicinity. Many of the rebel soldiers were lined up on Outram Road and publicly executed by a firing squad.

The lieutenant governor of Punjab, Michael O'Dwyer, now exercised special emergency powers to raid and arrest anyone suspected of being a Ghadarite. With his plans unravelling and his hideout already raided, Rashbehari had no choice but to escape to Varanasi in disguise. Many of the others were caught, sometimes after ferocious gunfights. Some such as Kartar Singh Saraba were hanged, while others were given long prison sentences. It should be noted here that the British received enthusiastic support from members of the Punjabi elite, including the Chief Khalsa Diwan. Indeed, many actively used their influence to gather information to hunt down Ghadarites.

Rashbehari knew that this time he would not be safe for long in Varanasi, as the government was expending every effort to locate him. One by one his associates were being hunted down. When Pingle was arrested in Meerut, he decided it was best to leave the country. He made his way back to his hometown, Chandernagore, and purchased a first-class ticket on a passenger liner leaving Calcutta for Kobe, Japan, via Penang, Singapore and Hong Kong. The reason for an expensive first-class ticket was that Rashbehari had decided to pose as P.N. Tagore, a relative of the famous poet Rabindranath Tagore. The poet was expected to visit Japan soon, and it would not be out of place if his cousin were to go ahead to make arrangements. Given the strongly hierarchical, class-conscious mores of the times, Rashbehari was betting that an aristocrat from a famous family would face less scrutiny. Indeed, he even managed to arrange for an identity card from the police commissioner in Calcutta!

On 12 May 1915, Rashbehari boarded the *Sanuti Maru* for Japan.[13] Sanyal accompanied him to the docks for a tearful farewell. Before leaving, Bose gave Sanyal his Mauser pistol and a pocket watch that he had specially purchased to mark the time of his now-failed revolt. Many years later, Sanyal would pass on this watch to one of his protégés, Bhagat Singh. The watch is said to be currently housed in a small museum collection in Hardoi.[14]

The ship set sail at 11 p.m. One can only imagine the emotions felt by the twenty-nine-year-old Rashbehari as he watched the city of Calcutta recede. His great rebellion had failed just hours before it was to be triggered, and his comrades had been arrested or were on the run. He was leaving India for the first time and had no idea when he would come back (as it turned out, he would never see India again). His disguise as P.N. Tagore required a confident exterior but the turmoil within would have been excruciating. He would go on to write later in his memoirs that he spent his time onboard reading the Bhagawad Gita for solace and talking to the Japanese captain. As the ship passed the Andamans, he thought about all the fellow revolutionaries, including Savarkar, who were held in the Cellular Jail:

Far distant in the sea, a faint light could be seen. The captain said, 'This is Andaman!' Hearing this, I felt a chill of horror. Many of my comrade-brothers were jailed there and were just waiting for their death in vain. These brave people did what Garibaldi and Washington did for their respective countries. But, they are destined to wait for their death, as they were unsuccessful. Thinking this, I shed tears of indignation.[15]

Rashbehari was briefly questioned in Singapore and Hong Kong; his fingerprints were also taken. However, he must have put on a convincing act as none of the officials seem to have doubted the bona fides of Tagore's cousin. It is also quite extraordinary that any link with the famous poet was enough to waive all suspicion. It is difficult to think of a writer or poet today who would command such respect. The ship reached Kobe on 5 June 1915, and a Japanese customs officer hurriedly walked up to Rashbehari and shook his hand. He told him that there were several letters waiting for him. After glancing through them, Rashbehari told officials that they were all addressed to the poet, not to P.N. Tagore. Nonetheless, he was exempted from screening and even a car was arranged to drop him off at a hotel.

THE SIAM SCHEME AND THE CHRISTMAS DAY PLOT

The very next day after arriving in Kobe, Rashbehari headed to Tokyo by train. He did not know the language and worried that he would soon run out of money. With some difficulty, he hunted down Bhagwan Singh, a Ghadarite who he hoped would help him. Bhagwan Singh turned out to be committed to the cause and immediately made arrangements for his stay. He also took Rashbehari to meet the Chinese leader Sun Yat-sen, who was in exile in Japan. They would meet at Matsumotoro Café in

Hibiya Park, a popular place for foreign exiles, rather like the cafés of Paris. It is often forgotten today that Japan was then actively encouraging the idea of pan-Asian unity and was home to rebels of many shades. Nonetheless, intelligence reports of that time suggest that the Japanese also kept a close eye on them.

Sun Yat-sen and Rashbehari seem to have got along well. One can imagine them passionately discussing world politics at Matsumotoro Café, even as Sun's wife played the piano in the background. The piano was one of the first produced by Yamaha and is still displayed in the café. It was Sun Yat-sen who introduced Rashbehari to Mitsuru Toyama, a powerful nationalist ideologue-politician in early-twentieth-century Japan. Toyama was a strong proponent of Pan-Asianism and took the young Indian revolutionary under his wing.

Even as Rashbehari was finding his feet in Tokyo, the British decimated the Ghadarite network back in Punjab. With the arrest of Sanyal a few months later, the network in the United Provinces was also neutralized. Sanyal narrowly escaped being hanged and was sentenced to life imprisonment at the Cellular Jail. Two of his brothers, Jitendra and Rabindra, were given milder sentences.

This left Bagha Jatin's Jugantar group in Bengal as the only surviving network with strike capability. Importantly, it was in touch with Indian revolutionaries who had come together in Berlin with support from the German government. Known formally as the Indian Committee for National Independence—and informally as the Berlin India Committee—it included Viren Chattopadhyay ('Chatto'), Champak Pillai and other Indian revolutionaries who had operated in Europe in the pre-war years. Many of them had been Savarkar's followers in London and Paris. After moving from the United States to Europe, Hardayal, too, contacted the committee. The German government provided the committee with financial support and accorded it diplomatic recognition.

As it became clear that it was going to be a long-drawn war, the Germans began to look for ways to undermine the British Empire. An obvious ploy was to instigate armed revolt in India—the Germans were willing to supply the guns. Thus, the Berlin India Committee reached out to the Jugantar group to find out ways to smuggle a large number of arms into India. They were also in touch with Rashbehari, who was trying to procure arms in Japan and Shanghai for the same purpose.

The first German attempt to supply arms to the revolutionaries was not to those in India but to Ghadarites operating from Siam (now Thailand) and Burma. The idea was to foment guerrilla strikes against the colonial administration in Southeast Asia as a way to draw away British resources ahead of the main uprising in India led by Bagha Jatin. An important objective of the Siam group was to land armed guerrillas in the Andaman islands and free the revolutionaries in the Cellular Jail. The original leaders of the movement, Vinayak Savarkar and Barin Ghosh, after all, were both imprisoned there.

The German consul in Shanghai arranged for a schooner, *Henry S.*, and had it loaded with arms. The ship was to pick up German military instructors arranged by the consul in Manila.[16] The Philippines was then under the control of the United States and was technically neutral (the US would formally enter the war in April 1917). The schooner next headed to Thailand through the waters of the Dutch East Indies, but developed engine problems and had to dock in the Celebes, where Dutch customs authorities inspected the ship and impounded the cargo.[17] They also alerted

British intelligence that something was afoot. The British chargé d'affaires in Bangkok pressured the Thai authorities to arrest key Ghadarites. A German agent, Vincent Kraft, was similarly arrested in Singapore and blurted out the plan. The whole scheme, therefore, ended in failure. Nonetheless, a small but dedicated group of Ghadarites continued to operate from Thailand for the next few decades and, as we shall see, played an important role in the Second World War.

TIGER JATIN

Jyotindra Nath Mukherjee was born in December 1880 in Nadia district of Bengal. He belonged to an educated and socially well-connected family. As a young man, he was a naturally gifted sportsman and a daredevil. In 1906, he and his friends were walking through the jungle near his village, when they were attacked by a royal Bengal tiger. Rather than run away, he decided to wrestle the tiger with his bare hands and even managed to kill it with a small knife he happened to be carrying. Although badly injured, he survived and earned himself the nickname Bagha Jatin (Tiger Jatin).

Bagha Jatin came in contact with Aurobindo Ghosh in 1903 and soon became part of the Anushilan Samiti network. As he was frequently in Darjeeling as part of his job as a government clerk, he was given the role of organizing units in north Bengal. After the original Anushilan Samiti became leaderless following the Alipore Bomb Trials, the movement broke up into many small units, which often worked at cross purposes. Bagha Jatin painstakingly brought together a core team—the Jugantar group—and built a working relationship with some of the better Anushilan Samiti units, such as the ones in Dacca, Barishal and

Chandernagore. He also orchestrated a number of targeted killings of police officers and their collaborators. The authorities suspected him of links with the revolutionaries, sacked him from his government job and arrested him—but they did not initially work out that he was the mastermind.

The meeting in Dakshineshwar with Rashbehari in 1913 drew Bagha Jatin into the Ghadarite plan of triggering a wider rebellion in the country. However, after the police raids and arrests in Punjab and the United Provinces, his was the only cohesive group left standing by mid-1915. The Germans were in touch with the Jugantar leadership through the Berlin India Committee. The failure of the Siam scheme had been a setback, but the Germans decided that they would still go ahead with the plan to land a large number of arms on the east coast of India. The Jugantar network began to clandestinely drill and train youth across Bengal, in many cases using the traditional akhadas. One of the local organizers in the Nadia–Murshidabad belt was a sixteen-year-old, Nalinaksha Sanyal. His elder brother, Anadi Kanta, had long been part of the Anushilan Samiti.

The plan was to land a large consignment of arms on the coast of Bengal and Orissa (now Odisha) in August–September 1915. Elaborate arrangements were made to distribute and disperse the guns to the drilled units across Bengal. The Rodda episode presumably provided a template for how this could be done. These armed guerrillas were to converge on Calcutta on Christmas Day, when senior British officials traditionally attended a lunch and a ball hosted by the viceroy; Calcutta was still the effective headquarters as the new capital of New Delhi was still being built. With the top colonial leadership trapped in a city that they no longer controlled, it was hoped that a wider rebellion would be triggered.

With this plan in mind, Bagha Jatin scouted the coast and decided on two landing spots—one near Balasore on the Orissa coast and one in Raimangal, a rivulet in the Sunderbans in Bengal. Feelers were sent out to engage with the Rajput troops then stationed at Fort William, Calcutta. Dynamite was procured for blowing up railway bridges to delay the arrival of relief troops.

In early 1915, Krupp Agency in New York purchased a large consignment of arms under instruction from Franz von Papen, the military attaché of the German embassy in Washington, D.C. It included 30,000 rifles and 400 rounds of ammunition per rifle—it was not a small consignment. These were loaded on a chartered ship, *Annie Larsen*, which was to transfer the cargo to another ship, SS *Maverick*, off Socorro Island in the Pacific. SS *Maverick* was supposed to take the shipment through neutral Dutch-controlled waters before entering the Bay of Bengal. Bagha Jatin sent Narendra Nath Bhattacharya to Batavia (now Jakarta) to coordinate the arms drop. Ram Chandra, the most senior Ghadarite leader left in North America, arranged for five trusted men led by Mangoo Ram to head to Batavia disguised as Persian waiters.

Unfortunately, when *Annie Larsen* arrived at the appointed place for the rendezvous, SS *Maverick* was not there. The captain waited for three weeks before sailing back to the United States, where its suspicious cargo was impounded by customs. When *Maverick* finally arrived a few days later, it found that *Annie Larsen* and its precious cargo had already left. Thus, the whole elaborate plan fell apart because of a coordination error. This is just another example of how the path of history can shift due to the smallest of reasons.

Meanwhile, Bagha Jatin was waiting for SS *Maverick* near Balasore. The revolutionaries had prepared a hideout, including a small house, outside a village. Unknown to him, not only was the arms consignment lost, British intelligence had a sound sense of the contours of the plan by the beginning of September 1915. Charles Tegart, widely regarded as the best anti-insurgency intelligence officer in the empire, took over the case in Calcutta. Multiple police raids were carried out in Bengal, and a lead brought them to Odisha.

On the evening of 6 September, Bagha Jatin received information from a local supporter that a large police contingent had arrived in the vicinity. He immediately realized that they were looking for him. He and his four companions picked up their Mausers and ammunition, and hid in the surrounding countryside. Tired and hungry, they crossed the Burri Balam river on the morning of 9 September. Unfortunately, the villagers mistook them for dacoits and informed the police. Very soon the police contingent arrived, and the fugitives were forced to flee. They crossed a rivulet and took up positions on a mound. A fierce gunfight followed, until two of the revolutionaries were killed and Bagha Jatin was fatally wounded. With ammunition running low, the remaining two surrendered. Bagha Jatin was taken to the nearby hospital but passed away the following day.[18]

This was followed by a series of raids across Bengal over the next three months. Hundreds of suspected revolutionaries were searched and arrested. Nalinaksha Sanyal's home in the village of Dhoradaha was also raided, but he managed to destroy all evidence before the police arrived. After being interrogated for several days, he was let off for lack of incriminating evidence. Others were not so lucky.

An important reason that the German arms shipments to India repeatedly failed was that British intelligence knew what the Germans were attempting to do, thanks to the capture of

German agent Vincent Kraft in Singapore. Maps of Bengal were found on him, in which certain points were marked along the coast. Kraft agreed to fully cooperate with the British in exchange for a substantial sum of money and being allowed to emigrate to the United States under a new name.[19] Papers related to Kraft's new identity are still not declassified.

An equally important source of information was a Czech nationalist and agent named Emanuel Viktor Voska, who was operating in the United States. Remember that at this stage the Czechs were trying to free themselves from the Austrians. Voska was close to Tomáš Masaryk, who would become the first President of Czechoslovakia after the war. The Ghadarite coordinator in New York was Chandra Kanta Chakravarty, who had an apartment at 364 West 120th Street. He had a Czech housekeeper, who had full access to the apartment and reported back to Voska about everything he saw and heard, especially about Chandra Kanta's dealings with German diplomats. Voska, in turn, reported this to British intelligence. Thus, the British were able to triangulate the various bits of information to get a clearer picture. One must admire their ability to gather information.[20]

Within India, Tegart's intelligence network was clearly hurting the revolutionaries. The latter struck back. Tegart survived several assassination attempts, but many of his colleagues were not so lucky. Sub-inspector Madhusudhan Bhattacharya was killed on 16 January 1916 and sub-inspector Jogendra Gupta was killed on 30 June. The biggest strike was the killing of Intelligence Branch Superintendent Basanta Chatterjee in broad daylight on the streets of Calcutta. Many people saw it but not a single witness came forward to give evidence.[21] As many as eleven intelligence officers were killed in quick succession—this was 20 per cent of the total strength of the department. The police responded with ever more arrests and repression. One of those arrested was Anadi Kanta Sanyal, who was taken to Rangpur Jail. He was subjected to such severe torture that he died from his injuries. He was barely twenty and his wife was expecting their first child. The child would die at the age of five, but his widow would live to see an independent India.

MISSION KABUL

The nationalist revolutionaries of India were not the only group that the Turko–German alliance were hoping to use to foment trouble in the British Empire. There were attempts, for instance, to supply arms to Irish nationalists. Given the claim of the Ottoman Sultans of being the Caliph of all Sunni Muslims, it should hardly be surprising that the alliance would seek to use pan-Islamic loyalties to trigger Muslims to revolt against British authority. The Sultan duly issued a fatwa, declaring a holy war against the infidels. Turks had an obvious claim to such Islamic loyalties, but German agents also fed the propaganda. This was occasionally taken to laughable extremes, with extravagant claims that Kaiser Wilhelm II had converted to Islam and was a 'haji'.

Just as the British were trying to get the Arabs to rebel against the Turks, the Turko–German alliance wanted to get the Muslim subjects of the British, French and Russian empires to rebel against their rulers. Tens of thousands of leaflets were printed in Istanbul, ordering Muslims in Egypt, India and Central Asia to rise up against colonial authority. The Germans dispatched a talented spy, Wilhelm Wassmuss, to southern Persia to instigate the local tribes—the German equivalent of Lawrence of Arabia. Rumours were spread that a large Turko–German army would soon march through Persia and Afghanistan to 'liberate' India.

Naturally, the German government wanted the revolutionaries of the Berlin India Committee, mostly Hindus, to collaborate with the pan-Islamic cause. Not everyone was entirely comfortable with the idea. After a trip to Istanbul, Hardayal decided that a Turkish-backed takeover of India would be worse than British rule. Then on he kept his distance from the Berlin India Committee and drifted away from the movement. Many of the other revolutionaries, however, decided to join hands in the larger interest of evicting the British.

Working with pan-Islamists against the British was not entirely a new idea. Some of Ajit Singh's supporters had been in exile for years in Persia. They were led by Sufi Amba Prasad, who was living near Shiraz under an assumed name, Muhammad Hasan Sufi. Wassmuss contacted him and was also able to attract several newly arrived Indian revolutionaries to his cause, which included Pandurang Khankhoje and Pramath Nath Dutta. Thus, we have one of those impossible combinations of history—nationalist Hindus fighting for the pan-Islamist cause in Persia, backed by Germany. Together they began to instigate the tribes of southern Persia and Baluchistan against the British.

Persia was technically a neutral country, but the northern half was under effective Russian control and the southern half under British control, as per a mutual understanding from the days of the 'Great Game' in the late nineteenth century. Therefore, there was already some pre-existing resentment against the British. Wassmuss had worked earlier in the German consulate in Bushire and was familiar with the region. Consequently, he was able to work the resentment into open rebellion, lubricated generously with bribes and promises.

The British and the Russians soon woke up to the danger and decided to cooperate in policing sensitive areas. Cossack units and British Indian Army cavalry were deployed along Persia's border regions with Afghanistan and Baluchistan. It was called the East Persia Cordon.[22]

The Turko–German alliance now started to look for a way to get Afghanistan to attack British India from the west. This would tie up a lot of British resources that were otherwise being deployed in the Middle East and Europe. The Germans reached out to the Berlin India Committee for a suitable candidate to lead a diplomatic mission to Kabul. They decided on Raja Mahendra Pratap Singh, who belonged to the ruling nobility of a small principality in the United Provinces. He had left India in 1914 and thrown in his lot with the Ghadarites. Although he did not hail from high royalty, it appears he spoke well and had an aristocratic demeanour, which was thought appropriate for the job of negotiating with the ruler of Afghanistan. Even the Kaiser met him to provide him with the right level of stature as 'Prince of India'.

Mahendra Pratap set off from Berlin with a letter from Kaiser Wilhelm II to Amir Habibullah of Afghanistan. He was accompanied by Maulana Barkatullah, a fiery pan-Islamist preacher from Bhopal who had old links with the Ghadarites of North America and Japan. The party also included Dr Werner Otto von Hentig, the German representative, and Captain Casim Bey, the Turkish representative. They armed themselves with a fatwa from Istanbul before heading east in May 1915.

Crossing the waterless deserts of east Persia in the height of summer was no easy task, especially when they also had to avoid being caught by cavalry units deployed along the East Persia

Cordon, as well as by tribal bandits. After four months of extreme hardship and near-catastrophe, the mission finally reached Kabul on 2 October. Amir Habibullah arranged for a royal reception and provided them with reasonable lodgings, but refused to commit to the Turko–German cause. One can understand why he would have been reluctant to start a war with his powerful neighbours—the Russian and British empires—on the basis of vague promises from distant powers. Besides, he had already been warned by Viceroy Hardinge to maintain strict neutrality.

Even as they waited for Amir Habibullah to make up his mind, Mahendra Pratap announced the formation of the Provisional Government of India in exile in December 1915, with himself as President and Barkatullah as Prime Minister. The duo also tried their best to reach out to key people in India, but all their letters appear to have been intercepted by O'Dwyer's police intelligence in Punjab. Barkatullah even tried to send a letter to sympathizers in Mecca, but this merely allowed the pro-British Sharif of Mecca to identify and arrest them.

After spending almost a year in Kabul, Mahendra Pratap and Barkatullah realized that Amir Habibullah was just playing them. They took their leave and headed back in September 1916. Amir Habibullah gave them polite letters for the Kaiser and the Sultan, but did not commit himself.

Meanwhile, constant pressure from the East Persia Cordon was wearing down Wassmuss's efforts with the Baloch and Persian tribes. The British further eroded his position by deploying Brigadier-General Reginald Dyer to bolster the southern end of the East Persia Cordon (yes, he is the same fellow). His reputation for ruthless brutality must have preceded him, for Dyer was able to use a small force to cause a 2,000-strong Baloch tribal raiding party to disperse. Amba Prasad died following the siege of Shiraz in late 1915, but some Ghadarites such as Khankhoje kept fighting alongside Persian partisans until 1918.

THE PERSIAN CAMPAIGN

Pandurang Sadashiv Khankhoje was born in 1886 into a Brahmin family that had been prominent in the Nagpur area (now in Maharashtra) for many generations. In the early seventeenth century, his ancestors had been military commanders of the local Gond kings and had led their resistance against Mughal incursions. This is how they earned their unusual surname 'Khankhoje', meaning 'the one who captured a Khan' (Khan was a common Turko–Mongol term for 'commander').[23] In the Maratha empire, the family served as officials of the Bhonsles of Nagpur. Not surprisingly, they were not pleased when the British replaced the Marathas as rulers. Pandurang Khankhoje's grandfather joined Tatya Tope's troops during the Revolt of 1857. When that was put down, he quietly returned to Nagpur and settled down (and is said to have later helped the tribal rebel Tantya Bhil). Thus, the young Pandurang Khankhoje grew up with legends of how his ancestors had put up a heroic resistance against foreign incursions.

When Khankhoje was in his teens, he joined a local akhada, where he learnt martial arts and imbibed revolutionary ideas. Soon, a group of boys in Nagpur organized themselves into a group that called itself Bandhav Samaj. They often held secret meetings in a house where, many years later, Keshav Hedgewar would found the Rashtriya Swayamsevak Sangh (RSS). The house still stands and is well preserved. As a cover for their activities, they decided to form a circus called National Circus! This is not as bizarre an idea as it may seem at first glance, as some other revolutionary groups were already using travelling circuses as a cover for their activities.[24]

The National Circus enjoyed a brief period of success until a fire destroyed their equipment, and the project had to be abandoned. Khankhoje started to explore ways to join the army of a princely state to be able to gain military training, but Tilak advised him to go abroad for the purpose. Thus, Khankhoje and a friend smuggled themselves out of India in 1906 on board a ship bound for Saigon (now Ho Chi Minh City). They then somehow made their way to Tokyo. When they arrived in Japan, they were penniless. This was long before Rashbehari Bose and the other Ghadarites had arrived in the country and created a network. Luckily, they were given some help by a poor student, Adhar Chandra Laskar, who had links with the Anushilan Samiti. Khankhoje eventually found a way to eke out a living by giving English lessons. Interestingly, he would make friends with some of Sun Yat-sen's Chinese revolutionaries in the city, who allowed him to take part in their military training.

The following year, Khankhoje made his way to San Francisco. The city was then recovering from a devastating earthquake. The young man from Nagpur started to earn a living by working on laying rail tracks and roads. This must have been hard physical labour, but somehow he found the strength to enrol in the agriculture department at Berkeley. This was an important decision, for he would go on to make major contributions in the field (we will revisit this in the last chapter).

While at Berkeley, Khankhoje was part of a growing Indian community that was developing increasingly strong support for liberating India from British rule. However, as we have seen, it was only with the arrival of Hardayal that the Ghadar movement gathered momentum in 1911. Meanwhile, the ever-enterprising Khankhoje managed to gain admission to Mount Tamalpais Military Academy, thanks to help from an Irish faculty member who was sympathetic to the Indian cause. For the first time he received formal military training.

With the outbreak of the First World War, Khankhoje wanted to use his newly acquired skills. Disguised as Persians, he and two other Indian revolutionaries boarded a Greek ship headed for the Mediterranean. They narrowly escaped being arrested when a British naval vessel searched the ship near Gibraltar. They eventually managed to reach Constantinople (now Istanbul), where they established contact with the Indian nationalists of the Berlin India Committee. Several other Indian revolutionaries had also assembled in the city. Barkatullah and Mahendra Pratap were sent on the Kabul Mission, while others such as Khankhoje were told to join Wassmuss and Sufi Amba Prasad in fomenting trouble in southern Persia.

Pramath Nath, Agashe and Khankhoje assumed Persian identities as Daud Ali, Mirza Muhammad Ali and Muhammad Khan, respectively, as they quietly slipped from Syria into Iraq and then into southern Persia. Using German gold, weapons and promises, Wassmuss and the Indians instigated local tribes against the British. They also recruited anti-British members of the Persian Gendarmerie, a paramilitary unit trained by Swedish officers. By the middle of 1915, the British had their hands full, dealing with hit-and-run attacks on their oil installations near Bushire (also spelt Bushehr). There was a mishap, however, that would prove costly for the Germans. One of the tribes loyal to the British captured Wassmuss. Although he managed to escape, he left behind the German codebook. This was picked up by the

British and sent to London, where the intelligence unit used it effectively to break into German communications across the war fronts.

By this time, the British had put a significant force of Indian troops under Captain Noel on their tail. Khankhoje and his band of guerrillas withdrew from Bushire to Shiraz, where they united with Sufi Amba Prasad, who had been operating from the city for some time. The combined force was able to put up a fierce opposition to the British for a while. Although they now had a motley army of about 5,000 men—tribesmen, Persian irregulars and a handful of Indians—their position was not secure, as the British were landing ever more troops under Brigadier General Percy Sykes at Bandar Abbas. Leaving Sufi Amba Prasad in Shiraz, Khankhoje was forced to move his troops to the north-east, towards Baluchistan. Although this presented an opportunity to directly attack British India, it also meant that he was trapped between British troops led by Sykes and Dyer. His communications links with the Germans were also disrupted.

Even as he weighed his options, Khankhoje received news that Sufi Amba Prasad had been captured in Shiraz and had died by suicide. With options dwindling, he decided to withdraw his army further into the mountains and deserts along the Baluchistan border. Unfortunately, they were ambushed and forced to fight in an impossible position. Khankhoje was shot in the leg and, with his horse being killed, he crashed to the ground and fell unconscious. When he opened his eyes, he realized he was a prisoner. Unbelievably, even with a bullet still lodged in his leg, he managed to escape into the barren desert, where he narrowly evaded death from thirst, thanks to a group of bandits who took pity on him!

Khankhoje spent some time with the bandits. He must have made quite an impression, as one of the leaders offered him his daughter in marriage! However, the Indian revolutionary was keen to get back to the war. Having lost his army, Khankhoje joined the remaining rebel groups. Despite occasional victories, it was clear by late 1917 that their cause was unsustainable. When the war ended, he was fighting as part of the Qashqai tribe. One of the conditions of surrender put forward by the British was that Khankhoje be handed over. The Qashqai agreed, but allowed him to escape. The problem was that he had nowhere to go. Returning to India would have been a death sentence.

For some time he wandered around Europe as an aide to a Persian nobleman (even visiting India in this guise). He then made his way to Russia, like many other revolutionaries, where he met Lenin twice. Khankhoje seems to have liked Lenin, but found the endless ideological and organizational debates of the communists tiresome. Eventually he made his way to Mexico, where he made a name as an agricultural scientist over the next few decades.[25]

THE HINDU–GERMAN TRIALS

The many different attempts by the revolutionaries during the First World War to end British rule in India all ended in failure. Some readers may take the view that their schemes were too far-fetched and doomed from the beginning. Others may take the view that the British were better than the Germans at intelligence-gathering, propaganda and logistics. The reality is that the war saw many such attempts by both sides succeed against all odds. The British, for instance, were able to instigate the Arabs to rise up against the Turks, despite their religious affinities (many readers will have seen the movie *Lawrence of Arabia*). The biggest success, however, was that of the Germans, who supported the Bolsheviks during the October Revolution of 1917. They even arranged for a special train to take Vladimir Lenin—no less—from Switzerland, through Germany, Sweden and Finland, to St Petersburg. Ex-ante, it would have been far from obvious that the Bolshevik Revolution was more likely to succeed than Rashbehari's attempted rebellion. This is consistent with the complex view of history, as history can go down many different paths and it is near impossible to predict the future—because the smallest of factors can cause a diversion.

The United States entered the war on Britain's side in April 1917. The Ghadarites had been under pressure from US authorities, but a formal declaration of war made things even more difficult. Repeated failures had already caused internal feuds within the Ghadar Party, with accusations of misappropriation of funds and incompetence. Dozens of Ghadarites were arrested along with their German and German-American associates for having violated American neutrality prior to the formal declaration of war.

The trials in California that started in November 1917 came to be known as the Hindu–German Conspiracy trials. Among the Indians sentenced were Taraknath Das for twenty-two months, Santokh Singh for twenty-one months and Bhagwan Singh for eighteen months. These were quite mild compared to what they would have faced if handed over to the British. However, the internal feuds were so bad by this point that Ram Chandra was shot dead by a gunman from Bhagwan Singh's faction.

The war ended in November 1918 with the defeat of the Germans. The members of the Berlin India Committee found themselves in a difficult situation as their former allies were no longer in a position to support or protect them. It was in this moment of acute uncertainty that some of them reached out to Soviet Russia. At least at first, this was not driven by any ideological affinity but by pure survival instinct, but several former nationalists would later become communists. We will catch up with them later in this book.

Despite the repeated failures to trigger a large-scale rebellion in India, the second generation of revolutionary leaders certainly ratcheted up the game. The movement had come a long way from the small number of idealists in India House and the Maniktola garden house. Their thinking was genuinely large-scale, they had links with major global powers and their support base was much wider. The British certainly took the threat seriously, judging from the resources they deployed to stamp them out. It is important, moreover, to appreciate the Ghadarite phase of the movement to be able to understand subsequent events from the Jallianwala Bagh massacre of 1919 to the formation of the Indian National Army in 1943. Indeed, as discussed in the last chapter, some of the consequences can be felt to this day.

LOYALISTS DURING THE WAR

When the war was declared, many sections of the Indian elite fell over themselves to offer help to the British cause. Nowhere was this more evident than in Punjab. The old Sikh nobility was more than keen to prove the loyalty of the 'martial race'. The Chief Khalsa Diwan condemned the Ghadarites and helped recruit soldiers. Even Gandhi, newly returned to India, joined the recruitment drive despite his avowed adherence to the principles of non-violence. However, the most enthusiastic supporters of the war effort were the contractors and agents who profited handsomely from arranging supplies and recruits. They fanned out across the province and used all means fair and foul to arrange recruits, supplies and contributions to war funds.

The demands became greater as the war dragged on and the death toll mounted. Recruitment quotas were set by district, or even individual village, and ever more young men were taken into the army using false promises and intimidation. In many places, the relatively wealthy purchased young men from poor families to replace their own children. In other places, they made large contributions to the Imperial War Fund. Lieutenant Governor O'Dwyer ramped up the incentives for the contractors. In addition to their monetary commission, they were given thousands of acres of irrigated farmland next to newly built canals. They were also given fancy imperial titles. O'Dwyer would later write that the system of rewards 'were such as would appeal to the Oriental mind, such as the Indian titles of honour from "Raja" and "Nawab" down to "Rai Sahib" and "Khan Sahib", robes of honour, swords of honour, guns ...'. He also states that the land grants could go up to 15,000 acres![26]

The contractors and agents quickly became a staunchly loyalist nouveau riche. In the early years, there may have been some members of the general population who voluntarily signed up for the army in exchange for regular pay or adventure. However, as the death toll mounted, voluntary recruitment all but disappeared. There are several eyewitness accounts of how local officials and agents colluded to 'herd' poor peasants into the army. They read like descriptions of slaving raids. Here is the statement of Tara Singh of village Chuharkana, district Gujaranwala:

> The Tahsildar used to come to our village for recruitment during the war. He used to have the village surrounded before sunrise and get everyone caught who came out, with the exception of Lambardars and Zaildars. Often, he would take them by surprise in the fields and ask them to enlist themselves on the threat of being shown up in a false case and put in jail. Being thus compelled, people had to assent; and he sent them to the Recruitment Officer who accepted some and rejected others. Those who objected were abused and punished. The Assistant Commissioner came many times to our village and harassed the people. One day, a Lambardar took away two of my tenants, named Manha, son of Ruldu, and Hira, son of Nathu, from my field. Being afraid they ran away and jumped into the canal. One of them reached the other side while the other nearly drowned. The Lambardar succeeded in getting hold of them. People were also forced to contribute towards the War Loan. A poor man who could afford to pay only one rupee was made to pay Rs 5.[27]

When the war was over, a 'grateful' colonial government built India Gate in New Delhi as a memorial for the tens of thousands of Indians who died fighting for someone else's empire. Many of their names are inscribed on it. One wonders if they include the names of Manha and Hira.

The Indian National Congress, meanwhile, had been mostly inactive in the immediate pre-war years. The split into two warring camps had significantly weakened it. It was the revolutionaries who had provided most of the political resistance during those years. Tilak returned from Mandalay Jail in mid-1914. Initially it appeared that he had mellowed in prison and even offered moral support to the war effort. However, a year later, he was back to his assertive self. Even as he tried to unite the Congress factions, he established the India Home Rule League in 1916, demanding full self-rule. The movement spread like wildfire and there was enthusiastic participation that cut across class and religion. Writings of senior British officials in 1918 show that they considered Tilak the most powerful Indian of that time.

Tilak left for London in late 1918, ostensibly to follow up on a libel case, but he would have been acutely interested in assessing Britain's post-war appetite for holding on to India. He returned to India at the end of 1919 and passed away a few months later, in August 1920. The momentum of the Home Rule League, however, was used by a new leader—Mohandas Karamchand Gandhi—to build up protests against the Rowlatt Acts in 1919 and eventually the Non-Cooperation Movement in 1920–21.

5

KALA PAANI

THE ANDAMAN AND NICOBAR ISLANDS ARE A STRING OF SMALL islands just north of Sumatra—the northern cluster is known as the Andamans and the southern as Nicobar. They were well known to ancient mariners plying the Indian Ocean. The name 'Andaman' derives from the Malay pronunciation of 'Hanuman', the monkey hero of the epic Ramayana. The islands were a Danish colony in the early eighteenth century, but the Danes were unable to make any use of them, so they passed into British hands by the end of the century. As early as 1789, the East India Company recognized the possibility of using one of the islands as a penal colony for convicts from the Indian mainland. The British already had a penal colony nearby in Bencoolen (in Sumatra), but it was decided to create an additional one on the Andamans. However, the settlement was abandoned after just seven years as the mortality rate among both prisoners and prison guards was found to be too high.

It was only after the Revolt of 1857 that the British revisited the idea of creating a penal settlement in the islands. Hundreds of rebels were sent there—many would be hanged while most of the others would die from diseases caused by unsanitary living conditions in an intensely hot and humid climate. Since few convicts ever returned alive, the penal colony came to be known popularly as Kala Paani, or the 'Black Waters'. To be sent to Kala Paani was considered a virtual death penalty. At the beginning of the twentieth century, there were 12,000 convicts scattered across the islands. An estimated 3,000 of these were political prisoners, including Wahhabi Islamists, members of the Manipuri nobility and followers of Vasudev Balwant Phadke.

THE CELLULAR JAIL

In the nineteenth century, convicts were kept in a number of scattered settlements. However, it was decided that those deemed the most dangerous would be locked up in a single large facility in Port Blair. The huge Cellular Jail was completed in 1906. It derived its name from the individual 'cells' that were 13'6" x 7'6". These were arranged in rows along seven radials. Where the radials met, there was a central watchtower. The design was based on the 'Panopticon' devised by the British utilitarian philosopher Jeremy Bentham as a mechanism for complete social and mental control. The idea was to keep prisoners in isolated cells so they could not interact with each other. They also could not observe the guards. In contrast, the guards could observe them at will from a central control tower and by walking down the corridor. The constant feeling of being watched, combined with a lack of social interaction, was meant to break the prisoner down mentally.

The Cellular Jail was soon the preferred place to send political prisoners deemed too dangerous to execute or imprison on the mainland. This included many of the revolutionaries mentioned in previous chapters—Barin Ghosh, Ullaskar Dutt, Vinayak Savarkar and Ganesh Savarkar. From 1915, Ghadarite leaders such as Sachindra Nath Sanyal were also sent here. Several survivors have left us vivid accounts of the horrifying conditions inside the facility. In his book *The Tale of My Exile*, Barin Ghosh describes, with a touch of dark humour, the tiny cell where he spent many years:

> Each room has a door closed by iron bars only, with no door leaf. On the back of the room, at a height of four cubits and a half, there is a small window, closed also with iron rails two inches apart. Of furniture in the room there is only a low bedstead one cubit and a half wide, and in one corner an earthen pot painted with tar. One must have a most vigilant sleep on such a bed, otherwise even the least careless turn will land the sleeper with a bang on the floor. And the tarred pot is the most marvelous invention to produce equanimity of the soul with regard to smell, for it is the water closet, and one has to share its delightful company during the whole night.[1]

Depressing as it was, the solitary cell was the least of the prisoners' problems. What turned life in the Cellular Jail into a living hell was the daily regime deliberately designed to constantly humiliate and physically torment the convict. The facility was run by a sadistic Irishman, David Barrie. In a classic example of divide-and-rule, he made sure that the mostly Hindu revolutionaries were put under Muslim jailors, who were encouraged to physically punish even the slightest transgression. Barin specifically mentions Khoyedad Khan, a religious Pathan who took special pleasure in tormenting the non-believers. By the time Savarkar arrived, Barrie's right-hand man was Mirza Khan, who was just as harsh.

The main meal was made of 'ganji'—boiled rice stirred into a gooey porridge. It had no salt and was consequently entirely tasteless. As a cruel joke, the goop was occasionally laced with a dash of kerosene, which rendered even this inedible. The prisoners were also sometimes served rotis that were as tough as leather, along with watery dal and half-cooked vegetables. The food often had insects and worms, and the half-cooked vegetables were not easy to digest. Any complaint was brutally punished and resulted in all food being withdrawn for days. Given the kerosene, the half-cooked vegetables and unhygienic conditions, almost all the prisoners suffered frequently from abdominal pain and diarrhoea. It was not uncommon to find a prisoner passed out in his cell in his own excrement.

The prisoners were expected to work during the day. Two kinds of tasks were commonly given. The first was that of coir rope-making. The prisoners were expected to use their bare hands to strip out the coir fibre, pound it to soften it and then braid it into rope. Each prisoner was expected to produce a minimum of three pounds of rope every day in this way. Hard as it was, it was considered better than the task of turning the *kolhu* (oil mill). The grinding oil mill was usually turned by yoked bullocks in the villages, but in the Cellular Jail it was done by humans. It required enormous strength and stamina to keep up the momentum, especially since this was done in the blazing tropical sun. Even a sip of water was not provided (unless one of the guards or the waterman was somehow bribed). If a convict was unable to keep up or fainted, his hands were tied to the handle and the others had to keep the mill turning. Not surprisingly, the oil mill caused the death of many by exhaustion while it drove others to insanity.

Some prisoners were mere teenagers. The jailors and their enforcers would routinely sexually exploit and rape them.

> There is a considerable number of boy prisoners in Port Blair whose ages vary from 17 or 18 to 20 or 22. They are kept under the charge of petty officers and tindals who are mostly unmarried and have no character. The revolting oppressions that they have to suffer in the hands of the latter cannot be described in any decent human language. The very shame of it prevents them from complaining to the authorities; and even if they do so, it is more often than not crying in the wilderness.[2]

The warders, of course, made use of sticks and whips to ensure compliance. However, if they wanted to break a mentally strong prisoner, they used fetters. One form was a crossbar fetter, which involved an iron bar between the ankles that held the legs apart. The prisoner would then have to walk, sleep and do his tasks with his legs stretched apart. Another form was an iron bar that hung from the waist and was riveted to the prisoner's feet. This prevented the prisoner from bending his leg. In both cases, the prisoner would be left in fetters for months and, after a while, would find it painful to do even small routine tasks.

Given this inhuman treatment, it is not surprising that many prisoners contemplated suicide. In 1912, Indu Bhushan Roy hanged himself in his cell. Barrie was furious when news of the suicide leaked out and caused a public uproar. A few weeks later, Ullaskar Dutt decided that he would no longer do his assigned work of climbing into a well and lifting buckets of water to the top. No amount of threats and beatings made him budge. Barrie ordered that his hands be put in chains and that he be suspended by them from the ceiling of his cell continuously for a week.

The pain made Ullaskar hallucinate, and his screams filled the Cellular Jail.

He was dragged out and found to be running a fever of 107 degrees Fahrenheit and in a state of delirium. But this did not stop his tormentors. Barrie insisted that Ullaskar was only feigning insanity to avoid work. He ordered that electric shocks be administered to see if the prisoner had indeed gone insane. As the electricity passed through his body, Ullaskar's heart-wrenching screams could be heard all over the Cellular Jail until he finally fell unconscious. Even after he regained consciousness after three days, he continued to have fits and convulsions, only occasionally regaining his senses.[3]

Just before he was arrested, Ullaskar had been engaged to Bipin Pal's daughter, Lila. Through the haze of his delirium, Ullaskar would see her image floating in front of him. This is what is said to have kept him going. We will return to their love story later in the book.

Vinayak Savarkar confronted Barrie about Ullaskar's condition, but he was still adamant that Ullaskar was just trying to shirk work. However, the jailor was concerned that the incident had been witnessed by too many people and news would get out. He eventually allowed Ullaskar to be shifted to a mental asylum in Madras, where he would remain for twelve long years.

The next act of resistance came from Nani Gopal, a seventeen-year-old revolutionary from Chinsura (now Chuchura) in Bengal. The boy refused to work the oil mill one day. Even though he was repeatedly beaten with a cane to within an inch of his life, he remained adamant. He was sent away for a while to another prison on Viper Island, but when he returned, he started a hunger strike. Barrie had him force-fed—milk through a pipe inserted through his nose—but Nani Gopal continued to rapidly lose weight. Meanwhile, several other prisoners also went on strike. With both the Ullaskar and the Indu Bhushan incidents by now in public knowledge, he did not want another casualty so soon. Savarkar realized this was a good time to extract some concessions. In return for convincing the prisoners to end their strike, Savarkar was able to negotiate small improvements in their lives—some time for social interaction between prisoners, access to books and papers, and a supply of slates, paper and pencils for teaching the less educated.[4] After this incident, Savarkar became the de facto leader of the convicted revolutionaries. This did not save him from being regularly subjected to torture—if anything, it made him even more of a target—but he had the satisfaction of being able to push back against some of the worst excesses.

Only two of the original radials of the Cellular Jail survive today, along with the entrance block and part of the central tower. These are now preserved as a national monument. A visitor can wander down the corridors of cells and even see the cell where Savarkar had been incarcerated. Another one has been recently dedicated to Sachin Sanyal. I sat alone for a long time in one of the bare cells on the second floor and tried to imagine how it would have felt to be a convict.

JALLIANWALA BAGH

The First World War ended in November 1918, and the Indian regiments began to come home. The colonial administration was nervous about this. They knew that the soldiers had been radicalized with Ghadarite ideas before they had been deployed and had come within an inch of revolt in 1915. As experienced war veterans, the demobilized returnees were now even more dangerous. Not only were they conversant with the latest military technology, they had stood shoulder-to-shoulder with European troops in the trenches. Therefore, they were not in awe of the white man. Nowhere was the nervousness greater than in Punjab, the province that had supplied a disproportionate share of Indian soldiers.

The British authorities decided that they needed to give themselves ever more draconian powers to deal with adverse developments. During the war, the administration had acquitted emergency powers under the Defence of India Act, but now something more permanent was to be put in place. An English judge, Sir Sydney Rowlatt, was put in charge of the committee to draft the legislation. The Anarchical and Revolutionary Crimes Act (popularly known as the Rowlatt Acts) were actually two bills. As should be clear from the nomenclature, the bills were specifically designed to target revolutionaries. The laws allowed for speedy trials by a special court that could meet in camera, take consideration of evidence not allowed under the Indian Evidence Act, and there was no appeal. The provincial government was given the power to search without a warrant and to confine any suspect without explanation 'in such place and under such conditions and restrictions as it may specify'.[5] In other words, it effectively removed all legal protection for the Indian population.

The first of the two bills was passed on 18 March 1919 and enacted before it was even published, despite the fact that only one Indian member voted in its favour. There was an immediate backlash. Three Indians resigned from the Imperial Legislative Council—Madan Mohan Malaviya, Mazharul Haque and Mohammad Ali Jinnah.[6] The political movement against the laws gathered pace under the leadership of Gandhi. This was the first time that his approach of passive resistance (*satyagraha*) was deployed on a national level.

Gandhi announced a general strike on 30 March and then again on 6 April. They were a success, with shops and other establishments being closed and a large number of protesters gathering. However, they were not entirely peaceful and there were clashes in Delhi and Ahmedabad—several people were killed in police firing. Gandhi went to Punjab but was forcibly made to deboard from a train near Delhi and sent to Bombay under escort before being freed.

Meanwhile, events were moving fast in Punjab. Lieutenant Governor Michael O'Dwyer was determined to quash any protests with an iron hand. Two local businessmen in Amritsar, Mahasha Rattan Chand and Chaudhuri Bugga Mall, had been setting up wrestling akhadas in and around the city. The colonial government was always suspicious of akhadas due to their association with revolutionary networks. Their suspicion was further aroused when the two organized a large Ram Navami celebration on 9 April, which attracted significant Muslim participation. A display of Hindu–Muslim unity was something that the authorities saw as a threat. It was also Rattan Chand and Bugga Mall who invited two well-known INC leaders, Dr Satyapal and Dr Saifuddin Kitchlew, to speak on the Rowlatt Acts.

At 7 p.m. on 9 April, the local administration in Amritsar received orders from O'Dwyer's office in Lahore to arrest Satyapal and Kitchlew. By the next morning, news of the arrest had spread across Amritsar and protesters began to gather at Hall Bazaar. Around 11.30 a.m., a group of protesters decided that they would walk to the office of the deputy commissioner to petition for their release. The group was unarmed and the protests were entirely peaceful. As they made their way across a railway overbridge, they were stopped by a military picket. Even as the protesters were arguing with the soldiers at the picket, more soldiers arrived and took up positions. At some point, two British soldiers lost their patience and fired into the crowd, killing about four protesters and wounding several more.

The crowd now fled back into the city and reassembled at Hall Bazaar. The sight of the dead and wounded had agitated the mood greatly, but the crowd was still peaceful. More and more people began to assemble, perhaps as many as 30,000. Some of the protesters decided to go back to the railway overbridge—some may even have thrown stones at the picket. The picket had received further reinforcements and was prepared to use force. Suddenly the soldiers let loose a volley of gunfire that killed another twenty people and left many more badly wounded.

News of the second massacre fed back to the main gathering at Hall Bazaar. As some of the bodies were brought back, the crowd grew ever more angry, until a mob decided to attack British-linked institutions in the vicinity—National Bank, Chartered Bank, Alliance Bank and the Church Missionary Society's Girls Normal School. Three European bank managers were killed, while the rest escaped with the help of Indian clerks. A female missionary was beaten, even as another British woman, a doctor, narrowly escaped. In all, five British civilians were killed by the mob.

The press reports of the time presented the mob attack as unprovoked. The names and personal details of all the European casualties were widely reported, but we have almost no information about the Indians killed. They are just described as 'the mob'.

By the evening of 10 April and throughout 11 April, more military contingents arrived in Amritsar from Lahore and Jullundur. They were mostly Baloch, Gurkha and European troops, since O'Dwyer was uncertain about how Punjabi troops would react to the situation. Funerals were allowed under strict restrictions on 11 and 12 April. Despite fears of renewed violence, the two days were relatively peaceful. Rattan Chand and Bugga Mall, however, were arrested on 12 April. They would be sent to the Cellular Jail and return to Amritsar only after seventeen years, in 1936! All for the sin of having organized a popular religious festival and having a meeting to discuss the Rowlatt Acts. Gholam Jilani, a local imam who had helped garner Muslim participation at the Ram Navami festivities, was picked up by the police and subjected to extreme torture, including having a sharpened pole forced into his anus. Another 200 locals were arrested and tried under martial law for the attacks on the Europeans.

On the night of 11 April, Brigadier-General Reginald Dyer arrived from Jullundur to take charge of the city. He was the son of a brewer and had grown up in Simla. He could speak Hindi and Urdu fluently. Dyer had spent the war running part of the East Persia Cordon. His experience with Baloch tribesmen was that a show of brute military power was a sure way to impress the natives. He intended to do the same in Amritsar. Military pickets were set up all over the city. Before dawn on 12 April, Dyer had cut off the water and electricity supplies to the city. Despite the inconvenience, the city remained peaceful. However, a group of local activists called a public meeting in Jallianwala Bagh on the afternoon of 13 April to discuss the situation. This was not unusual, as the park was used commonly as a place for meetings.

It was a Sunday as well as Baisakhi—a holy day for Hindus and Sikhs. Many people from the surrounding villages had come to visit the Golden Temple. Despite heavy military presence, the morning appeared peaceful, except that very few shops were open due to the strike.

Jallianwala Bagh is located in the old, crowded part of Amritsar, barely a stone's throw from the Golden Temple. It is a sizeable open area where local children played, people gathered for festivals and occasionally public meetings were held. Importantly, it only had one narrow entrance-exit. Around 4 p.m. on 13 April, there were 8,000–10,000 people in the park. Perhaps 2,000 or so were there to attend the public meeting, but the majority were there for other reasons—neighbourhood children playing, people resting before or after visiting the Golden Temple, and those out to meet friends and relatives for Baisakhi.

The first sign of trouble was a plane flying in circles above the city. This was an unusual sight in those days. Ground reports and the aerial survey gave Dyer a fairly good idea of the number of people in the park. He placed pickets on the roads leading to the park, with orders to shoot anyone escaping from it. Then, he arrived at the entrance of the Jallianwala Bagh with a contingent of troops armed with .303 Lee-Enfield rifles and two armoured cars with machine guns. The armoured cars were too big for the narrow passage, so Dyer left them outside to guard the entrance. He then marched the troops into the park and lined them up next to the only exit route.

Some of the people in the park would have noticed the soldiers, but would not have had the time to respond in any way. It all happened too quickly. Without any warning, Dyer ordered the soldiers to fire at the unarmed civilians. He had deployed two firing parties on either side of the entrance—Gurkhas to the right and Baloch to the left.[7] They fired 1,650 rounds, or 33 per person.[8] As one can expect, there was mayhem as people began to drop dead. In the stampede, several fell into an open well while others tried to escape by climbing the walls. Therefore, the casualties were not merely from the bullets but also from the stampede.

The official death toll was initially put at just 250 but later raised to 379, but most reliable estimates put it at around 1,000.[9] The number of the wounded would have been higher. Dyer was quite frank in the subsequent inquiry, that his act was deliberate and that he had been prevented from killing even more by the fact that the narrow passage did not allow the entry of his machine-gun-equipped armoured cars. All eye-witness accounts confirm that the casualties included a large number of children—the youngest was just seven months old. Several more were shot at the pickets as they tried to make their way out. There are accounts of grievously wounded people crawling out of Jallianwala Bagh a couple of days after the shooting. Most people, even those who were badly injured, did not seek medical help for fear that they would be summarily arrested for being at the venue.

Here is the testimony of Ratan Devi, who lost her husband in the massacre.

> I was in my house near Jallianwala Bagh when I heard shots fired. I was then lying down. I got up at once as I was anxious, because my husband had gone to the Bagh. I began to cry and went to the place accompanied by two women to help me. There I saw heaps of dead bodies and I began to search for my husband. After passing through the heap, I eventually found the dead body of my husband. The way towards it was full of blood and dead bodies. After a short time, both the sons of Lala Sundar Das came there;

and I asked them to bring a charpoy to carry the dead body of my husband home. The boys accordingly went home and I sent away the women also. By this time it was 8 o'clock and no one could stir out of his house because of the curfew order. I stood on waiting and crying.[10]

Dyer had not only disallowed any medical help, he had also imposed a strict curfew that prevented anyone from coming in to help. Ratan Devi stood next to her dead husband in the dark, listening to the desperate moans of the wounded all around. She found a bamboo stick, which she used to prevent stray dogs from eating her husband's corpse. There was a twelve-year-old boy in agony, lying nearby. He begged Ratan Devi not to leave him. She tried her best to comfort him. The boy kept asking for water, but there was no way to get him a sip.

Apologists sometimes try to put the entire blame of the massacre on the folly of one man—Reginald Dyer. However, it should be remembered that the events in Amritsar were not isolated. There was a broader attempt to batter the population of Punjab into submission. Lieutenant Governor O'Dwyer, for instance, ordered the use of military aircraft to bomb the civilian population. Thus, a day after the massacre in Amritsar, an aircraft flown by Major Carberry flew low over Gujranwala, dropping bombs and firing on any large group of Indians that he could see from the air. Many were killed and wounded in the aerial attacks. Arbitrary racist punishments were imposed in several towns. In Kasur, over a hundred suspects were forced into a public cage and left to the elements for several days. Schoolboys were randomly selected and publicly flogged. In Amritsar, Indians were forced to bend and crawl through the lane where an Englishwomen had been attacked.

Jallianwala Bagh still exists in Amritsar and is preserved as a national monument. One can walk through the narrow entrance used by Dyer. The walls on the opposite side still bear the bullet holes from the .303 Lee-Enfield rifles. On a bright afternoon, with flowers in bloom, tourists taking selfies and children running around, it was difficult to imagine the horror that had visited this place in April 1919. Perhaps this is the same reason why the victims, out to celebrate Baisakhi, were taken so completely by surprise.

THE AFTERMATH

The British initially tried to suppress news of the atrocities being perpetrated in Punjab, but the scale of events was too large to be kept hidden for long. It led to a wave of horror and revulsion across the country. The poet Rabindranath Tagore returned his knighthood in protest, with the words: 'Giving voice to the protest of the millions of my countrymen surprised in dumb anguish of terror.' The Congress instituted a committee of inquiry that collected eyewitness accounts of what had happened. Even a hundred years later, reading the testimonies is a very emotional experience for any Indian.

The colonial government, however, continued to support Dyer, and even gave him a promotion—albeit later reversed. The viceroy was ultimately shamed into instituting an official committee of inquiry under the chairmanship of Lord Hunter. It had five British members and three Indians. The Hunter Committee published its report in May 1920. It was far from unanimous, with the five Europeans issuing a mildly critical main report but with a dissenting note from the Indian members. It contains Dyer's own statements, which were unrepentant: 'I fired and continued to fire until the crowd dispersed and I consider this the least amount of firing which would produce the necessary moral and widespread effect it was my duty to produce ...'

The British government eventually pronounced a mild censure on Dyer and removed him from active service, while O'Dwyer was absolved of all responsibility. Even this was carried in the House of Commons only by 232 votes to 131. The House of Lords passed a resolution 129 votes to 89, deploring the removal of Dyer as unjust. The British press and prominent individuals such as Rudyard Kipling were almost entirely in Dyer's camp. A fund was opened by *The Morning Post* in London to collect money for him—it was supported by most English-language newspapers in India. The resident European community in India came out in full support of Dyer. English ladies in Mussoorie set up a Dyer Appreciation Fund and collected a large sum that they presented to the man.[11] The Bishop of Lahore made a statement to the authorities that the situation would have been far worse but for Dyer's prompt action. In short, the dominant British view was that Dyer had saved the empire from another 1857.

What was worse was the attitude of the loyalist Punjabi elite. Both the traditional elite and the newly rich contractor class were effusive in their support of O'Dwyer and Dyer. They organized farewell dinners for them and raised money for generous gifts. Just a few weeks after the massacre, the head of the Akal Takht, Arur Singh, invited Dyer to the Golden Temple and presented him with a *siropa* (robe of honour).[12] It is especially shocking, given that the Golden Temple is virtually next door to Jallianwala Bagh and that many of the victims were pilgrims. The British clearly understood the elite's hankering for titles, since many of the Loyalists found their names in the honour lists over the next few years. Glancing through the lists today makes for interesting reading.[13]

RETURN FROM HELL

By the end of 1919, it was obvious even to the most optimistic colonial official that the Jallianwala Bagh massacre had been a strategic mistake, as it had inflamed Indian nationalism. The government began to look for ways to soften the mood. One of the measures was to release some of the revolutionary leaders incarcerated in various jails. Among those released from the Cellular Jail were Barin Ghosh and Sachindra Nath Sanyal.

In his book *Bandi Jeevan*, Sanyal describes how he found out about his release in February 1920. He was in the jail hospital recovering from an illness when he was told to visit the main office. Sanyal tells us that he was quite afraid to go to the office, as all his previous encounters with jail officials had ended in arguments and punishment. Nonetheless, he had no choice and dragged himself there. To his surprise, the jailor gave him a big smile and said, 'Cheer up, man, you are released!'

Sanyal describes the initial exhilaration and then the somewhat mixed feeling on the realization that most of his fellow convicts would continue in prison. He felt almost guilty leaving them behind. It was another twenty days before the ship arrived. Sanyal had spent over four years in the hell of the Cellular Jail and asked if he could spend a few days wandering around Port Blair as a free man. Permission was not granted and he remained in his cell until he boarded the ship to Calcutta along with Barin and the others.

On reaching Calcutta, they were all taken to the police headquarters. They sat around for hours for some paperwork to get done. At some point, Sanyal lost his patience and just walked out. No one stopped him. The problem was that he did not have any money and did not have the address of a cousin who lived in Calcutta. He just knew that the cousin lived in the

Kalighat area. Along the way, he asked a young man for help with directions and made friends with him. Sanyal writes that he tried to ascertain his new friend's political views and to recruit him for the revolutionary cause. Note that he had been free for no more than a couple of hours and was already back to recruiting. He did not succeed, in this case. Nonetheless, he did manage to find his cousin's house and was given a warm welcome. Sanyal famously loved his food and tells us how much he enjoyed his first home-cooked meal in years!

He later went back to the police headquarters and finished the paperwork. A couple of days later, he took a train to Varanasi. His home had been confiscated by the government, and his mother and three brothers were living with relatives in the lanes of Bengali Tola, Madanpura. It was a joyful reunion. Nonetheless, Sanyal's main concern was to find a way to free the remaining political prisoners from the Cellular Jail, in particular Bhai Parmanand and Vinayak Savarkar. With this in mind, he met Madan Mohan Malaviya, who was then building Banaras Hindu University. Malaviya gave him a patient hearing but did not offer any concrete assistance.

Disappointed, Sanyal reached out to every INC leader who was willing to meet him. He recounts how he met Jawaharlal Nehru in Gorakhpur. After hearing him out, Nehru commented, 'At a time that we are planning to go to jail, you want us to help others come out of prison?'[14] This comment stunned Sanyal. He realized that most INC leaders simply did not appreciate the difference between conditions in a normal prison and those in the Cellular Jail. Despite the lack of support, he kept up his efforts and attended an INC special session in Calcutta. Lala Lajpat Rai, who was presiding over the session, met Sanyal and immediately offered his unconditional backing. Others such as Bipin Pal and Chittaranjan Das also offered help. They also arranged for a speaking slot at the Nagpur Congress in December 1920.

The Nagpur Congress is today remembered for the adoption of Gandhi's proposal for launching the nationwide Non-Cooperation Movement. Less remembered is the fact that Sanyal spoke at the event about the treatment of the political prisoners in the Cellular Jail. Narayan Savarkar, Vinayak's younger brother, was also present on the stage. A resolution was passed, asking for better treatment and release of the imprisoned revolutionaries. As a result of the sustained campaign by Sanyal, a few more revolutionaries were released but Vinayak Savarkar was still deemed to be too dangerous. He would be brought back to the mainland in May 1921 and held in Ratnagiri Jail for another three years. Thereafter, he would be kept restricted to the Ratnagiri district under strict conditions for thirteen more years.

KHILAFAT AND NON-COOPERATION

The post-war terms offered by the Allies effectively called for the dismemberment of the Ottoman Empire. As the Ottoman Sultan was considered by many Sunnis to be the Caliph, this led to discontent among pan-Islamists in India. Gandhi saw this as an opportunity to leverage Muslim resentment to increase the community's participation in the freedom struggle. The result was the Khilafat Movement, launched in August 1920. It was a controversial decision, since it made Muslim participation in a national freedom movement contingent on external loyalties. For the moment, however, there were loud proclamations of Hindu–Muslim unity and a palpable increase in Muslim involvement.

Gandhi now sought to use the momentum to launch the Non-Cooperation Movement. The idea was that Indians would progressively boycott all institutions related to the colonial administration—courts, offices, educational institutions, legislatures, titles/awards and so on. At the same time, Indians would adopt 'swadeshi', meaning they would boycott all foreign-made goods. This was conceptually similar to what had been done in 1905–06, except that Gandhi additionally insisted on traditional modes of production, such as hand-spinning and weaving. This was a break from the original emphasis on modernization.

Many senior leaders in the INC were sceptical of Gandhi's new methods. Madan Mohan Malaviya, Annie Besant, M.A. Jinnah and Chittaranjan Das initially opposed the proposals. However, Gandhi was able to carry the resolution at the Nagpur Congress with 1,886 votes against 884. With Tilak having passed away in August, this marked the emergence of Gandhi as the pre-eminent leader of the INC.

As the months of 1921 passed, it became apparent that Gandhi's new approach was attracting widespread public participation. Many revolutionaries, even those who may have been initially dismissive of the idea of passive resistance, joined the movement. The British suddenly found themselves in the awkward position of ruling a country where a sizeable section of the population simply did not listen to them. Optimists began to expect major concessions from the British before the end of the year. The colonial administration was certainly nervous when the Prince of Wales arrived on a state visit in November 1921 and repeatedly faced strikes.

Nevertheless, several key revolutionary leaders stayed away. Sanyal was not dismissive of Gandhi's movement and its popular impact, but remained sceptical about its ability to extract real concessions. He preferred to use this time to expand links with trade unions and peasant movements. Sri Aurobindo had withdrawn from political activity, but there were still many supporters who hoped that he would return, especially after Tilak's death. Even Gandhi sent his son, Devdas, to Pondicherry to elicit his support, but was refused. Sri Aurobindo was unconvinced by Gandhian methods. He would mock the extreme adherence to non-violence as 'getting beaten with joy'. When the Non-Cooperation Movement was launched, he predicted that it would end 'in great confusion or in a great fiasco'.[15]

Just as the Non-Cooperation Movement reached its climax in the second half of 1921, its internal contradictions also came to the fore. The Khilafat Movement had mobilized the Muslims along communal lines rather than along nationalist lines. In the Malabar, a section of the local Muslims—known as the Moplahs or Mapillas—directed their ire at the Hindu population. Temples were desecrated, women were mass-raped, houses were set on fire, thousands were killed, children were targeted and many were forcibly converted to Islam. C. Gopalan Nair, a retired civil servant, witnessed the events and published an account just two years later.[16] Here is a description of how kangaroo courts were set up in the villages by the Moplahs, who carried out the mass killings:

> More than 40 Hindus were taken to the Tangal with their hands tied behind their back, charged with the crime of helping the Military with supplying them milk, tender coconuts etc. and 38 of these Hindus were condemned to death. He superintended

the work of murder in person and seated on a rock near a well witnessed his men cutting at the neck of his victims and pushing the bodies into the well. Thirty-eight men were murdered, one of whom a pensioned head constable to whom he owed a grudge had his head neatly divided into two halves.[17]

The Hindu and Christian women of Malabar wrote desperate letters to the authorities and any senior person who would care to listen to their woes. Here is an extract from one such letter:

> Of the wells and tanks filled up with the mutilated, but often half-dead bodies of our nearest and dearest ones who refused to abandon the faith of our Fathers; of pregnant women cut to pieces and left on the roadside and in the jungles, with the unborn babe protruding from the mangled corpse; of our innocent and helpless children torn from our arms, and done to death before our eyes, and of our husbands and fathers tortured, flayed and burnt alive; of our helpless sisters forcibly carried away in the midst of kith and kin and subjected to every shame and outrage which the vile and brutal imagination of these inhuman hell hounds could conceive of; of the thousands of our homesteads reduced to cinder-mounds out of sheer savagery and a wonton spirit of destruction; of our places of worship desecrated and destroyed; of the images of the deity shamefully insulted by putting the entrails of cows where flower garlands used to lie, or else smashed to pieces ...[18]

There have been attempts by later writers and journalists to present the riots as 'peasant uprisings' but there is more than enough primary evidence that shows that it was a religious pogrom. Gandhi's responses were disappointing. He initially denied the violence and then tried to downplay its links to the Khilafat Movement. The Moplah riots were finally put down by government troops.

Despite the shock of the Moplah riots, the Non-Cooperation Movement was still going strong in January 1922. On 5 February, a police officer had an altercation with some volunteers manning a picket in front of a liquor shop in the village bazaar of Chauri Chaura, near Gorakhpur. The policeman had some of the volunteers beaten up, and in response several hundred villagers gathered at the police station to lodge a protest. Some local elders calmed the situation down and the crowd began to disperse. Things had been peaceful so far, but, for reasons that are not clear, the police decided to fire on some of the stragglers. At least two villagers were killed. This incensed the crowd, which now returned in full fury. The policeman bolted themselves inside the station but the mob set it on fire. About twenty-two trapped policemen were killed in the fire.

When Gandhi heard about the incident, he unilaterally decided to withdraw the Non-Cooperation Movement. Many Congress leaders felt that a single incident should not derail a national movement, but Gandhi was adamant that the movement would have to be strictly non-violent. His critics pointed out that his principled adherence to non-violence had not prevented him from helping the British during the Boer Wars, recruiting soldiers for the First World War or understating the brutality of the Moplah riots. The British took advantage of the confusion to make arrests and break down all opposition. Meanwhile, led by Kemal Ataturk, the Turks themselves deposed the last Ottoman Sultan and abolished the Caliphate. Sri Aurobindo sardonically commented that he had been wrong about the movement—it had ended in great confusion *and* in a fiasco.

CHITTARANJAN'S RECRUITS

The sudden withdrawal of the Non-Cooperation Movement and the subsequent arrests left the INC in disarray. Chittaranjan Das, a successful lawyer, became the effective leader of those opposed to Gandhi. Even moderates such as Motilal Nehru and Vithalbhai Patel joined him. They formed a group within the Congress known as the Swaraj Party. They took a somewhat different line from the Gandhian faction on several issues. They were willing, for instance, to participate in the provincial councils being set up by the colonial administration.

An important source of Das's growing political heft was the systematic absorption into the Congress of former revolutionaries or those with revolutionary sympathies. Readers will recall that Das was the young lawyer who had defended Aurobindo Ghosh during the Alipore trials of 1908–09 and, therefore, had a long relationship with the revolutionary movement. In the early 1920s, Das brought in two young men into the Congress who would play an important role in subsequent events—Subhas Chandra Bose and Nalinaksha Sanyal.

Subhas was born on 23 January 1897 in Cuttack to a lawyer, Janakinath Bose, and his wife, Prabhavati. Theirs was an upper-middle-class Bengali family, originally from Calcutta, and Subhas was the ninth child and sixth son of the couple. When he was around fifteen, he moved to Calcutta. This is also the time when he discovered the ideas and writings of Swami Vivekananda. This would have a profound impact on him, so much so that for a while he contemplated becoming a monk.

During the summer vacation of 1914, Subhas quietly left his home and travelled with a friend to various pilgrimage sites—Rishikesh, Hardwar, Mathura and Varanasi. At that time, Varanasi was the hotbed of Ghadarite activity, but there is nothing to suggest that Subhas was aware of it. He returned to Calcutta, having decided against becoming a monk, but would retain a strongly religious streak throughout his life.

After high school, Subhas joined Presidency College in Calcutta, where he was involved in an incident in 1916 that marks the first time he participated in an explicitly political activity. Edward Oaten, a history professor said to hold racist views, got into an altercation with a group of students. Led by Subhas, the student community demanded an apology and went on strike. Oaten and the principal met student representatives and settled the matter on the second day. However, the very next day, Oaten turned out ten of the twelve students from his class on the grounds that they had participated in the strike. He then 'manhandled' a student from the chemistry department. This enraged the students, and a group of them gave Oaten a beating. It is unclear if Subhas hit the professor, but he was certainly present. In any case, as the leader of the strike, he was blamed for the incident and expelled from the college.[19]

Subhas spent a year back in Cuttack before he enrolled in Scottish Church College to read philosophy. He got first-class marks and placed second in Calcutta University's order of merit. For his master's degree, he wanted to study experimental psychology, but his father persuaded him to go to England and attempt the Indian Civil Service examinations. Thus, in September 1919, Subhas sailed to England and, like Aurobindo Ghosh, enrolled in Cambridge while he prepared for the examination. When the results of the ICS examination of 1920 were published, he was surprised to find that he had stood fourth. At this moment, however, Subhas faced the same dilemma that Aurobindo Ghosh had a generation earlier—should he serve a colonial government that suppressed his people? To the great disappointment of his family, Subhas decided to follow Aurobindo and opt out. In April 1921, he wrote a letter of resignation. The British must have had an inkling that this young man was likely to be just as troublesome as his predecessor—several senior officials tried to dissuade him, but he remained adamant.

Subhas sailed back to India in July 1921. By coincidence, Rabindranath Tagore was on the same ship and they spent a lot of time discussing the evolving political situation. As it happened, the poet was not in favour of the Non-Cooperation Movement, as he felt that it would permanently damage and politicize institutions such as universities. He also felt that the movement was unnecessarily burdened by Gandhi's personal aversion to modern technology. The idealistic young man was not entirely convinced by Tagore's arguments. So, when he landed in Bombay, he immediately made his way to Mani Bhawan to meet Gandhi. Bose recalled the meeting in his book *The Indian Struggle*:

> But though I tried to persuade myself at that time that there must be a lack of understanding on my part, my reason told me clearly, again and again, that there was a deplorable lack of clarity in the plan which the Mahatma had formulated and that he himself did not have a clear idea of the successive stages of the campaign which would bring India to her cherished goal of freedom.[20]

Disappointed, Subhas returned to Calcutta, where he moved in with his brother Sarat at 38/1 Elgin Road, next door to his parents' house at 38/2 Elgin Road. A few days later, he met Chittaranjan Das, with whom he had been corresponding from Cambridge. Subhas immediately felt that 'here was a man who knew what he was about'. He would later write, 'I felt I had found a Leader and I meant to follow him.'[21]

Das was initially not in favour of the Non-Cooperation Movement but took to it enthusiastically once it appeared that a majority of the INC members were in its favour. Subhas became his chief organizer for strikes in Calcutta. There were great expectations that the accelerating momentum of the movement would force change. Looking back on the mid-1930s, Subhas would write, 'It is not possible at this distant date to understand how profoundly the people of India believed in 1921 that Swaraj would be won before the end of the year.'[22] In December 1921, both Subhas and Das were arrested. This was the first time that Subhas had been sent to prison, but the mood was optimistic. Therefore, the news that Gandhi had withdrawn the movement came as a shock, 'The Dictator's decree was obeyed at that time, but there was a regular revolt in the Congress Camp.'[23]

The British were jubilant at the turn of events and took full advantage of the confusion to make arrests. Prime Minister David Lloyd George made a speech in August 1922, where he congratulated the Indian civil service for suppressing the freedom movement and being a staunchly loyal 'steel frame'.[24] This phrase is usually attributed today to Vallabhbhai Patel, but was originally used by Lloyd George to describe how firmly the colonial administration had stood up through the World War, the Ghadar Movement, the Jallianwala Bagh massacre and finally the Non-Cooperation Movement. By a twist of collective amnesia, the bureaucracy of Independent India adopted the phrase 'steel frame' as a badge of honour.

When Subhas was released from jail in September, there was news of devastating floods in north Bengal. He immediately headed there, along with Nalinaksha Sanyal, to organize relief efforts. The relief work was widely appreciated and helped Subhas build a core team, but it did not change the fact that the wider movement was in a shambles.

The Swaraj Party now decided to break away from Gandhi's approach and contest elections, including those to the Calcutta Corporation. They won a comfortable majority in the municipal elections of 1924. Thus, Das became the mayor of Calcutta, Hussain Shaheed Suhrawardy became the deputy mayor and a twenty-seven-year-old Subhas became the chief executive officer of the administration. Subhas threw himself into administrative work, and it appears he rather enjoyed the responsibilities. Unfortunately, this did not last long as the intelligence agencies were convinced that he was secretly building an underground revolutionary network.

On 25 October 1924, the police arrested him under the Regulation III of 1818. Under this provision, the colonial administration could detain anyone indefinitely without a trial or even making charges against them public. He was briefly held in Berhampore and then shifted to Mandalay. This was the same prison where Lajpat Rai, Tilak and Ajit Singh had been incarcerated. Indeed, Subhas saw it as a rite of passage to be imprisoned in the same place as these stalwarts.

The prison cells in Mandalay were old wooden buildings that leaked when it rained and were full of dust when it was dry. They were also full of mosquitoes and other insects. However, unlike the Cellular Jail, the prisoners were not subjected to physical torture and humiliation. Subhas was allowed to use his time to read. Nonetheless, the untimely death of Das in June 1925 came as a blow. Subhas had lost his mentor and he would now have to evolve quickly into a leader in his own right.

In October 1925, the prisoners, led by Subhas, requested the jail authorities for permission to celebrate Durga Puja, the single-most important festival of Shakta Hindus. Permission was initially granted but abruptly reversed by the government—the jail superintendent was censured for granting approval. The Hindu prisoners were particularly incensed when Christian convicts were given full support for celebrating Christmas a few months later. In response, Subhas led a fifteen-day hunger strike in February 1926. Despite government efforts to keep a lid on this, news of the hunger strike was reported in the Swarajist newspaper *Forward* and caused an uproar. The government was eventually forced to back down and the hunger strike was withdrawn. Unfortunately, Subhas's health did not recover and kept deteriorating. The steady loss of weight led to concerns that he might have contracted tuberculosis, considered a deadly disease at that time.

Given his regular low-grade fever and continued loss of weight, the Bose family lobbied to have Subhas released. The government offered to release him on the condition that he would go directly to Europe for treatment and not return to India until 1930. Subhas knew that this was just a tactic to remove him from the Indian political landscape; the offer was rejected. In response, the government decided to shift him to Almora Jail in the Himalayas, where the weather was considered healthy for tuberculosis patients. He, accordingly, was brought back to Calcutta in May 1927, but when he arrived, the new governor Sir Stanley Jackson ordered his release. Thus, after two and a half years of detention without trial, Subhas was free!

THE REBEL SCHOLAR

Nalinaksha Sanyal was born in November 1898 in the village of Dhoradaha in the Nadia district of Bengal. His family was educated but not well off; they owned a patch of land and partly depended on agricultural income. His ancestral house in Dhoradaha is a modest single-storey affair and still exists, albeit in poor condition when I visited it in August 2021. Nalinaksha's elder brother, Anadi Kanta, was a member of the Anushilan Samiti.

During 1914–15, Nalinaksha was an active member of Bagha Jatin's Jugantar network and was involved in building a revolutionary network in the Nadia–Murshidabad belt. He was arrested during the police crackdown following Bagha Jatin's death, but was eventually let off as nothing incriminating could be found on him. However, he remained part of the surviving group of Jugantar revolutionaries led by Amarendra Nath Chatterjee in Nadia and worked closely with the Anushilan Samiti network run by Pratul Chandra Ganguli in nearby Murshidabad.

Not surprisingly, he was constantly on the radar of the police. In 1916, he was arrested at 4 a.m. on the last day of his intermediate of arts examinations, when he was to appear for his logic paper. Just hours earlier, Nalinaksha had seen a suspicious person loitering around his home and guessed that he might be an informer. Therefore, he had burnt all the papers and hidden his pistol. The authorities, nonetheless, were not going to let him off so easily and hauled him before the magistrate. After much begging, the magistrate let him appear for the paper under police surveillance and he was taken to the lock-up immediately afterwards. Despite the circumstances, Nalinaksha Sanyal would place eleventh in the overall order of merit at Calcutta University, and in logic he secured the highest marks![25]

Nalinaksha joined Presidency College and immediately became the leader of a group of students sympathetic to the revolutionary cause. Unlike Subhas, Nalinaksha was already a hardened activist when he joined college. He and his brother were soon arrested under the Defence of India Act for 'terrorist' activities after a number of intelligence officers were killed in Calcutta. Again, he was let off after weeks of severe interrogation for lack of evidence, even though the police were certain he had links with armed groups. His brother Anadi was not so lucky and died of internal injuries caused by torture in Rangpur Jail. This incident had a big influence on Nalinaksha.

On his release, Das reached out to Nalinaksha and brought him into the fold of the Congress. In 1920, he attended the INC session in Nagpur. The session included the first All India Students Conference, where Nalinaksha led the student delegation from Bengal. It was at this event that Nalinaksha met many national-level leaders, including Sachindra Nath Sanyal. The Nagpur session endorsed Gandhi's Non-Cooperation Movement, but, like many activists with a revolutionary bent, Nalinaksha remained sceptical. In common with intellectuals such as Tagore, he was not convinced by Gandhi's insistence on boycotting educational institutions or the unnecessary rejection of modern technology. Nevertheless, he loyally participated in the movement after Das endorsed it.

In 1921, Nalinaksha joined the MA course in economics at Calcutta University. By this time, he was the leader of a large network of student activists. Their work was not always related to the freedom movement. For instance, Bengal was then in the grip of a cholera epidemic and thousands were dying from it. The very poor, particularly Dalits, had no medical help. The fear of infection was so great that there were many instances when no one was willing to do the last rites when a person died. Nalinaksha organized a group of students who provided help to patients without support and performed the last rites when corpses were abandoned. In fact, he learnt Hindu funeral rituals and performed the last rites of scores of abandoned corpses himself.

There is an anecdote he would later recount about these times. It appears that Nalinaksha and his acolytes would do most of their relief work at night by escaping from the university boys' hostel. They would return before dawn by way of a window kept strategically open on the first floor. However, on one occasion, they were greeted by the hostel warden, who caught them red-handed. After a severe scolding, they were told to have a full bath and then marched off to the office of Vice Chancellor Ashutosh Mookerjee.

The vice chancellor was known as a strict, no-nonsense man, and the students were more than a little worried about the punishment awaiting them. Mookerjee cross-questioned them, and Nalinaksha told him the truth. The vice chancellor then told them to go to the meeting room and await his judgement. The students were sure that they would be rusticated. Half an hour later, the door opened and Mookerjee walked in with a retinue of attendants carrying *handi*s (earthen pots) of the very best-quality rasagollas. One handi was handed to each student and then Mookerjee gruffly told them that their punishment was that they could not leave until they had each finished their share of rasagollas!

Given his experience with organization and relief work, it is not surprising that Subhas took Nalinaksha along as his lieutenant when he was conducting relief efforts in north Bengal in 1922. After finishing his MA, Nalinaksha took up the job of a lecturer at Krishnath College in Berhampore. He was also the key coordinator of the Swarajist faction of the INC in the Nadia–Murshidabad belt. The college became a hotbed of revolutionary activity during this period. It was also during this time that the nationalist poet Kazi Nazrul Islam was held in Berhampore Jail. The poet and the activist became the best of friends, a relationship they would retain for the rest of their lives.

Das's death in 1925 was a blow to Nalinaksha. In common with Subhas, he had lost his mentor. However, a year later, he was able to secure a scholarship from a wealthy patron, Raja Manindra Chandra Nundy of Kasimbazar, who funded his PhD at the London School of Economics—no small matter at that time. His doctoral thesis, 'Development of Indian Railways', is still in print and considered a must-read for anyone interested in the early development of the railways in the subcontinent.[26]

RASHBEHARI'S BRIDE

Rashbehari Bose had arrived in Japan as Rabindranath Tagore's cousin, but his efforts to procure arms for Bagha Jatin did not escape the attention of British intelligence. All pretence was dropped after Rashbehari organized a public event for Lala Lajpat Rai in Tokyo on 17 November 1915. Japan was nominally a British ally at that time and came under intense diplomatic pressure to deport Rashbehari along with Heramba Lal Gupta, the representative of the Berlin India Committee in Tokyo. The Japanese government eventually issued orders on 28 November, stating that the two had to leave the country by 2 December. This was effectively a death sentence, as there were no scheduled ships to a neutral country before this date—all ships were routed through Hong Kong, Shanghai, Singapore and Vancouver.

The Japanese press was outraged, as it was seen as an insult to the country's sovereignty and the betrayal of a fellow Asian. Nonetheless, on 1 December, the Chief of Metropolitan Police issued a statement that the Indians would be handed over to the British if they did not leave the country by 10 a.m. the next day. Desperate, Rashbehari reached out to his friend Toyama, who invited them home for a farewell party that evening.

Both Heramba Lal and Rashbehari arrived at Toyama's house in the evening. They were tailed by a couple of policemen. As is customary, they took off their shoes and went inside while the policemen respectfully stood outside. Toyama was too politically powerful to force an entry. Once inside, the Indians were told that there was an escape plan. The two were herded barefoot through a kitchen backdoor that led into a neighbour's house. After exiting into a different street, they walked down the hill to where a getaway car was waiting for them. The policemen, meanwhile, kept up their watch in front of Toyama's house as they could see the shoes still lying outside the door.[27]

The escape route taken by Rashbehari can still be traced down Reinan Zaka Street, although most of the traditional buildings from the period were destroyed during the bombings of the Second World War and replaced by modern high-rises. Nevertheless, the road layout is the same. As one comes down the hill, Okura Hotel now stands on the right and the United States Embassy on the left. Take a left at the T-junction and keep walking along the perimeter of the embassy to a busy intersection with an elevated overpass running along it, and again take a left. Here there is an indentation in the pavement, where a single car or delivery van can park (when I visited it in 2018, there was a

7-Eleven store near it). This is the spot where the getaway car was waiting.

The Indians were now taken to the premises of Aizo Soma and his wife Kokko, the owners of a well-known bakery, Nakamuraya, at Shinjuku. Rashbehari and Heramba Lal were taken to a small stand-alone studio at the back of the bakery. They had to strictly stay inside all day, as there were many customers milling around. It was like a prison, but they were safe for the moment. Kokko, who knew some English, translated the numerous news reports that appeared over the next few days about their disappearance. They were full of conjecture about what had happened. It was also clear that public opinion was strongly in their favour.

After two months, however, Heramba Lal had had enough. He unilaterally escaped one evening through a window and moved to the home of a Japanese friend. This caused a temporary scare, until the Somas found out what had happened. Rashbehari was now all alone in the studio. He decided to learn Japanese and taught himself the basics using a bilingual textbook and help from Kokko. He also procured some Indian ingredients and started cooking curries for himself.

Life settled into a pattern until an almost-forgotten incident changed the situation. A British naval vessel fired on a Japanese ship, *Tenyo-Maru*, and forced it to dock in Hong Kong. Seven Indians were taken off and sent to Singapore, effectively kidnapped. The Japanese lodged a strong protest and retaliated by withdrawing the deportation orders against Rashbehari and Heramba Lal. They were now free to come out. Toyama even organized a suitable house for Rashbehari.[28]

A few weeks after moving into his new home, Rashbehari organized a dinner to thank everyone who had helped him. Everyone except Kokko was surprised when the Indian gave a speech in Japanese. They were also treated to an Indian meal prepared by Rashbehari himself. It is often said that this was the first time that the Japanese tasted a proper Indian meal, although this is unlikely since Tokyo was quite a cosmopolitan city by then.

Rashbehari now became an important member of the Pan-Asian movement, which was quite strong in Japan. Despite his changed status, however, he knew that agents hired by British intelligence were keeping an eye on him and tailing his Japanese friends. He changed homes several times, but the agents always found him. There was constant fear that they would harm him or that the British would find an opportunity to arm-twist the Japanese government into handing him over. This went on for two years. Toyama's solution was radical. He suggested that Rashbehari marry Aizo's daughter, Toshiko, and become a Japanese citizen.

Aizo and Kokko were taken aback, but it turned out that Rashbehari and Toshiko had fallen in love during the months that he was hiding in the studio at Nakamuraya. They would meet when Toshiko brought in food and other essentials for Rashbehari, although they had barely ever spoken. Therefore, they had never expressed their feelings to each other. It was only when Toyama made the suggestion that Toshiko confessed to her parents that she wanted to marry Rashbehari. The latter had similarly kept his feelings to himself as he had always believed that his revolutionary activities precluded family life. Now that the matter had been broached, he expressed his willingness to marry Toshiko. They got married in a private ceremony in Toyama's house on 9 July 1918.

The marriage would be a very happy one. A son was born in 1920 and a daughter in 1922. Rashbehari became a naturalized

Japanese citizen in 1923. Unfortunately, Toshiko came down with a severe case of pneumonia in 1924 and passed away at the young age of twenty-eight. In her final moments, they held hands and slowly chanted Vedic mantras that they used to chant together every morning. Rashbehari later wrote, 'Our married life was very short, but it was bliss. I had a feeling that I enjoyed total happiness during those years.'[29]

In the 1920s, the Nakamuraya bakery began to decline due to the entry of competition. The Somas responded by converting part of the premises into a café that served a new menu that included authentic Indian curries. This was Rashbehari's contribution, and it was a big success. Many of Tokyo's elite and intelligentsia came frequently to Nakamuraya to eat authentic curry. Rashbehari was probably not the first to introduce Indian cuisine to Japan, but he was certainly the person who popularized it. He soon became known widely as 'Bose of Nakamuraya'—Japanese writers of the inter-war period often mention the café.

The Nakamuraya restaurant still exists, although the original building was destroyed during the Second World War bombings. It is now in the basement of a modern high-rise, but claims to serve curries made from Rashbehari's original recipes. I tried the chicken curry and it tasted quite good—albeit much milder than the usual version in India. Perhaps Rashbehari himself had adjusted the spiciness to Japanese tastes, or perhaps the current cook had done so. Nonetheless, it was quite an experience to eat a meal directly linked to the extraordinary life of an extraordinary man.

6

THE HINDUSTAN REPUBLICAN ASSOCIATION

As the Non-Cooperation Movement gathered momentum in 1921, many revolutionaries left their initial scepticism and decided to join it. They were influenced by Chittaranjan Das's decision to support Gandhi as well as the general mood. Sachindra Nath Sanyal appreciated that Gandhi's softer approach made it easier for more people to join the national movement but decided to stay away from it himself. Instead, he briefly tried his hand at different things, including managing a brick kiln. However, his heart was not in any of these activities. Eventually, at the request of Das's brother-in-law, he took charge of the labour union in Jamshedpur.

Sanyal seems to have made quite a success of his time as a labour union leader. The Jamshedpur union was in a shambles when he arrived, but within a few months, its membership was up and the finances had improved. It is often assumed that nationalist revolutionaries such as Sanyal did not have links with the trade union movement because of their suspicion of Left-leaning ideologies. This is clearly untrue. He also got married to a spirited young lady, Pratibha, during this period. Nevertheless, Sanyal still yearned to re-ignite the revolutionary movement. In early 1922, he moved back to the United Provinces and began to re-establish contact with various groups. This time he established a base in Allahabad (now Prayagraj), although he also had operations in Varanasi.[1]

The collapse of the Non-Cooperation Movement after the Chauri Chaura incident in February 1922 dramatically changed the political landscape. Many revolutionaries were disillusioned with Gandhi's non-violent approach and decided to return to armed resistance. Sanyal also found a new generation of college students open to his message. He first started by recruiting new members in the United Provinces, including Ram Prasad Bismil and Ashfaqullah Khan. He also visited Punjab and re-established contact with the surviving Ghadarites, and visited several colleges. At National College, Lahore, Sanyal recruited Ajit Singh's talented nephew, Bhagat Singh. The college had been set up recently by Lala Lajpat Rai and Bhai Parmanand as an alternative to government-run colleges. It would prove to be an important recruitment ground for next-generation revolutionaries.

Sanyal soon reached out to the Anushilan Samiti network in Bengal. This was still the largest revolutionary network in the country but remained divided into numerous semi-independent groups. The Dacca–Barisal group was led by Pratul Ganguli, who was considered the senior-most active leader in Bengal in 1922. Sanyal established contact with him. To improve internal coordination with Sanyal's network, Ganguli sent a young representative, Jogesh Chandra Chatterjee, to Varanasi. Jogesh's autobiography, *In Search of Freedom*, is a useful eyewitness account of the world of revolutionaries.² Unlike Sanyal, Bismil and others, he published his book after Independence and, therefore, was more open about many issues that were deliberately obscure or left out of books written under British rule. Therefore, many of the writings of the 1920s revolutionaries can be better triangulated after reading Chatterjee's book, even though it was written from memory many years later and probably contains distortions caused by hindsight.

The autobiographical writings by the revolutionaries of this period reflect the fascinating internal debates regarding political strategy. The events unfolding in Ireland were of particular interest to them, as it became clear that the British were losing control. This was also the time that Sanyal began to write *Bandi Jeevan*, where he argues that a movement needs poets and writers just as much as it needs warriors and activists. Sanyal wrote his autobiography to inspire a new generation of freedom fighters, but he also specifically mentioned that he wanted to leave behind a first-hand account as he feared that future generations would not be told the truth about the revolutionary movement. This premonition is remarkable in the light of how this history would be edited out in later years.

WIFE'S PERMISSION

Even as Sanyal began ramping up his political activism, his mother began to get worried. She had been a rock of support all these years, but Sanyal was newly married and expecting his first child. Eventually, she went to meet a well-respected sadhu for advice. The sadhu told her that her son was destined to fight for dharma, but, nevertheless, Hindu tradition required that he could follow this path only if he obtained his wife's permission. Thus the young

Pratibha was brought before the sadhu and asked her opinion. She was in an impossible situation and initially remained silent, but in the end, she nodded her assent. This was no easy decision, as Sanyal himself admits.[3]

With the Swarajist faction breaking away from Gandhi, Sanyal reached out to Motilal Nehru and Chittaranjan Das. Both of them encouraged him and promised support. We have some evidence that Das may have initially funded a plan to assassinate the viceroy.[4] Sanyal's newly reconstituted unit in Punjab may have even scouted possible locations in Simla and Kashmir for the operation. It seems Das later backed out and the plan was shelved for the moment. Nevertheless, it is clear that there were close links between the Swarajists and the revolutionaries.

Sanyal simultaneously reached out to the younger emerging leaders in the Congress. He seems to have been impressed by Subhas Chandra Bose but appears to have found Jawaharlal Nehru too haughty. In *Bandi Jeevan*, he tells us that 'while I was speaking to Jawaharlal-ji, his attitude was that he was indulging a feeble-minded simpleton and was graciously wasting his precious time by listening to his foolish ideas'.[5]

At the same time, the revolutionary network in the United Provinces began to build close links with a peasant movement known as the Eka Movement, led by the charismatic Madari Pasi. Barely remembered today, the Eka Movement was a mass peasant movement that ran parallel to the Non-Cooperation Movement. Its leadership was drawn mostly from the lower castes, although its followers included small farmers and farm workers from a range of communities. The Eka protesters were generally peaceful, but not ideologically wedded to non-violence. Thus, they did not have any qualms about building close links with the revolutionaries. There is a possibility that the Chauri Chaura incident escalated because of its members. The colonial government cracked down on Madari Pasi in 1922–23, and he went underground. He continued to operate until 1931, however, using the revolutionary network to avoid arrest.

Mainstream narratives tend to leave the reader with the impression that the revolutionaries were niche operators with few links with mass movements and the wider freedom struggle. As should be obvious by now, they had close links with trade unions, peasant movements and with powerful factions of the INC itself.

THE RAMPA REBELLION[6]

The idea of armed resistance attracted admirers and allies not only in the urban centres but also among rural peasants and forest tribes. The Eka Movement by the peasants of the central Gangetic plains was just one example of a mass mobilization movement with links to the revolutionaries. Another is the Rampa Rebellion among the forest tribes of the Eastern Ghats in what is now Andhra Pradesh. Its leader was the charismatic Alluri Seetha Rama Raju. His romantic folk legend has inspired a lot of popular culture, although there is a surprising lacuna in serious research about him.

Rama Raju was born in a village near Visakhapatnam in 1897 in a middle-class family. His father is said to have been a photographer and died when Rama Raju was still in his teens. The teenager seems to have drifted away from formal education, although he was intellectually curious and read extensively in Telugu, Sanskrit and English. He was especially interested in Hindu religious philosophy. At this time, he also spent time wandering around in the forested hills of the Eastern Ghats, where he became acquainted with the local tribes, particularly the Koya community. This is how he developed a sympathy for their struggles against colonial forest laws and the incursion of Christian missionaries.

Around 1915, when he was about eighteen years old, Rama Raju decided to become a *sanyasi* (monk) and travelled across India. This was a time when the ideas of the Ghadar and Jugantar revolutionaries were widespread among the youth. Rama Raju would have encountered these ideas during his pilgrimages to Nashik and Varanasi. However, it was in Bengal that he met Anushilan Samiti members and crystallized his ideas of rebellion. It is said that it was in Chittagong (now Chattogram in Bangladesh) that he decided to return home and start a movement.

Like many young activists, Rama Raju was disappointed by the failure of the Non-Cooperation Movement and decided to strike back at the British with his own rebellion. He began to organize a band of tribesmen to carry out attacks against the colonial administration. Interestingly, they were armed mostly with traditional weapons such as bows and arrows (although they would later add muskets and rifles stolen from the police).

The first major attack was carried out against the Chintapalli police station in the Visakhapatnam district on 22 August 1922. Around 300 tribal warriors joined Rama Raju. This was followed by similar attacks in surrounding areas. The colonial authorities sent in a large number of armed police to counter them, but the rebels were able to evade them easily due to their knowledge of the hilly, forested terrain. Several government troops, including British officers, were killed in the skirmishes. Rama Raju became so confident that it is said that he pre-announced the place and time of his raid, and would leave behind a full list of the things he had taken. One of the things he took was a Webley revolver that he began carrying in his belt.⁷

Well-built and with a full beard, armed with traditional weapons and a revolver stuck through his belt, Rama Raju was a charismatic figure. He soon had a large following among both the tribal and non-tribal population.

As the rebellion reached its second year, the government decided to escalate their efforts. The British announced a bounty of Rs 10,000 on Rama Raju and Rs 1,000 each for his lieutenants Ghantam Dora and Mallu Dora. Hundreds of crack troops of the Malabar Special Police and the Assam Rifles were shipped in and put under the command of T.G. Rutherford. Their initial efforts were unsuccessful, as the locals refused to cooperate and provide information. However, they eventually managed to trap Rama Raju near the village of Koyyuru in May 1924. He was tied to a tree and summarily executed by a firing squad. Ghantam Dora was similarly hunted down and killed a month later. Mallu Dora, however, was sent to prison and survived. He would live to see Independence and become a member of Parliament.

THE CONSTITUTION OF HRA

It is important to understand Sanyal's aims and objectives at this time. While he was in favour of occasional targeted assassinations of senior British officials, he knew that random terror attacks would only lead to anarchy. He was especially uncomfortable with the practice of robbing Indian businesses to garner funds. Instead, he wanted to create an organization that could coordinate a large-scale armed uprising on the lines of the Easter Rising in Ireland, followed by the proclamation of an independent republic. He derived his thinking from events unfolding in Ireland as well as his own experience of organizing the Ghadar revolt. The first step was to create an umbrella organization for all the revolutionary groups operating across India. Importantly, this umbrella body would need to include the numerous Anushilan Samiti units of Bengal, as they collectively had the most developed network.

Thus, Sanyal travelled to Bengal and established contact with various groups. After several rounds of negotiations, Sanyal secretly met Pratul Ganguli and a couple of senior leaders in Bholachang village.[8] The place is now in Bangladesh but is close to Agartala, the capital of the Indian state of Tripura, and the famous Shakti temple of Tripura Sundari. The rebel groups agreed in principle to set up the Hindustan Republican Association (HRA) as an umbrella body and an armed wing called the Hindustan Republican Army. The choice of name is very likely derived from the Irish Republican Army.

During the monsoon of 1923, Sanyal made his way in a small country boat to a secret gathering in a remote village near Mymensingh. He beautifully describes the feeling of being on a small sailing boat on a swollen river amid torrential rain. The fields were flooded in many places and it was possible for the boat to sail right through villages. The meeting was held in a series of interconnected huts built on stilts. All the key revolutionary leaders were present. This included Surya Sen of Chittagong, who later led a major uprising. Sanyal and Ganguli explained the aims and objectives of the HRA. All the groups accepted it as the umbrella organization and endorsed Sanyal as the overall leader.

With authority clearly vested in him, Sanyal next started to expand and direct the network. Jogesh Chatterjee was told to shift to Kanpur to set up a unit there. Bismil and Ashfaqullah were asked to take charge of Shahjahanpur. Jitendra Nath Sanyal, one of Sachindra Nath Sanyal's younger brothers who was then working at Indian Press in Allahabad, was put in charge of the city. The youngest brother, Bhupendra Nath Sanyal, still a student, was to assist him. Sachindra Nath Bakshi was initially sent to Lucknow but was shifted later to Jhansi. Bhagat Singh was sent to Aligarh, where he was given a job in a new school. A recent recruit, Rajendra Lahiri, was asked to move back from Varanasi to Bengal to set up a bomb factory near Dakshineshwar. Lahiri came from a Bengali family that had settled in Varanasi and ran a shop near Dashashwamedha Ghat, which was a popular gathering place for local youth sympathetic to the revolutionary cause. His brother would later marry Sanyal's cousin. Jatindra Nath Das was based in Calcutta and functioned as Sanyal's effective right-hand man. The purpose of this long list of names is to provide the reader with a sense of the network. Many readers will be familiar with some of the names and may find it useful to get a sense of how they fit together.

Meanwhile, in Bengal, police intelligence was on high alert. The colonial authorities seem to have been aware that something was afoot and that Pratul Ganguli's Dacca group was involved in it. Realizing that Calcutta and Dacca were too dangerous, Sanyal created a new nerve centre at Krishnath College in the small town of Berhampur (Murshidabad district). Nalinaksha Sanyal was a lecturer at the college then and also the local representative of the Swarajist faction of the INC. He, too, became involved.

Despite the risks, Sachindra Nath Sanyal decided to shift his base to Bengal. Although he was himself a Bengali, his clout was stronger in Punjab and the United Provinces (UP), where he controlled about twenty-five units. It is possible that he felt that he needed to be physically present in this important province to weld the different groups together. The shift did not go smoothly. He arrived in Chandernagore with his wife, a two-year-old son and a three-month-old daughter. Unfortunately, after he arrived in the enclave, he discovered that his local contact was not keen to provide him shelter. The French authorities were no longer as open to giving refuge to fugitives as before, and there were many British agents operating there. Even though Sanyal was not on the run at this time, many did not wish to be openly associated with him. After wandering around the town with two tired and hungry children, he was finally welcomed into the home of Sirish Ghosh, an old associate of Rashbehari Bose and Aurobindo Ghosh.

The next step was to write out a formal constitution for the HRA. This was not merely to lay out the aims and objectives for its members but also to pave the path for a future Proclamation of Independence, presumably during an armed uprising. A meeting was held at the 'Pilikothi' Dharamshala in Kanpur in October 1924, where a draft constitution prepared by Sanyal was debated and adopted in the presence of Rajendra Lahiri, Jogesh Chatterjee, Ram Prasad Bismil and several others.[9]

The constitution of the HRA prepared by Sanyal stated:

The object of the association shall be to establish a Federated Republic of the United States of India by organized and armed revolution. The final form of the constitution of the Republic shall be framed and declared by the representatives of the people at the time when they will be in a position to enforce their decisions. The basic principle of the Republic shall be universal suffrage and the abolition of all systems which make any kind of exploitation of man by man possible.[10]

The above statement is remarkable in that it is the first clear exposition that post-Independence India should be a republic based on universal suffrage. The official demand of the INC was still for dominion status (self-government within the British Empire). Gandhi defined the word 'Swaraj' as 'self-government within the Empire if possible—and outside if necessary'.[11] In 1924 he argued, 'If the British government meant what they say and honestly help us to equality, it would be a greater triumph than complete severance of the British connection.'[12] Even those who advocated Purna Swaraj or full independence were not clear what form of government would replace the colonial system. Thus, it was the revolutionaries who first enunciated the goal of a fully independent democratic republic. When the HRA had debated various options in Kanpur, interestingly, the other option considered was for a constitutional monarchy, with Sayajirao Gaekwad III of Baroda as the king!

The constitution of the HRA soon began to circulate widely and provided a template for setting up local units. Bismil was put in charge of the armed wing. He and/or Sanyal then published a manifesto titled 'The Revolutionary' under a pseudonym, which explained the objectives of the revolutionaries. Copies were printed and distributed widely in many cities across north India on 1 January 1925. It is interesting to note that the revolutionaries disliked being called terrorists or anarchists. They saw themselves as putting up armed resistance to a foreign aggressor, and the pamphlet goes to lengths to explain the distinction:

> A few words more about terrorism and anarchism. These two words are playing the most mischievous part in India today. They are being invariably misapplied whenever any reference to

revolution be made, because it is very convenient to denounce the revolutionary under that name. The Indian Revolutionaries are neither terrorists nor anarchists. They never aim to spread anarchy in the land and therefore they can never properly be called anarchists. Terrorism is never their object and therefore they can never be called terrorists. They do not believe that terrorism alone can bring independence and they do not want terrorism for terrorism's sake although they may at times resort to this method as an effective means of retaliation. The present Government exists simply because the Foreigners have successfully been able to terrorise the Indian people.[13]

The above point is subtle but important to understand the self-image of Indian revolutionaries. Bismil and/or Sanyal were making a distinction between the use of targeted violence as resistance and the use of indiscriminate violence to spread fear or an ideology. This was neither violence for the sake of violence, nor was it hatred of the British as a people. This is why Indian revolutionaries never carried out the equivalent of the Beslan school massacre of 2004, despite the fact that there were tens of thousands of British children in India during this period. A large number of European businessmen, teachers, engineers, artists and other civilians continued to live in India largely unmolested; even wives of senior officials were almost never targeted. Therefore, their self-image was similar to that of members of the French Resistance under Nazi occupation.

In February 1925, Sanyal wrote an open letter to Gandhi that was published in *Young India*:

You wanted one year for your experiment, but the experiment lasted for at least four complete years, if not five, and still you mean to say that the experiment was not tried long enough? ... To say that non-violent non-cooperation did not work because the people were not sufficiently non-violent is to argue like a lawyer, and not like a prophet. The people could not be more non-violent than they were during the last few years. I would like to say that they were non-violent to a degree that smelt of cowardice.[14]

THE KAKORI TRAIN ROBBERY

Ram Prasad Bismil was born in 1897 into a poor family in a village in Shahjahanpur, the United Provinces. According to Bismil's autobiography, written on death row, his grandfather had migrated from the Chambal area to Shahjahanpur during a severe famine.[15] The family barely survived on subsistence wages. By the time he was born, however, circumstances had somewhat improved, as his father had managed to create a small business selling official stamps in the local court. By his own admission, Bismil was an energetic but unruly child, who regularly got into trouble. However, in his mid-teens, he turned to religion and started to conduct the evening rituals at the village temple. He was also influenced by the ideals of the Arya Samaj and a charismatic preacher, Swami Somdev, who strongly advocated nationalist ideas. (As an aside, the swami had also influenced Raja Mahendra Pratap.) It was under these influences that Bismil became an enthusiastic organizer in his district of *'shuddhi'*, or purification programmes (i.e., reconversion to Hinduism).

The young Bismil's initiation into political life was through the nationalist faction of the Congress. At a party meeting in Lucknow, he organized a small group of volunteers to give

Tilak a grand reception, despite the opposition from the Loyalist faction. This earned him the ire of the rival group. It was also in Lucknow that he first came in contact with the revolutionaries and soon got involved. Over the next year, he produced a number of underground pamphlets and posters in support of the freedom struggle; they were all banned by the colonial authorities. In due course, he started to explore ways to acquire small arms. His tract on this issue is quite illuminating about the difficulty faced by revolutionaries operating in central India to procure guns:

> Many people have the misconception that in the rural hinterlands, everyone carries a gun and no license is needed. One would presume, therefore, that such weapons were in easy circulation. While to some extent, it is indeed true that no license is required and everyone is free to keep a gun; still it is mandatory to keep the local police informed every time a bullet or explosive is procured. It is not like you walk into shops in open market and buy bullets and cartridges. Imported explosives or sealed cartridges have to be brought in from outside the princely states, which requires a permit from the Resident Officer (Government representative who is deputed to the princely state). To circumvent such a cumbersome procedure, shotguns are manufactured within the state, indigenous explosives are also produced by mixing Sulphur and coal. Even with a hypothetical freedom to keep the weapons, each village would have barely a person or two of affluent status or the rich landlord class who could afford to keep shotguns which they use with locally made bullets. The storage of the explosive charge too was difficult as they would go stale in the humidity and thus become useless beyond one season.[16]

Like many other revolutionaries, Bismil, too, joined the Non-Cooperation Movement and was deeply disillusioned when it was abruptly withdrawn by Gandhi:

> The Non-Cooperation Movement was in a state of inertness by then. We expected the veterans of the Non-Cooperation Movement to join us and work with passionate commitment. But when we explored deeper, we realized that there was something even more dead in the soul of the participants of the movement than the movement itself.[17]

Thus, Bismil drifted back to the revolutionaries. It was around this time, too, that he came in contact with Ashfaqullah Khan, who would become his closest friend and chief lieutenant. Some readers may find it difficult to understand such a close bond between a Muslim and an avowed Hindu revivalist, but one must understand that remarkable people are usually not monochromatic and entirely capable of looking beyond ideological straitjackets.

When the HRA was formally launched in Kanpur in 1924, Bismil and Ashfaqullah were put in charge of Shahjahanabad. Bismil was also put in charge of the armed wing, which meant that he was in charge of procuring guns. As we have seen, it was no easy task, especially since the revolutionaries were perpetually short of funds. A few sympathetic supporters did provide regular funds, but the growing organization was quickly stripped of resources. Many activists lived in abject penury and had to borrow for daily expenses. The revolutionaries did carry out a few robberies to garner funds but strongly disliked having to hurt the very people they wanted to liberate from foreign rule.

Even the victims often sensed that their heart was not in it, as they would just run away if confronted. On one occasion, the women of a merchant's house simply walked up to a newly recruited Chandrashekhar Azad and took away his pistol![18]

This was clearly not a tenable situation and Bismil began to scout for new sources of funding. It must have been especially frustrating, as he was now part of a network with national and international linkages that could be leveraged to acquire modern weapons, if only he could find the money. In early 1925, the revolutionaries arranged for a talented swimmer, Keshab Chakravarty, to go to Germany for a competition. His real job was to procure a large consignment of Mauser pistols. The pistols were brought by ship to the Bay of Bengal and secretly handed over by boat to Rajendra Lahiri on the high seas outside India's territorial waters.[19]

The need to pay for this large consignment of Mausers added to Bismil's financial urgency. He concluded that raiding the government treasury, although much more risky, would yield much larger dividends. This idea took concrete shape when he noticed on a train journey that bags of government funds were dropped into and taken out of the boxes in the guard's cabin. Using the timetable, Bismil decided to target a train travelling from Saharanpur to Lucknow (Train No. 8 Down). He estimated that by the time the train reached Lucknow, the treasury boxes would contain roughly Rs 10,000, a substantial sum at that time. The plan was to stop the train at Kakori, a small station about 20 km short of Lucknow (the station still exists).

Bismil began to put together a team of ten volunteers. It appears that Ashfaqullah was not too enthusiastic about the plan, as he considered it too risky. Even if the robbery was successful, he argued, it would attract too much premature attention to the HRA. Nonetheless, he seems to have eventually gone along with the plan.[20]

On 9 August 1925, the team together boarded the second-class compartment of the train. As planned, the train was brought to a halt using the emergency chain, just outside Kakori station. The guard was forced to the ground while the passengers were instructed to stay calm and remain on board. A couple of members of the team were assigned to stand along the train and regularly fire into the air to warn off any retaliation. The driver confined himself to the train while the engineer locked himself in the toilet. Meanwhile, the steel box was taken out of the guard's compartment but could not be opened with a chisel. Eventually, an axe was used to break it open. They found around Rs 4,600 (some sources suggest a higher amount), still a significant sum, and put it into three bags.

Bismil had strictly instructed his men to avoid shooting at anyone unless absolutely necessary. They would later find out that there were fourteen armed persons on the train, including two fully armed soldiers, but none of them fought back. Unfortunately, one unarmed passenger got off the train to see what was happening. He was shot dead in the confusion. Bismil was very upset by this as it was unnecessary. He admonished the shooter, but it was too late. This shooting converted a robbery into a homicide, a key legal point that the government later would use against them.[21]

The small, rural Kakori station still exists, surrounded by mango orchards. There is a small museum dedicated to the incident. On display is a money box such as the one in the incident. It is a heavy piece of equipment, and it is not surprising that it took so much effort for the revolutionaries to break it open.

Once the money had been taken out, the team members made their way to Lucknow, where they divided the money and split up. No one challenged them along the way. Aside from the single unintended casualty, the raid had been a big success from the revolutionary point of view. Personal debts were paid back, money was set aside for acquiring new weapons and so on. So far so good. However, the robbery became a media sensation and was reported across the country. Jogesh Chatterjee, then lodged in Berhampore Jail, read about the incident in the papers and guessed that it must be his HRA comrades. The British authorities, not surprisingly, deployed all available resources to find the culprits. This is exactly what Ashfaqullah had feared.

Very soon, some of the stolen currency notes began to circulate, and Special Superintendent Mr Horten traced them back to certain locations, including Shahjahanpur. As Bismil would admit in his autobiography, he had not anticipated this flaw in his plan. He was picked up for police questioning from home. Even this may not have been a shock for the wider network, but for what happened next. One member of the network, Banarasi Lal, was arrested from Rae Baraeli and cracked during interrogation. By turning approver, he revealed details of the entire HRA network.

Armed with this information, the police made numerous raids across the country, including on people that were not directly linked to the robbery. In Dakshineshwar, Rajendra Lahiri was arrested after the police found one live bomb, seven revolvers, one pistol, anti-British literature and a large amount of supplies for making explosives. Sachindra Nath Sanyal and his youngest brother Bhupendra Nath were also arrested. Ashfaqullah managed to evade arrest for some time, but eventually was caught too.

The authorities deliberately assigned Muslim officers to deal with him in the hope that religious affiliation would turn him into an approver, but he was not swayed.

The Kakori Conspiracy Case dragged on for a year and garnered a lot of media attention. The Swarajist faction of the INC even organized a defence team. Thirty-one persons were tried. At one point, the prisoners resorted to a hunger strike to protest against inhumane treatment. Less widely known were some daring attempts to escape. Sachindra Nath Sanyal's other brother, Rabindra, who had not been arrested, somehow managed to smuggle in a hacksaw inside a copy of the Tulsi Ramayan. Sanyal nearly managed to escape by cutting through the iron bars but was discovered. He was mercilessly beaten and put in fetters, before being put in solitary confinement.[22] Similarly, Jogesh Chatterjee tells us that a hacksaw was smuggled through to Bismil as well. He even managed to get out of his cell with two others, but was unable to find a way to scale the walls undetected. If they had managed to get out, they would have found Surya Sen, the unit chief from Chittagong, waiting outside to whisk them away.[23]

Even as they waited for the verdict in the spring of 1927, Bismil composed the famous revolutionary song *Mera Rang De Basanti Chola*—and all the other prisoners began to sing along. The lyrics found their way out of the prison they were in and soon became a popular anthem (note that Bismil's original lyrics are somewhat different from those later popularized by Bollywood). The verdict was read out at Lucknow's Ring Theatre amid elaborate security arrangements. Four were sentenced to death (Ram Prasad Bismil, Thakur Roshan Singh, Ashfaqullah Khan and Rajendra Lahiri); Sachindra Nath Sanyal, Jogesh Chatterjee and two others were given transportation for life; and a dozen more, including Bhupendra Nath Sanyal, were given sentences ranging from five to fourteen years. Banarasi Lal and Indubhushan Mitra were pardoned for turning approvers. There were widespread protests against the sentences and the elected members of the UP Legislative Council passed a resolution, asking the government to at least commute capital punishment to life imprisonment. Madan Mohan Malaviya even met the viceroy to push for reduced sentences. But the government did not budge.

Bismil spent his last days writing his autobiography—*The Revolutionary*. In it, he describes his death cell:

> The death cell of Gorakhpur prison lies in the middle of a barren ground. There is not even a hint of a shadow around. From morning eight till eight in the evening, the solitary cell smolders under the blazing sun; the heat further accentuated by the sandy earth. In the cell of nine feet by nine feet, there is a single exit—six feet high and two feet wide. To the rear end of the cell is a window, two feet long and a foot wide. Dining, bathing and even toilet, everything is within this cell. The nights are full of mosquitoes. It is hard to get sleep for three to four hours ... [24]

Bismil was hanged on 18 December 1927. His last words were: 'I wish the downfall of the British Empire.' Roshan Singh and Rajendra Lahiri bravely walked up to the gallows holding a copy of the Bhagawad Gita and singing *Vande Mataram*. Ashfaqullah similarly went to his death with a Quran tied around his neck. Just before the noose was put around his neck, he said, 'I tried to make India free, and the attempt will not end with my life.' He then smiled ... [25]

At the time they were martyred, Bismil was thirty, Ashfaqullah twenty-seven, Roshan Singh thirty-five and Lahiri barely twenty-six.

The Sanyal family was devastated by the Kakori sentences—Bhupendra Nath was imprisoned for five years, while Sachindra Nath was sent back to Port Blair for life, the only person to have been sent to the dreaded Cellular Jail twice. All the ancestral properties of the extended clan in Varanasi were either confiscated or forcibly acquired. This is why no member of the family lives in Bengali Tola, Madanpura, any more. The British were determined that the warren of lanes and interconnected houses would never again provide shelter to troublemakers. A few reminders of the times, nevertheless, can still be seen at Bengali Tola Intercollege, which has plaques for founders and freedom fighters that bear the names of several generations of the family. There is also the house of Sachindra Nath Sanyal's granduncle, Shyama Charan Lahiri, better known as the famous yogi Lahiri Mahashaya, which continues to be a shrine to the saint.

REGROUPING AFTER KAKORI

The Kakori arrests and the sustained raids against the Anushilan Samiti groups in Bengal had severely depleted the senior leadership of the HRA by 1926. This left the surviving network in the hands of an even younger group of activists, which included Sukhdev Thapar, Bhagat Singh and Chandrashekhar Azad. When they assumed control of the organization, Azad was barely twenty years old and the other two just nineteen!

Chandra Shekhar Tiwari was born in 1906 to a poor Brahmin family in Bhabhra village. The village was in the small princely state of Alirajpur, now part of Madhya Pradesh. The family had

The original Cellular Jail in the Andamans, circa 1910.

Subhas Chandra Bose while visiting the Cellular Jail, December 1943.

Photos courtesy: Cellular Jail Museum, Port Blair

Aurobindo Ghosh (extreme right) with Bipin Chandra Pal (extreme left) in Uttarpara, April 1908.

Aurobindo Ghosh in Alipore Jail, 1909.

Photos courtesy: Sri Aurobindo Ashram, Puducherry

Aurobindo's cell in Alipore Jail.
Photo courtesy: Sri Aurobindo Ashram, Puducherry

Bande Mataram
Photo courtesy: Sri Aurobindo Ashram, Puducherry

REGISTERED NO. C532.

SUBSCRIPTION RUPEES 5.

SINGLE COPY ANNAS 2.

A WEEKLY REVIEW

OF

National Religion, Literature, Science, Philosophy, &c.,

| Vol. I. | SATURDAY 7th AUGUST 1909. | No. 7. |

Contributors :—SJ., AUROBINDO GHOSE AND OTHERS

OFFICE :—14 SHAM BAZAR STREET,
CALCUTTA.

Karmayogin
Photo courtesy: Sri Aurobindo Ashram, Puducherry

Aurobindo Ghosh (seated) and Bal Gangadhar Tilak (to his left) addressing a stormy meeting of Nationalists in Surat in December 1907.
Photo courtesy: Sri Aurobindo Ashram, Puducherry

Photo taken soon after Sachindra Nath Sanyal's wedding in 1921. Standing (L–R): Jitendra Nath Sanyal, Rabindra Nath Sanyal and Bhupendra Nath Sanyal. Middle: Sachindra Nath Sanyal's mother (left) with two relatives or family friends. Bottom: Sachindra Nath Sanyal with his bride, Pratibha.
Photo courtesy: From the author's personal collection

The first edition of *Bandi Jeevan*, as written by Sachindra Nath Sanyal, circa 1923.

Sachindra Nath Sanyal with his wife, Pratibha, and newborn son, circa 1922.

Nalinaksha Sanyal, circa 1935.

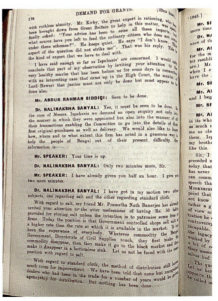

A record of questions raised by Nalinaksha Sanyal in the Bengal Assembly during the 1943 famine.

Photos courtesy: From the author's personal collection

Pandurang Khankhoje as a student in California.

In Japan in 1907.

Training with the Persian Revolutionary Army.

A photo of German officers that includes Wilhelm Wassmuss (probably the one seated on the right).

Photos courtesy: From the collection of Savitri Sawhney

Above and below: Photos from the Persian campaign taken by Pandurang Khankhoje

Photos courtesy: From the collection of Savitri Sawhney

Sohan Singh Bhakna, a Ghadar Party founder member

Ghadar Party members at a grand gathering in 1954. Bhakna is third from the left, and to his immediate right is Khankhoje.

The Bengali Tola Intercollege in Varanasi, established in 1854 by the Sanyal-Lahiri family.

Photo courtesy: From the author's personal collection

A plaque with the names of freedom fighters associated with the Bengali Tola Intercollege.

Photo courtesy: From the author's personal collection

Vinayak Damodar Savarkar in the late 1920s after his return from Cellular Jail.
Photo courtesy: Swatantryaveer Savarkar Rashtriya Smarak

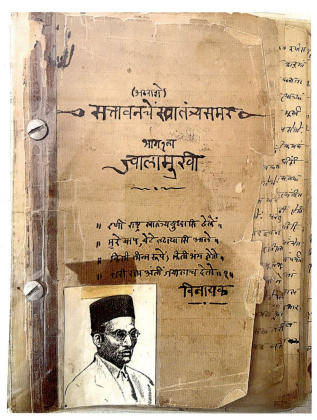

The original manuscript of Vinayak Savarkar's 1857 book in his own handwriting.
Photo courtesy: From the author's personal collection

Group photo at India House, London, taken in early 1909. Standing (L-R): Mitra, M.P.T. Acharya, Harnam Singh, Syed Haidar Raza, Dr Rajan and housekeeper Jack. Sitting (L-R): V.V.S. Aiyar, Gyanchand Verma, Vinayak Damodar Savarkar, Niranjan Pal, Khan, Lala Govind Amin.
Photo courtesy: Swatantryaveer Savarkar Rashtriya Smarak

The entrance to the wholesale market of Chandni Chowk's Katra Dhulia, from where Rashbehari Bose and Basant Kumar Biswas threw a bomb at Lord Hardinge in 1912.
Photo courtesy: From the author's personal collection

Prison cells in the Red Fort baoli, where INA officers were kept.

Caxton Hall, where Udham Singh killed Michael O'Dwyer.

Photos courtesy: From the author's personal collection

A view of the barracks at Salimgarh Fort where INA soldiers were kept.

The door to the room where the INA trials were held.

Photos courtesy: From the author's personal collection

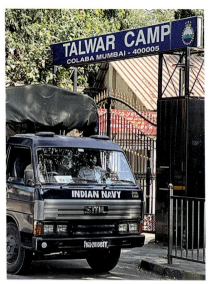

The present-day entrance to the navy facility in Talwar, Colaba. Now a nondescript transport depot, this was the hub of the Naval Revolt in 1946.
Photo courtesy: From the author's personal collection

Keshav Baliram Hedgewar's house in Nagpur, where the Rashtriya Swayamsevak Sangh (RSS) was founded.
Photo courtesy: Sameer Gautam

Gallows in Alipore Central Jail, Kolkata, where many revolutionaries were hanged.
Photo courtesy: From the author's personal collection

The porch of the family home in Kolkata from where Subhas Chandra Bose embarked on his great escape. (The car is preserved to the right.)
Photo courtesy: From the author's personal collection

The death row cell where revolutionaries were kept in the days leading up to their execution in Alipore Central Jail.
Photo courtesy: From the author's personal collection

moved here during the famine of 1899. As one can see, repeated famines had caused large-scale migrations in the colonial period. In common with Bismil, Azad was a restless teenager and, at the age of fourteen, left his village and took a train to Bombay. He knew no one in the city and earned by washing dishes in a restaurant and then working in the docks as a ship painter. It was hard work, but it gave him a wider view of the world. After a year or so, he decided on a whim to accompany a co-worker going to Varanasi. Here he decided to learn Sanskrit, and enrolled himself at a Sanskrit *pathshala*. The school provided meals and a place to stay, but it also introduced him to the charged political milieu of Varanasi.

Like many other students in the city, Chandrashekhar also participated in a number of protests during the Non-Cooperation Movement and was arrested. When produced before the magistrate, he was asked his name and replied 'Azad', meaning 'free'. This is how he ended up with this moniker. The magistrate, however, was not amused and awarded him fifteen strokes of the cane. Azad bore the punishment without flinching, crying out 'Vande Mataram' at each stroke. The news of his bravery soon spread and was reported in some Indian-language papers. Thus, Azad became a minor celebrity.[26]

By 1923, Sachindra Nath Sanyal had established a hub in Varanasi that operated clandestinely out of a religious institution called Kalyan Ashram. Rajendra Lahiri was the key organizer of operations in the city and it was he who recruited Azad. Over the next two years, the teenage revolutionary played a minor part in the activities of the newly formed HRA.

The arrests following the Kakori incident threw the organization into turmoil. Azad escaped to Jhansi, where he lived for a while as a car mechanic and then disguised as a sadhu in a forest temple. There is an amusing anecdote from that time that Azad would later relate: The ruler of the nearby princely state of Orchha had come on a hunt to the forest, and Azad had accompanied them. When the party finally spotted an animal, the prince fired his rifle and missed. The accompanying officials, too, aimed and fired, but missed. At this point, Azad picked up someone's pistol and shot the beast dead. The prince was most surprised and realized that this was no ordinary sadhu. To his credit, he did not express his suspicions to anyone.

It was clear by mid-1927 that the HRA needed new leadership as most of the experienced revolutionaries had been killed, were on death row or in jail with long sentences. Azad travelled to Maharashtra to meet Vinayak Savarkar for guidance. Savarkar had been freed from jail with severe restrictions and was kept under constant surveillance. Thus, this was a risky meeting for both of them. Azad came away inspired by the veteran and threw himself into building a new network. One of the first things he did was garner funds. There is evidence that many leading figures of that time contributed money to the cause and may have included the likes of Motilal Nehru, Purushottam Das Tandon and the writer Sarat Chandra Chatterjee.[27]

One of Azad's key allies in this rebuilding effort was Bhagat Singh. He was the son of Ajit Singh's brother Kishan Singh and was born in 1907 in the village of Banga in the Lyallpur district of Punjab (now in Pakistan). The family were wealthy landowners descended from one of Maharaja Ranjit Singh's chieftains. Although practising Sikhs, they were closely associated with the Arya Samaj movement. The family decided not to send Bhagat Singh to Khalsa High School, where many well-to-do

Sikhs sent their sons, as they were suspicious of the school's Loyalist leanings.[28] Instead, Bhagat Singh was sent to Dayanand Anglo Vedic School in Lahore. After matriculation, he joined the National College, which had been newly established by Lala Lajpat Rai and Bhai Parmanand. His family links to the early revolutionaries probably predisposed him to this path, but it was in college that he met other young men who dreamt of an armed insurrection against the British. The Non-Cooperation Movement had collapsed and the disillusioned youth of Punjab were open to Sachindra Nath Sanyal's ideas when he visited Lahore during 1922–24. An early underground version of Sanyal's *Bandi Jeevan* was circulating widely among students and inspired many to join the HRA.

After joining the organization, Bhagat Singh spent some time in Allahabad, Kanpur and Aligarh. Like Azad, Bhagat Singh was left a political orphan after the Kakori arrests and decided to shift back to Punjab. In October 1926, a bomb was thrown into a Ram Leela procession in Lahore, killing many, including children. The police blamed it on the revolutionaries and arrested Bhagat Singh. He was later freed for lack of evidence, but it shows that he was already being watched.

It was during this period in limbo that the young man began to read more about Marxism. Following the Russian Revolution of 1917, there had been some curiosity in India about communism and the Soviet socioeconomic experiment. However, there was little available literature on the topic until the late twenties, and few Indians, including the well-educated, would have had a clear idea of the Marxist frame of thinking. The dominant intellectual influences ranged from Irish nationalism to Hindu revivalism, even Japanese Pan-Asianism. Bhagat Singh was among the first in India (ignoring, for the moment, expatriate Indians) to take a systematic interest in Marxist ideas. Nonetheless, not everyone was impressed with what they read.

Around the same time, sitting in jail, Sachindra Nath Sanyal was also reading up on Marxism. Although he found some of the egalitarian ideals of communism appealing, he was not impressed by its soulless materialism. Sanyal would not have known at that time about the economic and human cost of Stalinist and Maoist social engineering, but his writings suggest an inherent dislike of an ideology that does not make space for individual striving, intellectual freedom or civilizational continuity. He was also not convinced by the Marxist theory of dialectic materialism and constant class struggle as an explanation of history. *Bandi Jeevan*, written mostly in the 1920s (albeit later revised), hints at his discomfort with Marxism, but *Vichar Vinimay*, written in the late 1930s, is quite explicit about his objections.[29] By that time, Sanyal was also worried that both Russian and British communists were using ideology to infiltrate India's Independence movement.

From the middle of 1927, the revolutionaries began to regroup. A clandestine meeting of the surviving units took place in Kanpur in July 1928. The groups in Punjab and UP were keen to re-establish a centralized leadership, but the groups in Bengal disagreed and wanted a more decentralized approach. Thus, the Bengal revolutionaries kept away from the second meeting, which took place in September 1928 in the medieval ruins of Ferozshah Kotla in Delhi. A central leadership was constituted with two members each from Punjab, UP and Bihar, and one from Rajputana (Rajasthan). There was no representative for Bengal. Azad, who was not present, was unanimously elected as head of the armed wing. This effectively made him the senior-most leader of this generation of revolutionaries.

At this meeting, Bhagat Singh also proposed a change of name to Hindustan Socialist Republican Association (HSRA). The insertion of the term 'socialist' was initially opposed by several attendees, who felt that the founders, such as Sachindra Nath Sanyal, would not approve of the change. In the end, however, Bhagat Singh prevailed and the new name was adopted. Nonetheless, it should be pointed out that the word 'socialism' was fluidly used in that period as a generic term for radical political change and did not always have the connotations of a clear socioeconomic framework. Even the 'Left–Right' dichotomy was often seen as one between radicals and gradualists. This explains why Subhas Chandra Bose would write of Tilak and Aurobindo Ghosh as belonging to the Left![30] Note that the fluid use of these terms was not restricted to India—the Nazis are usually depicted today as the far Right, but they considered themselves socialists, and the full form of the Nazi party is National Socialist German Workers' Party. Thus, one needs to be careful when imposing today's ideological lens to the use of these terms in an earlier era.

AVENGING LALA LAJPAT RAI

The Government of India Act of 1919 had a provision that required political reforms and greater representation of Indians to be reviewed after ten years. Thus, there was an expectation that a commission would be formed to look further into the matter. However, the British establishment feared that a Labour government would come to power and make too many concessions to the Indians. Thus, rather in a hurry, a commission was announced under the chairmanship of Sir John Simon. It included seven British members of Parliament and had no Indian representation. When Viceroy Lord Irwin made the announcement, he justified it by stating that 'the two chief requisites of a member of the Commission are that he should be unbiased and unprejudiced. An Indian member cannot be expected to possess these two qualities.'[31]

Not surprisingly, the commission faced stiff opposition from Indians from the very start. When the commission travelled to India in 1928, it was met with vociferous protests at every location. Large processions marched through major cities, carrying black flags and banners, stating 'Go Back, Simon'. Expatriate Indians also organized protests across the world. Nalinaksha Sanyal was in London at the time, pursuing his PhD, and was an active member of the London branch of the INC. He was one of the main organizers of a large demonstration at Victoria station against the Simon Commission. Press reports of protesters in the middle of the capital of the British Empire led to a lot of consternation in the establishment. Nalinaksha was arrested, but, as a student, did not have the money to hire a lawyer. However, he argued his case so well in court that he was freed after being fined just £2 for 'obstruction of traffic' outside the station!

On 30 October, the Simon Commission faced a very large gathering of protesters led by Lala Lajpat Rai in Lahore. A large police contingent pushed them back. In an impromptu speech, Lajpat Rai mocked the government: 'If the government did not wish the Commission to see the demonstrators, the best thing for it to do was to put blindfolds over the eyes of the members and take them straight to Government House.' As tempers rose, the Superintendent of Police James Scott ordered a lathi charge. The crowd initially dispersed, but on seeing Lajpat Rai standing alone, they came back in force. Scott decided to target the leader, and a group of policemen, led by Scott, beat him mercilessly.

They kept hitting Lajpat Rai on the head until he collapsed, bleeding profusely. All this was done in full public view, as the purpose was to instil fear—the same mindset that had led to the Jallianwala Bagh massacre. There is evidence that Bhagat Singh witnessed the event.[32]

Lala Lajpat Rai never recovered from the injuries and died on 17 November 1928. His death sent shock waves across India. He was no ordinary leader, but had been at the forefront of the freedom movement for three decades. The repeated use of lethal force against unarmed protesters ignited public opinion. Chittaranjan Das's widow, Basanti Devi, publicly urged India's youth to avenge the killing: 'I, a woman of India, ask the youth of India: What are you going to do about it?' On 10 December, key revolutionaries, including Shivaram Rajguru, Bhagat Singh, Sukhdev Thapar and Chandrashekhar Azad, met in Lahore in the house of Bhagwati Charan Vohra. The mood was angry. Vohra was away in Calcutta, but his wife, Durga Devi (affectionately called Durga Bhabi), played host. The revolutionaries unanimously decided to kill Scott to send a message that violence would be met with violence.

Sukhdev was given the role of mission planner. He chose a team consisting of Rajguru, Bhagat Singh, Jai Gopal and Azad. The date was fixed for 17 December 1928. Each member was given a role: Bhagat Singh was given the job of shooting Scott, Rajguru was to accompany him to provide covering fire and Azad was to cover the escape. Jai Gopal, the most junior member of the team, was given the job of keeping a lookout and letting the others know that Scott had arrived at the police station. He was not part of the main operation.

Over the next few days, the revolutionaries scouted the location. It was decided that the Dayanand Anglo Vedic (DAV)

College (now Government Islamia College, Lahore) provided the best escape route. A new recruit, Hans Raj Vohra, helped Bhagat Singh make handwritten posters.

As it happened, Scott did not come to the police station on 17 December, as he had taken the day off. Jai Gopal mistook Assistant Superintendent John Saunders for Scott and informed the waiting team. Note that Saunders had also been involved in directing the lathi charge on the protesters, but it is not clear whether he was involved in beating Lajpat Rai. When Saunders came out of the premises in the afternoon and was mounting his motorcycle, Bhagat Singh realized they had the wrong man. However, Rajguru had already pulled out his Mauser and started to fire. Bhagat Singh also pumped a few bullets into the dying police officer before they ran towards the college. Another British officer, Inspector W.J.C. Fern, came out to see what was happening but ran back in when Azad shot at him. Only the head constable, Chanan Singh, gave chase. The revolutionaries begged him to turn back as they did not want to spill Indian blood, but when he kept running after them, Rajguru shot him dead too. Several people witnessed the shootings, including the famed Urdu poet Faiz Ahmad Faiz.

The three revolutionaries now ran into DAV College and scaled the walls into the hostel. Here they picked up their bicycles and left immediately. The police later surrounded and ransacked the college premises, but it was soon obvious that they had escaped. Bhagat Singh next edited the handwritten posters hurriedly to change the name. It appeared as:

Hindustan Socialist Republican Army Notice
J.P. Saunders is dead; Lala Lajpat Rai is avenged.

It was followed by a short text signed by 'Balraj, Commander-in-Chief'. It is often mistakenly stated that Balraj was a pseudonym used by Bhagat Singh, but it was Azad who used it. As the chief of the armed wing, the attack was officially done in his name.

Holed up in their hideout on Mozang Road, the three revolutionaries knew that the police was systematically combing the city and would eventually knock on their door. They needed to get out of Lahore. They made their way before dawn to Durga Devi's house to consult with her and Sukhdev. It was decided that they would leave that very day for Calcutta, with Bhagat Singh and Durga Devi disguised as a well-to-do couple—Ranjit and Sujata. Her three-year-old son would be their child and Rajguru would act as their servant. Azad opted to make separate arrangements.

Dressed in European clothes, including an overcoat and a felt hat, Ranjit walked confidently into Lahore station. He was accompanied by his well-dressed wife and followed by a servant, dressed in old clothes, carrying a child. The station was being closely watched, but no one suspected the family that walked into the first-class compartment. Having settled them in, the loyal servant went to his seat in the third-class compartment. Unknown to them, Azad was on the same train as a member of a party of pilgrims headed for Mathura!

Bhagat Singh and Durga Devi changed trains at Lucknow for Calcutta. This was important, as the police in Bengal was keeping a close watch on direct trains from Lahore. In Calcutta, Durga Devi and her son were reunited with Bhagwati Charan. Given his old family links with the Arya Samaj, Bhagat Singh made his way to the city's Arya Samaj temple. It is also likely that the revolutionaries secretly met the wealthy Haryanvi businessman Chajju Ram and received some funds before Bhagat Singh returned to Punjab a few days later. Chajju Ram is today barely remembered even in Haryana, but he was an important financier of many sociocultural and political movements of the early twentieth century, particularly the Arya Samaj.

BOMBING THE ASSEMBLY

Once the initial furore over the Saunders killing had died down, the revolutionaries rented two small houses in Agra's Hing ki Mandi neighbourhood. This became the new headquarters. Azad, Bhagat, Sukhdev and Rajguru used it as their base. They were soon joined by a number of new recruits as well as old HRA activists from the pre-Kakori years—Jatindra Nath Das (shortened henceforth to Jatin Das), Batukeshwar Dutt and Ram Saran Das. Jatin Das had been Sachindra Nath Sanyal's key lieutenant during his stint in Calcutta and was an explosives expert. Batukeshwar was from Bengal but had been recruited when he was studying in Kanpur. Ram Saran had been sentenced in the Kakori case and had recently returned after serving a sentence in the Cellular Jail (the experience had clearly not changed his mind).

The revolutionaries, as usual, were desperately short of funds, but they would occasionally receive help from the strangest of sources. For example, Azad once received a bearer cheque from Bengal's advocate general Sir N. Sircar. Azad immediately had it encashed so as to leave no trace. As they discussed the next course of action, they also debated new ideas and ideologies. Bhagat Singh was, by now, increasingly swayed by Marxism, but most of the others were still nationalists driven by older sociocultural views of nationhood. The tension can be seen in a commentary that Bhagat Singh wrote about Ram Saran Das's book *Dreamland* about his experiences in Kala Paani:

His interpretation of the world is metaphysical and ideological, while I am a materialist and my interpretation of the phenomenon would be causal. Nevertheless, it is by no means out of place or out of date. The general ideas that are prevailing in our country are more in accordance with those expressed by him ... mysticism that has been originated and developed by Hindu sages, such as Sankaracharya and others. But in the materialist philosophy this mode of thinking has absolutely no place.[33]

In early 1929, Viceroy Irwin introduced two bills for discussion. The first, the Public Safety Bill, was designed to empower the government to detain anyone without trial. The second, the Trade Disputes Bill, was designed to deter trade unions from going on strike. The revolutionaries decided that they would express their opposition to these laws by throwing a bomb into the Central Legislative Assembly in Delhi on 8 April, when the bills would be debated. The idea was not to hurt anyone but to make a big splash that would attract public attention. Unlike in the Saunders assassination, the activists would make no attempt to escape but would court arrest to make a strong statement.

Batukeshwar Dutt and Ram Saran Das were initially chosen to carry out the operation. However, an argument arose between Sukhdev and Bhagat Singh, where the former accused the latter of being too cowardly to do it himself. This stung Bhagat Singh and he now insisted on leading the mission. Azad realized that this was a bad idea as the police would soon work out his link to the Saunders killing. The throwing of a non-lethal bomb would result in a prison term, but the killing of a police officer meant capital punishment. Unfortunately, Bhagat Singh was adamant.

One must remember that for all their bravery, these were very young men, who often argued, disagreed and acted impetuously. The Central Legislative Assembly building, built for the new imperial capital of New Delhi, is an impressive structure. It would later house Independent India's Parliament, but in 1929 it had been in use for only a few years. Bhagat Singh and Batukeshwar Dutt visited the public gallery of the main hall on 6 April to do a dry run. They did not arouse any suspicion and came away without being questioned. On the morning of 8 April, Durga Devi, Bhagwati Charan and Azad met Bhagat Singh for a 'picnic' in Qudsia Park in Old Delhi. This park still exists, although part of it is now occupied by the ever-busy Inter-State Bus Terminal and a wide road. Nonetheless, wandering around the park on an April morning, I tried to imagine the mental state of all the participants. Few words were exchanged as Bhagat Singh ate oranges and his favourite sweets. Everyone knew that this would be the last time he would be seen free.[34]

Bhagat Singh left the park and headed directly to the Assembly, where Batukeshwar was waiting for him. They were dressed in khaki shorts and shirts. An Indian member quickly gave them passes at the entrance and then disappeared into the crowd. A few minutes before 11 a.m., the two made their way into the public gallery. The gallery was crowded. They could see many well-known people below—Motilal Nehru, M.A. Jinnah, Madan Mohan Malaviya and even Sir John Simon. Bhagat Singh carefully threw his bomb away from the seated members, but the explosion led to utter confusion. Then a second bomb thrown by Batukeshwar exploded, followed by a shower of leaflets. The low-intensity bombs were designed to be loud rather than deadly, but pandemonium broke out as people rushed in panic for the doors.

The two revolutionaries had fully loaded revolvers and could have killed several policemen and senior officials if they had wished. Not only did they not attempt to escape, they calmly put down the revolvers on adjoining chairs when the police sergeants arrived. Even as they were arrested, they were heard shouting 'Long Live the Revolution' and 'Down with Imperialism'. The idea was to make a political statement, and the leaflets made the point quoting Auguste Vaillant: 'It takes a loud voice to make the deaf hear.'

Meanwhile, Bhagwati Charan and his family had hired a horse *tonga* and were circling the area. When Bhagat Singh was dragged out, he looked up and saw them. Durga Devi's four-year-old son suddenly shouted out to 'Lamba Chacha (Tall Uncle)', but thankfully no one noticed in the din.

The British were aware that the revolutionaries intended to use the attack as a way to stir up public opinion. Hence, the police restricted information and instructed the press to play down the events. Most papers initially complied but *Hindustan Times* ran the story prominently. The chairman of the newspaper, Madan Mohan Malaviya, publicly maintained a distance from the revolutionaries but employed several journalists such as reporter Chaman Lal and editor J.N. Sahni, who were sympathetic to their cause. While the editorials carefully toed the government line, the story was given full front-page coverage on 10 April. This broke the 'omertà' and other papers began to cover it more openly.[35]

What further stoked public interest was the publication, a few days later, of photographs of the two revolutionaries. This included the well-known image of Bhagat Singh wearing a hat. The photograph had been taken on 4 April at Ramnath Photographers at Kashmiri Gate, Old Delhi. Batukeshwar was separately photographed at the same studio. It was common for revolutionaries of this period to get themselves photographed just before a dangerous mission. It was partly driven by the human longing of being remembered, but also as a possible propaganda tool, should they be martyred.

Unfortunately, the photographs were not ready by the time the two were arrested. Two HSRA members, Jaydev Kapoor and Shiv Verma, were given the job of retrieving them. The problem was that Ramnath Photographers also worked with the police and had taken the official photographs of the prisoners. Thus, Kapoor and Verma were nervous when they went to the studio. One of them asked for the photographs while the other stood at the door with a finger on the trigger of a concealed revolver. The photographer, who almost certainly knew what was going on, handed over the package and even gave them the negatives for no extra charge. The HSRA network now sent copies to several friendly reporters. *Hindustan Times* and a small Lahore-based paper, *Bande Mataram*, published the photographs prominently, much to the chagrin of the colonial authorities. Within a few days, the images spread across India and began to be reproduced both in mainstream newspapers and underground publications. Bhagat Singh's cool hat made him instantly recognizable, and it became what would today be called a viral meme. Similarly Batukeshwar's dreamy, boyish look elicited a lot of sympathy. The two of them became instant national heroes.

Meanwhile, the British had a growing suspicion that Bhagat Singh was somehow involved in the Saunders killing. Thus, a special investigation was initiated to look into possible links between the events in Lahore and Delhi. The trial for the Assembly Bombing Case began a few weeks later under unprecedented security. The two defendants were unfazed and kept interrupting the proceedings by shouting slogans. Bhagat Singh even took a dig at Gandhi: 'We have only marked the end of the era of utopian non-violence, of whose futility the rising generation has been convinced beyond the shadow of doubt.' After a show trial, both of them were sentenced to fourteen years in jail.

British officials, however, were not satisfied as they wanted to establish who had killed Saunders and shut down the wider network. Therefore, the number of police raids in Lahore was increased and several suspected HSRA members were arrested. One of them, Jai Gopal—who had mistaken Saunders for Scott— agreed to turn approver. This was a major breakthrough as he revealed the names of the others. Hans Raj, who had helped make the posters, turned approver a few days later. Based on information from the approvers, Sukhdev, Rajguru, Jatin Das and several others were caught and brought to Lahore. One of Sachindra Nath Sanyal's brothers, Jitendra Nath, was also arrested. He would later write an underground biography of Bhagat Singh, published in 1931, that provides a valuable eye-witness account of what followed.[36]

The prisoners soon began to complain about the appalling conditions in jail. They pointed out how European prisoners, often common criminals, were treated much better. The complaints eventually resulted in a hunger strike, demanding better treatment. The news of the hunger strike leaked out and some newspapers even began to publish a daily health bulletin of individual prisoners. Protests were held across the country, including a large meeting at Jallianwala Bagh in Amritsar. Eventually, the government was forced to appoint an inquiry committee. Most of the protesters withdrew from the strike, but Jatin Das refused. Given the increasingly charged political situation, the government even arranged for Bhagat Singh to visit Jatin Das and persuade him, but the latter was adamant.

Jatin Das died on 13 September after sixty-three days of fasting. Subhas Chandra Bose paid Rs 600 to bring his body from Lahore to Calcutta. Six hundred thousand people turned up at Howrah station to receive the body. As the funeral cortege made its way to the cremation ground on the banks of the Hugli river (a distributary of the Ganga), crowds lined both sides of the road and showered flowers. The British were unnerved by the demonstration of solidarity.

THE SECOND LAHORE CONSPIRACY CASE

The trial began in the intense heat of May 1930. It is now remembered as the Second Lahore Conspiracy Case, not to be confused with the First Lahore Conspiracy Case of 1915 involving the Ghadarite generation of revolutionaries. In the audience was Bhagat Singh's father Kishan Singh, who, despite his son's objections, had constituted a defence team. It must have been quite a moment when the prisoners entered together, singing '*Sarfaroshi ki tamanna ab hamare dil mein hai ...*', a song popularized by Bismil, which meant 'The dream of self-sacrifice now fills our hearts'. Many members of the audience began to sing along.[37]

The judges had only just managed to re-establish order when Rajguru stood up and made a statement that the viceroy did not have the authority to try them by a special tribunal and that the trial was invalid. This was followed by a statement read out by Jitendra Nath Sanyal on behalf of the prisoners. The statement, co-authored with Bhagat Singh, argued that the defenders of India's honour and freedom could not be tried as criminals.

Given the crimes against humanity committed by the British, it was the colonial administration that should be put on trial.

Justice Coldstream tried several times to stop Jiten Sanyal, but he continued reading, undeterred. At the end of the statement, he stated on behalf of the accused: 'We decline to be party to this farcical show. We shall not take part in the proceedings.' In other words, the revolutionaries did not recognize the legitimacy of the colonial government and the court, and would not participate in the trial in any way. As one can imagine, the authorities did not know how to react and the case was adjourned for the day.

For the next several days, the prisoners were brought to the court, but the trial could not proceed as the accused would either shout out slogans or sing. Eventually, the two British judges, Coldstream and Hilton, asked the police to use force. The police entered the box and mercilessly beat the prisoners. There was utter pandemonium in the court as the accused were dragged away. Agha Haider, the only Indian member of the tribunal, made a statement disassociating himself from the actions of the police. The revolutionaries henceforth boycotted the trial, and the tribunal had to proceed without them. All of this was widely covered in the press and had the whole country riveted.

Even as the courtroom drama was playing itself out, Azad and Bhagwati Charan were at large. They decided to increase the pressure. In mid-December, a team led by Bhagwati Charan rigged explosives to the railway tracks entering Delhi from the south, not far from Purana Qila. Then they waited for the viceroy's special train that was supposed to pass this section while entering Delhi on the 23rd of the month. A mid-level HSRA member, Yashpal, was given the job of pressing the switch. Unfortunately, the trigger was mistimed and the explosion took place a few seconds after the viceroy's carriage had passed the segment (some versions suggest it was too early). The viceroy was unhurt, although the explosion caused extensive damage to some of the other bogies. It was foggy and it is possible that Yashpal had genuinely misjudged the speed, but Azad had a suspicion that he may have deliberately mistimed it. For the moment, however, he kept his suspicions to himself.

The attack was widely condemned by both the government and the INC moderates. Gandhi wrote an article, 'The Cult of the Bomb', in *Young India*, strongly criticizing the revolutionaries. In response, Bhagwati Charan published a widely circulated pamphlet titled 'The Philosophy of the Bomb', which argued:

> What has the Congress been doing? It has changed its creed from Swaraj to Complete Independence. As a logical sequence to this, one would expect it to declare a war on the British government. Instead, we find it has declared a war against the revolutionaries ... As to Gandhi's contention that violence impedes the march of progress and directly postpones the day of freedom, we can refer him to many contemporary instances where violence has led to the social progress and political freedom of the people who practice it ... It is mainly the mania for non-violence and Gandhi's compromise mentality that brought about the disruption of the forces that had come together at the call of Mass Action.[38]

Azad and Bhagwati Charan must have been disappointed by their failed attempt on the viceroy—they had missed by seconds. Not to be deterred, they started to plan a daring rescue attempt to free their comrades. The date was set for 1 June 1930, as this was the day when Bhagat Singh and Batukeshwar Dutt were supposed to be taken from Central Jail to Borstal Jail. Two teams were set up to carry out the operation at the gates of Borstal Jail. Unfortunately, the plan went horribly wrong when Bhagwati Charan was killed as a bomb went off accidentally during the preparations. Whatever her internal turmoil, Durga Devi was outwardly stoic about the death of her husband and remained an active member of the movement.

The tribunal delivered its judgment on 7 October 1930. Bhagat Singh, Sukhdev Thapar and Shivaram Rajguru were sentenced to death by hanging; eight others were sentenced to long jail terms. Jitendra Nath Sanyal and two others were freed for lack of evidence.

The hangings were scheduled to be carried out on 24 March 1931. A popular clamour was growing to have the sentences commuted. As one can imagine, there was a lot of pressure on Gandhi to push for clemency during his extensive meetings with Viceroy Irwin in the first week of March. To this day, there is a lot of debate over whether Gandhi did indeed discuss the matter with the viceroy at all. The best available evidence suggests that he briefly raised the matter but did not press it, and there is a possibility that he was subtly misled by the viceroy to believe that the executions were not imminent.[39] Given how heated this issue can get even today, let me quote what Subhas Chandra Bose wrote about the matter in his autobiography:

> I was reminded of a similar incident during the armistice between the Sinn Fein Party and the British government, when the strong attitude adopted by the former, had secured the release of an Irish political prisoner sentenced to the gallows. But the Mahatma who did not want to identify himself with revolutionary prisoners, would not go so far and it naturally made a great difference when the Viceroy realized that the Mahatma would not break on that question.[40]

Bhagat Singh, Sukhdev and Rajguru were hanged on 23 March, a day ahead of schedule. The bodies were then smuggled out in sacks by the police through a hole in the back wall of the jail and secretly burnt on the banks of the Sutlej in Hussainiwala. The local villagers found the half-burnt remains and cremated them properly a day later. The news of the hangings cast a pall of gloom over the country, including the INC session held in Karachi. It became worse when attempts by Congress workers to organize a protest in Kanpur spiralled into a Hindu–Muslim riot, which resulted in 400 deaths.

The place where the three were cremated ended up in Pakistan after Partition, but was taken back by India in 1961 in exchange for twelve villages. A National Martyrs' Memorial was built in 1968, but was ransacked by Pakistani armoured units during the war of 1971. The memorial was then rebuilt in 1973.[41]

THE BATTLE OF ALFRED PARK

After the death of Bhagwati Charan and the announcement of the sentences in Lahore, Azad must have felt isolated and lonely. However, he carried on travelling across north India to keep the network going. In late January or early February 1931, he moved to Allahabad and started operating from a house in the Katra area of the city. A few HSRA members, including Durga Devi and Yashpal, met him there to discuss the future course of action. Sachindra Nath Sanyal was in the Cellular Jail at this time, but his extended family had moved to Allahabad and was living in the Colonelgunj neighbourhood. His wife Pratibha and brother Rabindra Nath were aware that Azad was in the city.

There is evidence that Azad and Yashpal met Jawaharlal Nehru around 20 February. Motilal Nehru had passed away just days earlier. Since he had been supportive of the revolutionary cause in his later years, it is likely that Azad wanted to convey his condolences to the son as well as elicit some help. Yashpal would later claim that the meeting did not go well, as Jawaharlal was generally dismissive of the revolutionary approach. Jawaharlal would also briefly recall the incident in the first edition of his autobiography.[42] Curiously, he dropped it in later editions.

On the morning of 27 February, Rabindra Nath Sanyal was teaching a niece in a rented house in Colonelgunj when he noticed that there were a large number of plain-clothes policemen on the street below.[43] The Sanyal home was often used by revolutionaries as a place to get a quick meal and change laundry. Since it was constantly under watch, the women of the family had worked out a drill, which allowed the fugitives to quickly eat, pick up their laundry and leave through a neighbour's terrace before the informer could walk to the nearest police station and return with a raiding party. Long accustomed to being under surveillance, Rabindra knew that something special was afoot but was wondering how to warn Azad, who was expected to drop in that day.

A stone's throw away, in Alfred Park, Azad and Sukhdev Raj were casually walking towards the Indian Press gate of the park. They had spotted an old comrade, Veerbhadra Tiwari, a few minutes earlier. Veerbhadra had been arrested for the Kakori case but had escaped punishment. Since then he had re-established contact with the revolutionaries, but Azad had generally kept him at arm's length. Suddenly seeing him in Allahabad made Azad suspicious. Sukhdev and Azad were still in conversation when they saw an armed police officer, Visheshwar Singh, enter the park along with another policeman and walk past them. Clearly something was going on.

All of a sudden, a car came to a halt and the city's crime branch chief, John Nott-Bower, jumped out. He asked the two men to put their hands up. Azad pulled out his pistol and shot out the car's tyres, but was shot by Nott-Bower in the thigh. Sukhdev and Azad now ran into the park and hid behind a jamun tree. By this time, Visheshwar Singh and several other armed policemen had taken up positions and were firing at them.

Azad realized that he could not escape with a badly injured leg. So he ordered Sukhdev to escape while he provided covering fire. The gunfight lasted for quite some time; Visheshwar Singh was hit in the jaw while Nott-Bower was hit in the wrist (both survived, although the former was forced to take premature retirement). Azad was a good shot and the police could not get closer, but he was surrounded, injured and running out of ammunition. When he had only one bullet left, he shot himself through the head. Thus, he kept his promise that he would never be taken alive.[44]

A few hundred metres away, the Sanyal household listened to the gunfight in horror. Once the shooting had died down, Rabindra Nath and Pratibha carefully made their way to Alfred Park. The police cordon did not allow them to get close, but they could recognize their comrade's body in the distance. The colonial administration was aware that Azad's heroic last stand had made him a potent martyr. The body was hurriedly taken to the river and cremated. However, senior Congress leader Purushottam Das Tandon arrived in time to witness the cremation and collect the ashes. He then took the ashes into the city, where a meeting had been organized by the Allahabad Students' Association. Kamala Nehru and Pratibha Sanyal addressed an emotionally charged audience. Several students smeared Azad's ashes on their foreheads and swore that they would avenge his death.

Alfred Park is still there but has been renamed Chandrashekhar Azad Park. The jamun tree that he used for cover, however, no longer exists as the British soon cut it down to stop it from becoming a shrine. Today there is a martyr's memorial and statue on the spot where he fell fighting. Locals still like to point out bullet holes in the trunks of nearby trees, but frankly, it is unclear if they are authentic. There is also a pistol in the nearby museum that is said to belong to Azad. While it probably belonged to Azad, there is some reason to believe it is not the one used in the gunfight. The pistol in the museum is a Colt, whereas the one used in the gunfight was almost certainly a Mauser.

There has long been a controversy about who provided the information about Azad's whereabouts to the police. Veerbhadra Tiwari is usually assumed to be the only source, but the fact is that he had been kept out of the loop by Azad for some time. Therefore, he is unlikely to have had precise information about Azad's location and activities. There is now strong evidence that there was another source—Yashpal. In the 1960s, an intelligence officer, Dharmendra Gaur, came across incriminating documents in UP police records in Lucknow that strongly suggest that Yashpal was a police informer from 1930. The British had taken care to destroy such records before the handover of power in 1947, but a couple of official letters related to Yashpal somehow survived.[45]

We know that Azad was becoming increasingly suspicious of Yashpal in the months before his death. Jai Gopal and Hans Raj may have turned approver, but they did not know the whereabouts of many of the arrested HSRA leaders—but Yashpal did. The failed attempt on the viceroy was also a source of suspicion. Azad had conveyed his suspicions to some of his colleagues, and the British were aware that the surviving revolutionaries might try to kill him. It is likely, therefore, that they staged an arrest and put him in Bareilly Jail for his protection. Suspiciously, he was allowed to get married in jail and keep his wife with him. Such a privilege was unheard of in an age when even junior revolutionaries were routinely sent to face the horrors of Kala Paani.[46]

7

CHITTAGONG

EVEN AS THESE DRAMATIC EVENTS WERE PLAYING OUT IN LAHORE and Allahabad, the revolutionaries in Bengal had not been quiet. Following the arrests of senior leaders in the mid-1920s, a new generation had emerged here as well. Perhaps the most charismatic of these leaders was Surya Sen.[1] He was born in 1894 in Chittagong. He was initiated into the world of the revolutionaries when he was pursuing undergraduate studies at Krishnath College in Berhampur. As we have seen, the college was a hotbed of the Jugantar group.

Surya Sen returned to Chittagong and became a mathematics teacher at National High School. This is why he came to be known widely as 'Master-da' (schoolmaster). The Easter Rebellion in Ireland in April 1916, particularly the capture of Dublin by a few hundred men, had a deep impact on him. The rebellion itself was crushed, but it had triggered a sequence of events that led directly to Irish independence. Surya Sen planned to instigate a similar revolt in India.

In the early 1920s, Sen was part of the Anushilan Samiti network in east Bengal and was witness to the formation of the HRA as an umbrella body. However, like most of the Bengali groups, his unit did not join the HSRA when it was reconstituted by Azad and Bhagat Singh. Instead, the easternmost wing of the HRA was rebranded as the Indian Republican Army. It is unclear why it opted for this name, but it is possible that it was done simply to acquire the same acronym as the Irish Republican Army. Yet again, one can see how the impact of the Irish on the Indian struggle for Independence is underappreciated today.

THE ARMOURY RAID

On the morning of 18 April 1930, Good Friday, the Indian Republican Army struck in Chittagong. Around 10 a.m., an advance party hijacked two taxis and attacked the telegraph office and telephone exchange, so that communication with the rest of the world was severed. Meanwhile, the main body of activists, dressed in khaki, raided the police armoury. The revolutionaries only had a few pistols among them, but they took the police completely by surprise. The same happened at the auxiliary forces armoury. There were several hundred trained auxiliary troops in the barracks, but they did not know how to respond. A British sergeant major, who lived in the compound, was shot dead when he tried to challenge the insurgents.

The rebels now collected rifles and a couple of machine guns from the armoury but could not find the appropriate ammunition as it was kept on separate premises. A frantic search for ammunition turned up nothing. Thus, the revolutionaries had to be satisfied with smooth-bore muskets, for which they found plenty of ammunition. These were single-shot guns with relatively poor range, but there was no choice.

One party was sent to the local European club to look for any officials who might be there, but found it empty. Another chased away a group of Europeans that had organized a response team with weapons from the Chittagong port armoury. Nonetheless, it was obvious to the leaders Surya Sen and Ganesh Ghosh that they could not hold the town for long with barely fifty-six men armed with muskets. Thus, the rebels decided to head into the hills beyond the town. They carried as many arms and ammunition as they could.

For the next three days, Surya Sen led his men further into the hills. Weighed down by the guns and ammunition, the going became slow. They were also desperately hungry and thirsty. Some sympathetic villagers provided them with meals along the way, but they could not linger at any one place for too long. They knew that the British administration would have restored communication by now and would be looking for them. On more than one occasion, they saw a plane flying low over them.[2]

On 22 April, the group took up positions on a hillock known as Jalalabad. It was around 5 p.m. when they saw a large number of troops gathering some distance away, including Gurkha armed police, some companies of the Eastern Frontier Rifles and some Europeans of the Surma Valley Light Horse. The government troops now tried to encircle the hillock. Subodh Roy, who participated in the defence of the hill, later described the intense feelings that the revolutionaries experienced as they watched the professionals systematically take their positions.

The British officers planning the assault probably felt that the revolutionaries would realize their impossible situation and quickly capitulate when faced with a frontal assault. They were probably also encouraged by the lack of response as they closed in. However, recognizing the limitations of the muskets, Surya Sen had ordered his men to hold their fire until the enemy was very close. Then, all of a sudden, the revolutionaries opened a volley at close quarters. The government troops were forced to fall back, with several casualties. This was followed by a few more waves of frontal assault with the same result. The British now withdrew and positioned some machine guns on a hill that overlooked Jalalabad. From here, they kept up constant fire that proved more effective. Several revolutionaries were killed at this stage.

As it became dark, the revolutionaries realized that firing from the opposite side had stopped. They would later find out that the authorities were unsure of the number of rebels and did not want to leave the town unguarded in case there was a second unit that could outflank government troops. Therefore, the troops were withdrawn. Surya Sen and the surviving men used the opportunity to escape. Figures are disputed, but a later statement by Charles Tegart, Calcutta police commissioner, suggests that twelve revolutionaries died on Jalalabad hill while the government lost sixty-four men. This was quite a performance by a ragtag group against well-armed professionals.[3] Surya Sen remained at large and kept directing guerrilla attacks until he was betrayed and captured in February 1933. He was hanged a year later.

The Chittagong armoury raid was never going to succeed as a military operation. All the participants knew this. The objective was to inspire a wave of unrest—and it succeeded. In the next two years, Bengal saw a large number of attacks on government officials, which paralysed the colonial administration. On 25 August 1930, Tegart narrowly escaped being killed when Dinesh

Majumdar and Anuj Sen tried to throw a bomb at his car. Dinesh escaped but Anuj was killed in the encounter. Four days later, Benoy Basu shot dead Inspector General Lowman in Dacca. Benoy then escaped in disguise from Dacca and headed to Calcutta, where he planned an even more audacious attack.

On 8 December, Benoy Basu, Badal Gupta and Dinesh Gupta entered Writers' Building, the secretariat, and shot dead Inspector General of Prisons J.J. Simpson. This was followed by a famous gunfight in the corridors of the secretariat, remembered as the 'Battle of the Verandah'. Benoy and Badal shot themselves with their last bullets while Dinesh was hanged in 1931. Dalhousie Square—the open area in front of Writers' Building—is today known as Benoy–Badal–Dinesh Bagh in their memory.

Alipore Central Jail is now a museum dedicated to the freedom movement. One can see the gallows where so many revolutionaries were hanged. Just beyond the gallows are the depressing cells where the condemned spent their last days before execution. This is where Dinesh Gupta was hanged, aged just nineteen.

Even as political violence in the rest of Bengal increased, the district magistrate of Midnapur, James Peddie, ordered the police to shoot down peasants refusing to pay taxes. The revolutionaries not only killed him but two of his successors as well.[4] Inevitably, the British responded by arresting large numbers of young men and women suspected of having links with the revolutionaries. Many of them were housed in a new detention centre at Hijli in Midnapur. The buildings of the Hijli Detention Camp still exist and are part of the Indian Institute of Technology in Kharagpur. The main building is used today as a technology museum and administration offices. Visitors should also see the women's ward and the solitary-confinement cells built separately. One should remember that the revolutionaries detained here in the 1930s were about the same age as the engineering students using the buildings today.

Dinesh Gupta, the only survivor of the trio that had attacked Writers' Building, had been sentenced to death by J.J. Gerlick, the sessions judge at Alipore court. On 27 July, Gerlick was shot dead by the revolutionaries. This news was reportedly received with jubilation by the inmates at Hijli. The authorities were even more enraged when three inmates escaped. The British officials in the district decided to teach the inmates a lesson, and, on the night of 16 September 1931, the guards were ordered to wreak vengeance. In an unprovoked attack, fifty armed guards entered the facility and fired at the prisoners. Two of the inmates died and twenty-nine were badly injured.[5]

The news of the unprovoked attack on unarmed inmates soon leaked out and caused public outrage. Subhas Chandra Bose visited Hijli to collect the bodies of the martyrs. Yet again, large numbers gathered at Howrah station as the bodies were brought in. Many prominent Indians, including Rabindranath Tagore, condemned the government. Political prisoners across Bengal went on hunger strike, demanding an inquiry. The government inquiry concluded: 'In our opinion, there is no proper justification for the indiscriminate firing by the sepoys at the Detention Camp which killed two political prisoners and injured many others.'[6]

Following the Hijli incident, the authorities began to monitor Subhas Bose's links with the revolutionaries with renewed suspicion. Not only was Bose showing a great deal of public sympathy for their martyrs, but some of the new breed of revolutionaries were found to have links with the Bengal

Volunteers, rather than the old revolutionary groups. The Bengal Volunteers had been set up by Bose for the Calcutta session of the INC in 1928 as an organizing corps for the event. However, it subsequently developed a life of its own. The trio that attacked Writers' Building, for instance, had links with the organization.

Nalinaksha Sanyal, who had recently returned from London with a PhD in economics, was also connected to the Bengal Volunteers and had been one of its key organizers at one stage. Given his long history of revolutionary links, he was clearly a suspect. As a result, Calcutta University withdrew its offer of a lecturer's position, forcing him to embark on a business career that would prove successful (to their credit, the commerce department defied the authorities to give him an adjunct position, which he held until 1964). Meanwhile, his wife Tunu became close friends with a female revolutionary Bina Das and her sisters (daughters of Subhas Bose's schoolteacher Beni Madhab Das). They would practise pistol-shooting in the open fields of the newly developing suburb of Hindustan Park (near Gariahat). Nalinaksha's house in the area still stands, although it is today a densely packed neighbourhood.

In February 1932, Bina Das attempted to shoot Bengal Governor Stanley Jackson in the convocation hall of Calcutta University. She fired five shots but missed, and was sentenced to nine years in prison. Unsurprisingly, Nalinaksha and Tunu were soon arrested and subjected to weeks of severe interrogation at the Elysium Row headquarters of Calcutta Police. They were eventually released due to inadequate evidence, but a hint of suspicion lingered.[7]

The sharp escalation of revolutionary activity across India, however, lost steam by 1933. Almost all key leaders such as

Surya Sen and Chandrashekhar Azad had been either killed or put in prison. Moreover, the movement was degenerating from organized armed resistance to anarchic acts of violence that were not sanctioned either by founding principles or by public support. As often happens, common criminals made claims of being revolutionaries to justify armed robbery.

For all his sympathies for the revolutionary cause, Subhas Bose was not yet ready to pick up the leadership under these circumstances. Thus, there was a lull for a period of about six years in the mainstream revolutionary movement. This was a period of expansion for two offshoots, at opposite ends of the ideological spectrum, that had emerged out of the revolutionary movement—the Communist Party of India and the Rashtriya Swayamsevak Sangh. Both of them were started by survivors from the attempts at insurrection during the First World War.

THE MANY ADVENTURES OF M.N. ROY

Some readers may be under the impression that the communist movement in India began with Bhagat Singh. Although it is true that he increasingly took to Marxism towards the end of his short life, he was not part of a Marxist organization. As Bhagat himself points out in the tract 'Why I Am an Atheist', which he wrote on death row, he was almost alone among the revolutionaries in adhering to this ideology in 1930. The real founder of the Communist Party of India is another fascinating character— Manabendra Nath Roy, usually remembered as M.N. Roy.

He was born Narendra Nath Bhattacharya in Bengal in 1887, and joined the Anushilan Samiti during the protests against the Partition of Bengal in 1905.[8] After the arrest of Aurobindo and Barin Ghosh, he drifted into Bagha Jatin's Jugantar group. He had been part of the meeting that had planned the Rodda arms heist but had opted out as he felt it was too risky. When Bagha Jatin was negotiating with the Germans for a large arms consignment in 1915, he sent Narendra to Batavia to coordinate the logistics with the German consul-general. As we have seen, the consignment never reached India and Bagha Jatin was killed while waiting for it on the Balasore coast. The British then proceeded to arrest many members of the Jugantar group. Thus, Narendra found himself stranded in South East Asia.

Unsure of what to do next, he decided to go to California in the hope of joining the Ghadarite community. He also changed his name to M.N. Roy in the hope of throwing British intelligence off his scent. Here he met and married Evelyn Trent, a graduate student at Stanford University with a passion for radical politics. The United States joined the war in 1917, and it immediately became a dangerous place for Indians with revolutionary links. So Roy and his wife escaped to Mexico. The couple was soon part of a circle of ultra-Left radicals, which included several American draft dodgers. This is how Roy met Mikhail Borodin, who had been sent by Moscow as the emissary of the Communist International. They became close friends and together founded the Communist Party of Mexico in 1919. In this way, a fugitive from India became the father of Mexican communism!

On Borodin's recommendation, Roy was invited to Moscow to meet Lenin. The latter was then looking for someone to advise him on how to think about Asia, and specifically British India. By all accounts, Roy impressed Lenin and was given access to the top Soviet leadership. He was then sent to Tashkent with orders to set up a Marxist indoctrination school for Indians. There were several Indian activists who had sought refuge in the Soviet Union after the Turko-German alliance had surrendered. Lenin wanted to use them to create a group steeped in Bolshevik ideas, which could be deployed to pressure the British in India when necessary. This is how the Communist Party of India was founded in Tashkent on 17 October 1920.

Interestingly, the British were aware of these developments through their agent, Frederick Bailey. He had disguised himself as an Austrian officer who had been taken prisoner by the Tzarist regime during the war and subsequently been marooned in Central Asia. He must have been very good at his job, because the Bolsheviks hired him to help identify British agents, including himself! Bailey kept a close watch on the Indians. He even spent several days in Samarkand's only hotel, in a room across from the one occupied by Mahendra Pratap, who was also a refugee in the Soviet Union. The former leader of the Kabul mission does not seem to have suspected anything, as he freely discussed his plans with the spy.[9]

Back in India, the Muslim population was growing restive over the treatment of the last Ottoman Sultan. A significant number of Muslim radicals decided to make their way through Afghanistan and Iran to Turkey to fight for the Caliph's cause. However, after the defeat in the Third Anglo-Afghan War of 1919, the Afghans were not in a position to help them. Kemal Ataturk was in the process of seizing power in Turkey and was also not keen on hosting radicals from India. Thus, they were stranded, destitute and desperate in Afghanistan when Lenin decided to take them in. It appears that Lenin felt that they could be used to destabilize British India and create conditions for a future Soviet expansion.

Roy's training school for Indians in Tashkent was soon dominated by these Islamic radicals. If this Marxist–Islamist mix looked complicated, it became even more so when Enver Pasha, the charismatic wartime leader of Turkey, escaped to Central Asia. Lenin asked Roy to collaborate with Pasha to plan a 'war of liberation' in India. However, Roy soon realized that Pasha was enamoured with the idea of creating an empire for himself in the original Central Asian homeland of the Turkic people. Plans of military operations in India began to look increasingly like the medieval Turkic invasions of the subcontinent. Therefore, Roy distanced himself from Pasha. This was just as well, as the Turkish leader shortly afterwards led a bloody revolt against his Russian hosts and was eventually hunted down and killed.[10]

As one can see, M.N. Roy's personal journey is so fantastic that it would be scarcely believable in a novel. Nonetheless, he was rather less successful in spreading communism in India. The British arrested most of the indoctrinated groups that were sent back to India. The individuals who evaded arrest showed little interest in spreading the message. Nonetheless, the colonial authorities issued a warrant against him in 1924.

When Stalin grabbed power after Lenin's death, Roy found that he no longer had a sympathetic supporter. The activities of the Tashkent school were transferred to the ominously named University of the Toilers of the East. Roy and Borodin were then sent off to China to spread communism, but their mission failed. Stalin characteristically blamed them. Recognizing the Soviet leader's volatile nature, Roy quietly left Moscow for Berlin in April 1929. He clandestinely returned to India in December 1930. He was already in touch with some senior leaders and, on the invitation of Jawaharlal Nehru, he secretly attended the Karachi session of the Congress. The police eventually traced him to a house in Bombay and arrested him on the basis of the warrant of 1924. He was sentenced to twelve years in prison.[11]

Meanwhile, the Communist Party of India was finally gaining some traction. Ironically, this did not happen due to the efforts of M.N. Roy or any Indian communist, but two British communists, Philip Spratt and Benjamin Bradley. With financial support from Moscow, Spratt managed to organize a small number of units before the British arrested several of the activists in 1929. Known as the Meerut Conspiracy Case, the accused were defended by no less than Jawaharlal Nehru and K.N. Katju. The trial went on until 1933, and twenty-seven persons were given sentences of various lengths. More importantly, it provided a great deal of publicity to the communists and created interest in their ideas. Similarly, Roy's colourful life also attracted a lot of admirers.

The other reason for the spread of Marxist ideology is even more intriguing. There is a fair amount of first-hand evidence that the British deliberately encouraged the spread of Marxist literature among political prisoners in the early 1930s. Subodh Roy, sent to the Cellular Jail for taking part in the Chittagong rebellion, wrote in his memoirs:

> Readers would be surprised to know that we also got books on socialism at government cost. The government thought that they would be able to divert the minds of political prisoners by making them interested in socialist ideas, which they thought were a lesser evil than 'terrorist' actions such as the murder of oppressive British officials. Thus, the government had some hand in making political prisoners in the Andamans interested in socialism. They had unknowingly sowed the seeds of communism among political prisoners detained in other jails as well.[12]

We can only speculate why colonial authorities would deliberately spread potentially dangerous ideas. One possibility, as suggested by Subodh Roy himself, was that communism was considered less dangerous than the revolutionary nationalism that had spread among the youth in the previous three decades. At the very least, it would create cleavages that could be exploited. They certainly succeeded in the case of Subodh Roy, who broke away from his earlier affiliations and joined the communists on his release from jail:

> I was granted candidate membership of the Communist Party of India, a section of the Communist International. My joy was no bounds. Oh, what an honour for me! Forsaking past beliefs and discarding old ideals, I had been accepted as a member of the Communist Party of India.[13]

Another reason could be that the British had infiltrated the Indian communist movement and felt that they could misdirect its energies (there is some evidence that Yashpal was used for this as well). This was entirely in character with colonial tactics. We have already seen how the British had set up the INC as a 'safety valve' and later infiltrated the Sikh gurudwaras in Canada to wean them away from Ghadarites. Thus, it was not uncommon for the British to divert politically aroused youth to join a movement that they indirectly controlled. Whatever the original thinking behind the strategy, there is no denying that it turned out to be useful during the Second World War. Subodh Roy, a former member of Surya Sen's Indian Republican Army, returned to the Chittagong hills during the Second World War as an irregular guerrilla, fighting for the British cause against the Japanese and Subhas Bose's Indian National Army!

A key conduit for foreign influences on the CPI was the Communist Party of Great Britain, and specifically a nebulous activist Rajani Palme-Dutt. He was born in Cambridge, England, to an Indian doctor and a Swedish mother (who was the grand-aunt of future Swedish Prime Minister Olof Palme). He and his brother Clemens were part of a small but influential circle of intellectuals supported by the Russians in Britain. In the early 1930s, Palme-Dutt became heavily involved in the development of the movement in India. Together with Benjamin Bradley, he developed the Dutt–Bradley thesis that defined the CPI's political strategy of that time. The basic idea was that Indian communists should not expend their energy fighting British imperialism independently. Instead, they should focus on infiltrating the INC, so that it could influence the policies of the 'bourgeoisie-led' freedom struggle. In other words, their energies were to be directed at an internal takeover rather than at an external enemy.

M.N. Roy, meanwhile, had appealed against his sentence and managed to reduce the prison term to six years. He was released in November 1936 and joined the Congress. With Nehru's help, he was even elected to the All India Congress Committee.[14] This may have initially looked like a success for the Dutt–Bradley strategy, but Roy's commitment to the communist cause was wavering. Not only was he uncomfortable with foreign influences in the CPI, but he was also beginning to question several accepted Marxist ideas. Eventually, he drifted off to develop his own complex ideology—'radical humanism'. Even as he plunged deeper into theoretical nitty-gritty, his followers left him over time, and Roy became largely irrelevant by the 1940s. One of the consequences of his ideological drift is that Indian communists would later be embarrassed by their founder. As a result, they would latch on to

Bhagat Singh, even though, his personal views notwithstanding, he had little role in building the communist movement in India.

THE FOUNDING OF THE RSS

Keshav Baliram Hedgewar was born into a family of modest means in Nagpur in 1889. He lost both his parents to an epidemic when he was just thirteen. Thereafter, he was supported by family members and a charismatic local leader, Dr B.S. Moonje. When he was in high school, Hedgewar was deeply influenced by the nationalist ideas being spread by Tilak and became the leader of a band of students. When the inspector of schools visited, he arranged for the whole class to shout 'Vande Mataram' when the official entered the room. The principal attempted to find out the name of the main organizer but was stonewalled. Thus, the whole class was suspended. The news spread and it led to students in several Nagpur schools boycotting class. The authorities eventually accepted back most of Hedgewar's classmates on the basis of a written apology, but he adamantly refused to write one. Thus, young Keshav Baliram ended up being expelled.[15]

Hedgewar was now forced to move to Pune to complete his studies. The disruption meant that he only completed high school at the age of twenty. With the blessings of Dr Moonje, he next moved to Calcutta to pursue a medical degree at National Medical College in 1910. This was one of several nationalist institutions that had been recently set up to bypass the control of the British on the education system.

Given his political leanings, it is not surprising that Hedgewar was soon initiated into the Anushilan Samiti. Evidently, he even learnt to speak Bengali and dress like a local. He was given the code name 'Cocaine' and assigned the job of delivering messages, pamphlets and revolvers to different units. By 1913, he had earned himself a licentiate in medicine and surgery—although this degree was not yet recognized formally by the colonial administration, as it was issued by a 'native' institution. The newly minted doctor moved back to Nagpur with instructions to set up an Anushilan Samiti unit there. He quickly reconnected with his old friends and set up an organization named Kranti Dal (Revolutionary Party). The mother organization in Bengal seems to have supplied guns and propaganda material.

Like most other revolutionaries, Hedgewar saw the First World War as an opportunity to strike against the British Empire. The Kranti Dal attempted to smuggle in German small arms through the Portuguese enclave of Goa. Unfortunately, the attempt was foiled when the British seized the ship at sea. This is not dissimilar to what had happened to the consignments meant for Bagha Jatin on the east coast. Deprived of an adequate supply of arms, Hedgewar and his group decided to throw in their lot with Tilak, who had returned from Mandalay and started to re-energize the Congress.

The INC session was held in Nagpur in 1920. As a local trusted by Tilak, Hedgewar was involved in raising a volunteer force of over a thousand to manage the event. It was to be Tilak's moment, but he passed away a few months before the session. The event, instead, saw the launch of Gandhi's Civil Disobedience Movement. Again, like most revolutionaries, Hedgewar was not entirely convinced either by the insistence on strict non-violence or by the mobilization of Muslims using a communal cause such as Khilafat. Nonetheless, he seems to have participated with enthusiasm and, in 1921, was arrested and charged with sedition. He decided to plead his own case, so that he could make a bold statement:

> India belongs to Indians. We therefore demand Independence ... That the British have been carrying on their despotic rule in our beloved country is obvious to everyone. What law is there that gives one country the right to rule over another? We demand nothing short of Complete Independence. Till we achieve it, we cannot be at peace.[16]

Hedgewar was found guilty and sentenced to a year in prison. By the time he was released, however, Gandhi had withdrawn the movement. Although he returned to a hero's welcome in Nagpur, he was deeply disillusioned. There were two broad reasons for the disillusionment among those of a revolutionary bent. First, they were shocked that Gandhi was willing to call off a movement in full flow due to what they saw as a stray incident of violence. Second, they were unhappy with the Congress leadership playing down large-scale attacks on Hindus during the Moplah riots. While most mainstream revolutionaries placed greater weightage on the first grievance, some such as Hedgewar were impacted equally, if not more, by the second.

This was the milieu when Hedgewar decided to set up an organization that could weld together the Hindu community (defined broadly to include all Dharmic groups such as Buddhists, Jains and Sikhs). The RSS, meaning the National Volunteers' Organization, was founded on Vijaya Dashami in September 1925. Hedgewar's small traditional wooden-frame house in Nagpur, where it was founded, is well preserved and worth a visit (do not miss the secret chambers in the attic for keeping fugitive revolutionaries hidden).

The RSS was soon establishing branches (called shakhas) across the country. The organizational structure was likely influenced by the idea of a network of akhadas, as had been envisaged by the original Anushilan Samiti. Importantly, the organization was designed strictly as a sociocultural body that would keep away from active politics. Hedgewar was clear that members were welcome, even encouraged, to participate in the freedom movement but the RSS as an organization would not participate in anything political. Indeed, he was himself arrested and jailed for taking part in a personal capacity in protests against colonial forest laws in 1930, but still refused to allow the outfit to get involved.

The adamant refusal to let the RSS get involved directly in politics displeased many of his potential allies. Vinayak Savarkar, finally fully freed in 1937, had decided to take up the Hindu cause and was trying to expand the Hindu Mahasabha as a political party to represent the community. He appears to have been both puzzled and annoyed by the RSS's insistence on keeping an arm's length from politics.

There is considerable debate to this day on why a long-term activist such as Hedgewar was so vehemently against letting the RSS participate directly in politics. A likely explanation is that Hedgewar saw Gandhi's support for the Khilafat Movement, and the brushing aside of the victims of the Moplah pogrom, as the consequence of letting short-term political expediency override legitimate Hindu interests. He probably feared that the same would happen to the RSS if it became engaged directly in politics. Therefore, he set about creating a network that could act as a united bloc, irrespective of immediate expediency.

By the time Hedgewar passed away in June 1940, the RSS had grown beyond its Maharashtra heartland and established shakhas across the subcontinent—Lahore, Karachi, Delhi, Rawalpindi, Calcutta, Madras and so on. It had an estimated 60,000 members by this time and was attracting the attention of British intelligence. However, no one at this stage would have imagined that this particular offshoot of the revolutionary movement would become an important influence in Indian public life in the twenty-first century.

THE REBEL PRESIDENT

After the Hijli incident, Subhas Bose had been touring the country. It was quite clear that he had inherited the legacy of C.R. Das and Tilak. Combined with his links to the revolutionaries, he was emerging as the most important national-level leader after Gandhi. In December 1931, he travelled to Maharashtra, where he presided over the Maharashtra Youth Conference held at the Shivaji Mandir in Pune. He then travelled to Satara, Karad and Sholapur, where he was met by large crowds.[17]

Following his unsuccessful negotiations in London, Gandhi returned to India on 28 December. The public mood was charged with disappointment and Viceroy Willingdon saw Subhas as fanning the flames. On 3 January 1932, he was arrested at Kalyan on his way back to Calcutta. A day later, Gandhi and other senior leaders of the INC were also arrested.

Yet again, Subhas fell seriously ill in prison and lost some 14 kg by May. He was also in severe pain from a gall bladder inflammation. The colonial authorities dithered about what to do as pressure built to release him. It was only in mid-January 1933 that the government agreed to let Bose travel to Europe for treatment. He was given a passport that was only valid for France and Switzerland (although it was later extended to other countries). Bose sailed out from Bombay on 23 February on SS *Gange*. On board he spent his time catching up with the latest writings of Sri Aurobindo and conversing with a young medical student, Dhiren, a cousin of Sachin Sanyal, who was also on the ship. The latter would later recall that the ship had a couple of intelligence officers deputed to keep an eye on the nationalist leader. Their attempt to look inconspicuous while hanging about on the deck amused Subhas no end.

While undergoing treatment in Clinique La Lignière in Geneva, Switzerland, Bose spent a lot of time with Vithalbhai Patel, the elder brother of Vallabhbhai, who was also undergoing treatment there. Vithalbhai was the last of the senior Swarajist leaders, and his views were more closely aligned with Bose's rather than Gandhi's. The two grew close, and Subhas diligently attended to the older man in his last days. After his death, it emerged that Vithalbhai had bequeathed a significant portion of his assets, valued at that time at Rs 1 lakh, to Subhas.[18] This would lead to an ugly legal dispute with the Patel family.

Although Bose was away from India, he was constantly thinking about developments back home. It was in Vienna in mid-1934 that he began to write *The Indian Struggle*, where he provided a first-hand account of events in the country. He hired a young Austrian woman, Emilie Schenkl, who knew English, to help him type and edit the book. The two would fall in love and, years later, get married.

By mid-1934, the non-violent branch of the freedom movement had also got stuck in a quagmire. As Subhas put it, 'By that time, civil disobedience was as dead as a doornail ... the only way out was for the Congress leaders to eat humble pie.'[19] He then goes on to make a strong pitch for the two branches of the freedom movement to come together for their common cause: 'Is it possible in the circumstances to come to an understanding with the revolutionaries? Yes, it is. Provided the approach is made in the right way and the intentions are really sincere.'

Recall that this was a time of intense ideological turmoil in the world and Bose witnessed a Europe caught up in it. Two ideologies—fascism and communism—were on the rise and everyone was expected to take sides. In a press statement in December 1933, Jawaharlal Nehru made it clear which way he stood: 'I do believe that the choice before the world today is one between some form of Communism and some form of Fascism, and I am all for the former, that is Communism.'[20] In contrast, Bose was unconvinced that the future of the world was so black-and-white or that history would come to a halt at some definite destination. He expressed his doubts as follows: 'Unless we are at the end of the process of evolution or unless we deny evolution altogether, there is no reason to hold that our choice is restricted to two alternatives.' He then goes on to speculate that one could even imagine a synthesis between the two. Some present-day commentators interpret this to mean that Subhas was in favour of some mix of fascism and Marxism. This is not correct. The original text is quite clear that Subhas was merely arguing against ideological straitjackets.

Reading this debate a century later, it is quite amusing that some leading public figures of the early twentieth century genuinely believed that they had found the end state of the world. This is not so different from Francis Fukuyama's 'End of History' thesis, after the fall of the Berlin Wall and the collapse of the Soviet Union, that the Western 'liberal' system was the end state of the world. In both cases, Bose's view about constant evolution would prove to be prescient.

From his various speeches and writings, one can see that Bose was essentially a pragmatist, who did not want ideology to divert him from his main mission of freeing India from foreign domination: 'There are many reasons why Communism will not be adopted in India. Firstly, Communism today has no sympathy with Nationalism in any form and the Indian movement is a Nationalist Movement—a movement for the national liberation of the Indian people.'[21] At the same time, Bose was in favour of large-scale public-sector investment to modernize the economy. Nonetheless, today's readers should recognize that the real issue in his mind was not so much private-versus-public investment, but the rapid industrialization of India, in contrast to Gandhi's near-Luddite traditionalism. His view at that time, possibly coloured by Soviet propaganda, was that state-led investment would modernize the economy faster than private investment.

While in Europe, Subhas Bose also had the opportunity to visit fascist Italy and Nazi Germany. He was not pleased with what he saw. In a letter written in March 1936, he expressed his misgivings:

> The recent speech of Herr Hitler in Munich gives the essence of Nazi philosophy ... The new racial philosophy which has very weak foundation stands for the glorification of the white races in general and the German race in particular. Herr Hitler has talked of the destiny of the white races to rule over the rest of the world ... Apart from this new racial philosophy and selfish nationalism, there is another factor which affects us even more. Germany, in her desire to curry favour with Great Britain, finds it convenient to attack India and the Indian people.[22]

The above writings should be seen in the context that the Nazis in general, and Hitler in particular, were admirers of the British Empire, as it fit their view of Germanic racial superiority. Indeed, *Mein Kampf* explicitly mentions support for British domination of India. It is well documented, moreover, that the Third Reich was directly inspired by the empire and that Hitler wanted to recreate on land what the British had done by sea.

Subhas also attempted to visit the Soviet Union, but was repeatedly refused a visa. The reason is unclear, but his biographer Sitanshu Das is of the opinion that 'it is more likely the Soviets in the 1930s saw Jawaharlal and Subhas as two rising stars of the Congress movement, and preferring the former, they did not want to make a gesture that could be interpreted as Soviet approval of Subhas in India's domestic politics'. This is likely an accurate assessment, as Comintern officials such as Virendra Chattopadhyay ('Chatto') were known to be suspicious of Bose.

The Irish proved to be more welcoming. President Eamon de Valera warmly received Subhas Bose and hosted several events. This was not unexpected, as the Indian and Irish revolutionaries had long established links. The two leaders formed a close personal bond and exchanged notes on how external support could be mobilized for an anticolonial movement. The Partition of Ireland along religious lines would also have played on the Indian's mind as demands for something similar for India had recently gathered momentum.

Bose landed in Bombay on 8 April 1936. He was arrested on the docks and taken away to Arthur Road Prison. He was later kept under house arrest in his brother's house in Kurseong, in northern Bengal. Subhas had been away for four years and, in the intervening period, the political situation in Bengal had become very complicated. A new system of separate electorates had been introduced for the Bengal provincial assembly, where Muslims were given 119 seats, Hindus 80 seats and Europeans/Anglo-Indians 39 seats. Moreover, the Hindu allotment was further divided into 50 seats for the 'general' category and 30 seats for designated scheduled castes.[23] In one sweep, the colonial authorities had reduced the political power of the rebellious Bengali Hindu community.

The countrywide provincial elections held in early 1937 went well for the INC—it had a clear majority in six out of eleven provinces, and was in a position to form the government in two more. In Bengal, the party had swept the Hindu seats under the leadership of Sarat Bose, while the Muslim seats were divided between the Muslim League, the Krishak Praja Party and independents. No single party had a majority. After negotiations between the Krishak Praja and the Congress broke down, the former teamed up with the Muslim League to form a coalition government headed by Fazlul Huq. This was the situation when Subhas Bose was released from house arrest in March 1937.

Bose made a short trip, on a KLM flight, to London in late 1937. When he returned in mid-January 1938, he was informed that Gandhi had chosen him as the next president of the INC. There are good reasons why Gandhi chose Subhas Bose for the post despite their differences. He had earlier successfully tamed Jawaharlal Nehru by making him president, and thereby converted him into a Loyalist. It is likely he hoped to do the same with Bose.

The Haripura Congress held in February 1938 was quite a grand affair. A temporary city of huts and tents called Vithal Nagar came up at the venue, named after Vithalbhai Patel. A two-lane motorable road was built to connect it to Navsari, and electricity connections were provided. A large fleet of new Ford cars was made available for senior leaders. The newly anointed president arrived on a royal chariot drawn by fifty-one bullocks. He then unveiled an eight-foot-tall bust of Vithalbhai. More than 2 lakh people attended the open session. Gandhi, however, expressed his unhappiness at the ostentatious display of modern amenities such as cars and electricity.[24] The gap between the visions of the two leaders was apparent.

One of the issues that Subhas championed as president was the proper treatment and early release of political prisoners. Many of these prisoners were from the revolutionary movement. It was probably in this context that he met the old revolutionary leader Sachin Sanyal, who had recently returned from his second stint in the Cellular Jail (recall that he had been sent there following the Kakori case more than a decade earlier). They met in October on the sidelines of the Durga Puja celebrations on Lucknow's Hewitt Road, the city's oldest puja. Sanyal was living in the area with relatives and yet again trying to re-establish his network. We know from surviving letters that Sanyal had already re-established contact with his old comrade Rashbehari Bose in Japan. We do not know exactly what Subhas and Sanyal discussed, but it is likely that they discussed the gathering clouds of war and the possibilities it presented. A few days later, they together visited Lucknow District Jail to meet the political prisoners lodged there.

It was also around this time that Subhas Bose made up his mind to seek a second term as INC president. There was significant support for this among the rank and file of the party, and several prominent individuals such as Rabindranath Tagore were in favour of it. In contrast, Gandhi and his Loyalists were adamantly against this. They wanted Maulana Abul Kalam Azad as the next president. Hectic meetings took place within the Gandhian camp in December as it became obvious that Bose was not going to back down from a contest. Eventually, Abul Kalam announced on 20 January 1939 that he was stepping aside for Pattabhi Sitaramayya, a staunch Gandhi loyalist from Andhra Pradesh. A few days later, the Gandhian group—Vallabhbhai Patel, Rajendra Prasad, Jairamdas Doulatram, J.B. Kripalani, Jamnalal Bajaj and others—wrote to Subhas Bose to step down in favour of Sitaramayya. Bose responded by issuing a statement:

> If the President is to be elected by the delegates and not be nominated by influential members of the Working Committee, will Sardar Patel and other leaders withdraw their whip and leave to the delegates to vote as they like? ... Otherwise why not end the elective system and have the President nominated by the Working Committee.[25]

There was no escaping an electoral contest. Bose's confidence drew from a broad pool of support that included the youth, various Left-leaning groups, former revolutionaries, the remnants of C.R. Das's Swarajists and so on. Most Left-leaning groups, meanwhile, had coalesced around the newly created Congress Socialist Party (CSP), which functioned as a loose bloc with the INC. The CSP also had the support of the communists. Thus, Bose had the direct or indirect support of a strong coalition.

It is important in this context to understand the condition of the revolutionary movement at this time. As already discussed earlier, it had been mostly moribund since 1933, but its followers were now ideologically split into many factions. A small number had joined the Communist Party of India. Another small group had become part of M.N. Roy's faction (let us call them Royists). A larger group, including former HSRA and Anushilan Samiti members, had accepted Marxist or socialist ideas to some degree but were suspicious of Russian and British influence in the communist movement (let us call them the Anushilan Marxists for convenience). Jogesh Chandra Chatterjee was the key leader of this faction. Then there was another large group of former revolutionaries, including Nalinaksha Sanyal, who remained nationalists and unswayed by the spread of Marxism (let us call them the Jugantar nationalists, as some of its leaders had been part of Bagha Jatin's original group). Yet another group had drifted towards Hindu nationalism and were joining Vinayak Savarkar's Hindu Mahasabha. Finally, there were revolutionaries who were still active and wanted to re-ignite the armed struggle. They were scattered around the country and the world. After returning from his second stint in the Cellular Jail, Sachin Sanyal was trying to reconnect them. It was his third attempt at instigating an armed rebellion.

Despite their internal differences, the revolutionaries threw themselves into drumming up support for Subhas Bose. When the ballots were counted, Bose beat Sitaramayya 1,580 to 1,377 delegates. The revolutionary strongholds of Bengal, Punjab and United Provinces had voted overwhelmingly for Bose. It was clear to everyone that it was a personal defeat for Gandhi. As he himself put it: 'And since I was instrumental in inducing Dr. Pattabhi not to withdraw his name as a candidate when Maulana Saheb withdrew, the defeat is more mine than his.'[26]

Despite the clear election defeat, the Gandhi Loyalists were not willing to cede control or cooperate. Twelve members of the Working Committee resigned. Bose was especially hurt that it included Jawaharlal Nehru, who he had felt would be an ally against the old guard. The Tripuri Congress in March, therefore, began in an atmosphere of intrigue. What made it worse for Subhas was that he was very unwell and had to be carried to the venue on a stretcher.

Gandhi did not attend Tripuri, but his Loyalists had come prepared to disrupt the president's agenda. At the outset, Govind Vallabh Pant stood up and proposed a resolution to 'request the President to nominate the Working Committee in accordance with the wishes of Gandhiji'.[27] This was followed by a heated debate. Subhas's supporters pointed out that it was unfair to ask an elected president to select his team based entirely on the wishes of a person who was not present and was not even formally a member of the INC. In many ways, this was like a repeat of the unseemly spat between the Nationalists and the Loyalists a generation earlier.

Subhas Bose had hoped that he would be able to get his way as he had, after all, won the election comfortably. At this juncture, however, the Congress Socialist Party convener Jayaprakash Narayan decided suddenly to turn 'neutral'. Whatever his later contributions as an opponent of Indira Gandhi's Emergency in the 1970s, Narayan's actions in 1939 were ethically questionable, even if they were politically expedient. M.N. Roy described the CSP's actions as 'abject surrender' to Gandhi.[28] The communists similarly withdrew their support following a directive from British Communist Party leader Harry Pollitt.[29]

Without support from the CSP, Bose's position was suddenly weak. He again reached out to Jawaharlal Nehru but it only resulted in a caustic exchange of letters. With no room to manoeuvre, Subhas was forced to resign, and Rajendra Prasad succeeded him. As soon as Prasad became president, he nominated Dr Bidhan Chandra Roy and Prafulla Chandra Ghosh, both from the Gandhian faction, as the Bengali representatives in the Working Committee.

From here on, nothing that Subhas did in the political sphere seemed to go right. He decided to unite the various Left-leaning groups within the INC under the umbrella of a new group called the Forward Bloc. He held meetings with the Anushilan Marxists, the Royists and the CSP to elicit their support but received a mixed response. The communist leader P.C. Joshi explained the CPI's reluctance to help the Forward Bloc as an unwillingness to support 'the disruptive agency of the bourgeoisie'.[30] Subhas Bose's increasing emphasis on the Left, meanwhile, alienated his non-Left supporters such as the Jugantar nationalists. They had been fellow travellers from the C.R. Das era and felt that they were being taken for granted.

Under the influence of his elder brother Sarat, Subhas also began to get deeply involved in the politics of the Calcutta Municipal Corporation. This was a tactical mistake, as it merely diminished his stature from that of a national-level leader to that of a local politician. With the Forward Bloc and Gandhian factions of the Bengal Congress not on speaking terms, Nalinaksha Sanyal emerged as the Chief Whip of the INC in the provincial assembly. He was associated with the Jugantar nationalists but had good personal relations with the Bose brothers and Dr B.C. Roy. He would go on to play an important role in opposing British policies during the Second World War, particularly those that led to the Bengal famine of 1943.

PREPARING FOR A SECOND GHADAR

Subhas Bose had begun 1939 in triumph but ended the year in a shambles. The escalating war in Europe, however, changed the political dynamics yet again. Here was another opportunity to ignite an armed rebellion in India. Subhas always had a soft corner for the revolutionaries, but now he decided to join them.

After returning from prison in 1937, Sachindra Nath Sanyal had been gradually re-establishing his network across India as well as reconnecting with remnants of the international Ghadarite network through Rashbehari Bose. This was not easy, since he was constantly under surveillance. With train stations under constant watch, he was using some of his cousins to ride long distances on horseback to deliver secret messages! Interestingly, we know that Sanyal was in touch with the Japanese consul well before the war. His son would later recount how he had been witness to late-night meetings between his father, Subhas Bose and Japanese officials in 1939–40.

Sachin Sanyal's writings from this period suggest that he still retained his distrust of Marxism, and was distressed by how ideological differences had divided the movement in his absence (even his brother Bhupendra had become a Royist). Nonetheless, the smell of a possible armed rebellion attracted some of the former revolutionaries back to the fold. The Anushilan Marxists, who had drifted away from nationalist revolutionaries on grounds of ideology, now drifted back. Jogesh Chandra Chatterjee wrote: '[The] Second World War was our second chance ... The revolutionaries rose through the struggle from the soil and hence they are indigenous and were always with the nationalist movement.'[31]

Using the reconstituted revolutionary network, Subhas Bose and Sanyal reached out to a large number of old revolutionary leaders. Feelers were sent out to Akbar Shah in the North West Frontier, Bhai Parmanand in Lahore, Keshav Hedgewar in Nagpur, Ganesh Savarkar and so on.[32] The revolutionaries were heartened by the overall response. Interestingly, Jogesh Chandra Chatterjee mentions in his biography that the famously apolitical Hedgewar went as far as to offer the 44,000-strong RSS cadre if an armed insurrection could be triggered during the war.[33] The revolutionary fervour of the former Anushilan Samiti activist was still alive, but he passed away in June 1940.

Unfortunately, British intelligence was also aware that something was cooking. An intelligence report from 1940 reads as follows:

> Its aim is to bring about an all-India armed revolution, and it is with this object in view that so much attention is being paid to the spreading of its influence in other provinces ... The leaders of district parties were instructed to recruit vigorously and prepare for an armed rebellion, to have shelters in readiness for absconders, and not risk the disorganization of the party by participating in demonstrations that might entail arrest and prosecution.[34]

Intelligence officials soon found out that Subhas had met soldiers of the 1/15 Punjab Regiment several times in 1939 with the help of Niranjan Singh Talib. They also discovered that Trailokyanath Chakraborty, a well-known Anushilan Samiti operative, was in the Chittagong hill tracts collecting arms and building a network. Remember that at that time, the British colonial administration was desperately galvanizing resources in India to help the war effort, and these discoveries came as a shock. Four soldiers from the Punjab Regiment were arrested. So was Chakraborty. The revolutionaries had primed Naik Indar Singh, the key contact in the regiment, to raise the national flag in Calcutta's Fort William as a sign of revolt. Sensing that something was afoot, the authorities moved the regiment out of Calcutta, and the plan was never carried out.[35]

For Sachin Sanyal, all of this would have felt like déjà vu. They had come so close to causing an 1857-style revolt in 1915 but failed. The effort in 1939–40 seemed to be unravelling at an even earlier stage. Unknown to him, however, a lone HSRA operative in London was about to carry out a major strike.

AVENGING JALLIANWALA

Udham Singh was born in December 1899 as Sher Singh in the home of a poor peasant in Sunam, Patiala State (today in Sangrur district of Punjab). His mother died when he was three and his father when he was five years old. Thus, he and his brother became orphans at an early age, and were admitted into an orphanage in Amritsar run by the Chief Khalsa Diwan. It was here that the boy was rebaptized and given the name Ude Singh.[36]

Ude Singh's brother died of pneumonia in 1913. At the age of seventeen, Ude briefly joined the British Indian Army and was sent to Basra. Although it was only a brief stint, it gave him a taste for travel that he retained for the rest of his life.

Ude was back in the orphanage in Amritsar by the end of 1918 and was in the city when the Jallianwala massacre took place on 13 April 1919. Some accounts suggest that he may have actually seen the shooting, but more likely he heard the shots and visited the site a couple of hours later. The scene of death that he witnessed would have a profound impact on the young man. Ude and some others from the orphanage tried to help the victims as best they could, but given the lockdown, there was little they could do other than provide drinking water and help relatives carry the bodies of the dead and dying.

Like many others, Ude was outraged when several leading Punjabis came out in support of the British after the massacre, some even conferring a 'siropa (robe of honour)' to the perpetrator at the Akal Takht. It is said that Ude went a few days later to the Golden Temple and swore while taking a dip in the holy tank that he would avenge the massacre.[37] It would take him two decades.

Over the next couple of months, Ude came under the influence of Lala Lajpat Rai. He attended political meetings and avidly read nationalist literature. It was during this time that he met his hero Bhagat Singh, who was then at National College, Lahore. Nonetheless, he was now a young man expected to earn a living outside the orphanage. As a trained carpenter, he got a job with the Uganda Railway Workshops and left for Africa. Using his earnings from working there for two years, Ude decided to travel the world—Mexico, the United States and Europe. While in California, he connected with the Ghadarites and witnessed veteran revolutionary Mahendra Pratap deliver a fiery speech at the gurudwara in Stockton in early 1924.

After living and working in many other places, Ude Singh returned to India in July 1927. By the time he reached Amritsar a few weeks later, police intelligence seems to have marked him out as a potential Ghadarite. He was arrested in late August and charged for the possession of two revolvers and an automatic pistol. He had purchased them in the United States but did not have a gun licence for India. He was sentenced as Sher Singh, his birth name, to five years of rigorous imprisonment. He was still in jail when he heard of the deeds and hanging of Bhagat Singh—which served as a reminder of his own oath.

On being released from jail, he applied for a passport under the name Udham Singh in March 1933. The clerks in Lahore seem not to have realized who he was and issued him a passport—No. 52753—which allowed him to head for Europe. After extensive travels, Udham Singh ended up in Coventry, England. He seems to have taken up many different jobs to earn a living. By mid-1939, he had shifted to London, where he frequented the gurudwara at 79 Sinclair Road, Shepherd's Bush. His occasional nationalist statements, however, made the gurudwara management wary of him. Over the past few years, the British authorities had systematically replaced Ghadarites in gurudwara management committees with Loyalists across the empire. They were uncomfortable with people such as Udham Singh, who expressed revolutionary sentiments.

There is reason to believe that Udham had originally planned to kill Reginald Dyer, but the latter had died several years earlier. Therefore, he turned his attention to Sir Michael O'Dwyer, who had been the lieutenant governor of Punjab at the time of the Jallianwala massacre. His notes later showed that he was aware of where O'Dwyer lived but had decided against assassinating him at home. This was to be a political act done in full public view.

Udham eventually decided on an event organized by the Royal Central Asian Society at Caxton Hall on 13 March 1940. This was the same venue where Vinayak Savarkar had stood up to defend

Madanlal Dhingra's actions three decades earlier. As a bonus, Lord Zetland, secretary of state for India, was also going to be present at the event.

The meeting started at 3 p.m., as scheduled. The hall was packed with around 400 people. No one seemed to have paid attention to a well-dressed Indian looking like a banker in a blue pin-striped suit and red tie.[38] Lord Zetland was seated on the stage to chair the session. Sir Percy Sykes spoke for forty-five minutes about Afghanistan. This was followed by Sir Michael O'Dwyer, who spoke about how Muslims around the world were likely to support Britain's war efforts.

The event had just been brought to an end when Udham Singh pulled out a revolver and fired six bullets in quick succession. The first two shots were aimed at O'Dwyer, who died almost instantly with a bullet through his heart. The next two were aimed at Zetland, who fell from his chair but was only mildly grazed. The next shot went through the arm of Sir Louis Dane while the last shot shattered Lord Lamington's right hand.

At this point, Udham Singh's revolver was out of ammunition. He had more bullets in his pocket but did not have time to reload as several members of the audience jumped on him. When the police handcuffed him a few minutes later and took him away, Udham Singh was photographed smiling. He had finally avenged Jallianwala.

When the Scotland Yard interrogators asked Udham his name, he replied, 'Ram Mohammed Singh Azad'. This mixed name is significant in the context of communal tensions back in India and the growing demands for Pakistan. Of course, further investigations soon revealed his real identity.

Udham Singh was initially sent to Brixton Prison and then shifted to Pentonville Prison. He was hanged at Pentonville on 30 July 1940 from the same gallows as Madanlal Dhingra. These two men from Amritsar, separated by a generation, gave their lives at the same spot for the same dream of a free India. Udham Singh's remains were brought back to India in July 1974 and received a hero's welcome. The *kalash* with his ashes is kept on display at the Jallianwala Bagh museum in Amritsar.

8

'ONE MORE FIGHT. THE LAST AND THE BEST'

GERMANY INVADED POLAND IN SEPTEMBER 1939 AND OCCUPIED the western half within two weeks. The eastern half was taken over by Soviet forces a few days later. Hitler and Stalin were uneasy allies at this stage. With Britain and France declaring war, Germany now turned its attention westwards. By April 1940, the Nazis had taken over Denmark and Norway, and were bearing down on Belgium and Holland. By late May, the British Expeditionary Force was trapped in Dunkirk and had to be evacuated in a desperate effort. On 14 June, the Germans entered Paris without opposition.

This rapid sequence of events was watched closely by all political groups in India. The general pre-war feeling in the Congress was that India should not be dragged into another war: 'India cannot fight for freedom unless she herself was free.'[1] Nevertheless, when Britain declared war in September 1939, Viceroy Linlithgow unilaterally issued a proclamation that India was a party to the war against Germany.

Even as Gandhi vacillated, two views emerged in the INC. On one side was Nehru, who declared:

> We do not approach the problem with a view to take advantage of Britain's difficulties ... In a conflict between democracy and freedom on one side and Fascism and aggression on the other, our sympathies must inevitably lie on the side of democracy ... I would like India to play her full part and throw all her resources into the struggle for a new order.[2]

The alternative view was that of Subhas Bose, who remained adamant that India should keep out of the war and focus on liberating itself from foreign occupation. Why should Indians die to preserve the freedom and democracy of their oppressors? The Congress leadership soon realized that the mood of the rank and file swayed towards the latter view. A party resolution on 10 October states: 'India must be declared an independent nation, and present application must be given to this status to the largest possible extent.'[3]

Faced with such intransigence on the one hand and a rapidly deteriorating military position on the other, the viceroy made the 'August Offer' on 8 August 1940, which promised to set up a body to frame a new constitution after the war. At the same time, it used language that seemed to provide a veto to the Muslim League in the name of protecting minority rights. The colonial authorities then played for time by stoking the League's growing demands for a Partition of India along religious lines.

Former and active members of the revolutionary movement had a variety of views on the evolving situation and India's participation in the war. Vinayak Savarkar, now leader of the Hindu Mahasabha, was of the view that Hindus should enthusiastically enlist in the army. This was not a newly found loyalty to the British, as some of his detractors may claim today. Savarkar was of the view that the British would be too weak to hold India after the war and would inevitably leave. His concern was that if they left behind an Indian army that was dominated by Muslims, it would result in yet another Islamic conquest of India. This was not an idle concern in the context of the increasingly shrill demands for Partition and growing communal tensions. Thus, Savarkar wanted to make sure that there was an adequate number of well-trained Hindu/Sikh regiments available for post-Independence exigencies. He would be proved right when India and Pakistan would go to war over Jammu and Kashmir within months of gaining freedom.

The Anushilan Marxists, led by Jogesh Chandra Chatterjee,[4] meanwhile, had formed a new party called the Revolutionary Socialist Party (RSP) of India in 1940. They remained opposed to the British throughout the war. In contrast, the Communist Party of India was initially unsure of its position, as the British and Russian-controlled factions disagreed with each other. With the Stalin–Hitler pact in 1939, most communists initially became supporters of the Axis cause and accused Britain and France of being imperialist warmongers. However, when Germany invaded the Soviet Union in mid-1941, the views of British and Russian factions converged, and the CPI enthusiastically collaborated with the British authorities. Jogesh Chatterjee wrote in his biography about how his group was different from the communists: 'The revolutionaries rose from struggle from the soil and hence they were indigenous and were always with the nationalist movement while the Communist were always anti-national and pro-Russian.'[5]

The revolutionary network, being revived by Sachin Sanyal and Rashbehari Bose, had remained committed to the old idea of fomenting a revolt in the British Indian armed forces. They saw the Second World War as a chance to complete what they had started in the previous war. Despite their discomfort with Nazism and Japanese imperialism, they were focused on ending the British occupation of their motherland. Similarly, they were willing to work with the Anushilan Marxists despite their ideological differences.

As we have seen in the previous chapter, the intelligence agencies were aware of the active revolutionaries and keeping a close watch. When they found out that Sanyal had met the Japanese envoy in Varanasi in 1940, he was arrested once again and sent to Deoli Detention Camp. Although he was a well-known and senior political leader, who normally would have been accorded a private room, the British put him in a cramped cell with a dying tuberculosis patient. It was quite likely that the colonial authorities did this deliberately. Sanyal nursed the man until his last breath but himself contracted the disease, which was considered incurable at that time. Repeated appeals for his release were rejected, even as his health deteriorated sharply.[6] When it was clear that he would not survive, his relatives were allowed to take him away. He died a few days later in Gorakhpur on 6 February 1942. It was the passing away of a patriot who had inspired, recruited and organized several generations of revolutionaries. Given that Japan had entered the war by this time and the flow of information was disrupted, it is unclear if and when Rashbehari Bose learnt about the death of his closest ally and friend.

THE ESCAPE

Subhas Bose was arrested again on 2 July 1940; he had just returned after meeting Rabindranath Tagore. The Battle of Britain was raging and the outcome was far from certain. The colonial authorities were not taking chances with a man who could sway a large segment of the population. However, they could not hold him down for too long. In November, Subhas swore on the Goddess Kali that he would fast unto death unless he was released. The viceroy soon realized that this was no empty threat and, as the case of Jatin Das had demonstrated, force-feeding often did not work. The last thing he needed was a leader of Subhas Bose's stature dying in custody. Thus, Bose was released on 5 December and allowed to go home to Calcutta.

A frail Subhas was taken to 38/2 Elgin Road and lodged in his late father's bedroom on the middle floor. It is a large and airy room that visitors can still see. At that time, the room had Janaki Bose's large four-poster bed, a smaller cot, a painting of Goddess Kali, a tiger-skin rug for meditation, a low table with books (including the Bhagawad Gita) and some family photographs. Several members of the extended family occupied rooms in the rest of the house. Outside the house, the government had deployed a large number of policemen in plain clothes to keep watch, and all his correspondence was intercepted and monitored by the post office; intelligence reports suggest that the British even knew about his meal menu.

Subhas had no intention of spending the war stuck in limbo. The fluid geopolitical situation provided an opportunity that was too good to be wasted, but he knew he would immediately be re-arrested if he did anything within India. He needed to find a way to get out of the country. So he approached his nephew, Sisir, and took him into confidence.

In mid-December, the Forward Bloc's provincial head for the North West Frontier Province, Akbar Shah, visited Calcutta. Sisir accompanied him to Wachel Molla's department store and purchased some baggy salwar trousers and a black fez cap. He also purchased a suitcase, toiletries, a bed roll and so on. Finally, he went to a printing shop and ordered visiting cards that read: 'Mohd. Ziauddin, B.A., LL.B., Travelling Inspector, The Empire of India Life Assurance Co. Ltd., Permanent Address: Civil Lines, Jubblepore.'[7]

From his window, Subhas could observe the policemen assigned to keep watch. During the day, they walked around, but at night they huddled in blankets around a charpoy at the crossing of Elgin Road and Woodburn Park Road (this is in front of what is now a popular bookstore).

By 16 January 1941, Subhas was ready to execute his plan. He announced to his family and friends that he was going into religious seclusion for a while, as he wanted to spend time meditating. Since everyone knew of his religious disposition, it came as no surprise. At 1.35 a.m. the plan was put into motion. Subhas transformed into Mohammad Ziauddin in a long coat, baggy salwars and a black fez. Sisir and another nephew quietly carried the luggage to Sisir's car—a Wanderer BLA 7169. The car went out of the gate, took a right and then another right into a narrow lane named Allenby Road to avoid the huddled policemen at the crossing further ahead. Sisir next took a left on to Lansdowne Road (now named Sarat Bose Road after his father) before he breathed a sigh of relief. They had escaped the immediate cordon.

The authorities did not seem to have noticed anything—the duo travelled unimpeded until they reached the home of a relative near Dhanbad by 8.30 a.m. After a brief period of rest, Subhas was dropped off at Gomoh railway station, where he boarded the Delhi–Kalka Mail. Still disguised as Ziauddin, he next boarded the *Frontier Mail* from Delhi to Peshawar, where he was met by Akbar Shah on 19 January. He was taken to the Taj Mahal Hotel. The staff must have been impressed by their scholarly and devout guest, for they specially provided him a room with a prayer rug!

The next stage of the journey into Afghanistan needed a new disguise. Subhas was now transformed into a deaf and mute Pathan, who was going on a pilgrimage to the shrine of Adda Sharif to cure him of his affliction (the pretence of being deaf and mute was necessary as Subhas did not know Pashto). He was accompanied by Bhagat Ram Talwar, a local communist, disguised as a relative named Rahmat Khan.[8]

Meanwhile, back in Calcutta, the police and most of the Bose household continued to be oblivious to the escape. Food was dutifully taken into the seclusion room but was eaten by the two nephews and a niece. It was only on 26 January that the disappearance was discovered by the cooks, who raised an alarm, and it immediately led to a sensation. The viceroy was furious when he heard the news and the press reports turned the Bengal provincial authorities into a laughing stock. By this time, Subhas and Bhagat Ram had crossed into Afghanistan. He had pulled off one of the most audacious escapes in Indian history—perhaps matching that of Shivaji from the clutches of Aurangzeb.

Subhas and Bhagat Ram arrived in Kabul on 31 January and initially lodged at a small *serai*, but the next move was unclear.

Bose knew that he could not linger there for too long, as there were many British agents in the city. Once they had identified him, it would not be difficult to bribe a few tribesmen to kidnap him and bundle him back to British-controlled territory. Thus, after a few days in hiding, he decided to barge into the German embassy. The German officials cabled Berlin for instructions.

While he waited for a reply, Bose knew that his disguise would not hold for long, and decided to move into the home of an Indian shopkeeper named Uttam Chand Malhotra. Impatient with the Germans, he also contacted the Italian embassy. Pietro Quaroni, the Italian minister in Kabul, turned out to be especially helpful. He arranged for an Italian passport for Bose under the name Orlando Mazzotta, a diplomatic courier. The Italian, German and Soviet diplomats then worked out an escape route. Subhas made his way on foot through the Hindukush passes to the Soviet frontier on the Oxus river, where he was picked up and driven to Samarkand. From there he went by train to Moscow and reported at the Italian embassy. He eventually flew to Berlin on 2 April 1941.

Interestingly, British intelligence had got wind by late February that Bose was in Kabul and trying to get to Germany or Italy. They expected him, however, to take the route through Iran and Turkey. Britain's Special Operations Executive had alerted its agents in Istanbul to make arrangements for his assassination.[9] Their expectations were perhaps shaped by the routes taken a generation earlier by Mahendra Pratap's Kabul mission. By taking the northern route through Russia, therefore, Subhas Bose escaped the assassination plan. Just two months later, this route would close as Germany would invade Russia.

QUIT INDIA

From the very beginning of the war, Prime Minister Winston Churchill had been trying to coax a reluctant President Roosevelt to join the war on the Allied side. Eventually, Britain and the United States issued the Atlantic Charter in August 1941, which declared that: 'They respect the right of all people to choose the form of Government under which they will live; and they wish to see sovereign rights and self-Government restored to those who have been forcibly deprived of them.'[10] Indians were aware that President Roosevelt had been pushing the British to make concessions to the colonies, but this declaration made it concrete. All hope was dashed, however, when Churchill clarified a few weeks later in the House of Commons that the Atlantic Charter did not apply to India. This was blatant hypocrisy and caused a breakdown of trust.

Events then took a sharp turn after Japan entered the war in December 1941 by simultaneously attacking Pearl Harbor and the Malay Peninsula. By 15 February, they had taken Singapore, hitherto considered an impregnable fortress. This naturally weakened Britain's position in India and the War Cabinet realized that some concrete promises had to be made. In March 1942, Sir Stafford Cripps was sent to India to discuss the terms of a draft declaration. The draft accepted that self-government would be introduced as soon as possible and that a constitution-making body would be set up 'immediately upon cessation of hostilities'. This was a big step forward.

The declaration, however, also included a provision that provinces and princely states that did not want to join the Indian Union were free to frame their own constitution. This was included as a way to assuage the Muslim League and the various Indian princes, but INC leaders saw it as a cynical move to facilitate Partition as well as to encourage the princely states to chart an independent course. The breakdown of trust was complete.

It was under these circumstances that the old revolutionary Aurobindo Ghosh reappeared on the political stage after being absent for three decades. During these years, he had turned into Sri Aurobindo, a much-revered spiritual guru in French-ruled Pondicherry, and his earlier career as a freedom fighter was just a faint memory. Thus, everyone was taken aback by his sudden political intervention.

In an open letter, Sri Aurobindo welcomed the Cripps Mission and urged the political class to take it seriously. He then sent Duraiswami Iyer as a special emissary to the Congress Working Committee, urging the members to take up the proposals. His arguments were twofold. First, he felt that India needed to stand with the Allies against Nazism, an ideology that he felt was an even greater evil than British colonial rule (one wonders if he still held this view after the Bengal famine and the brutal suppression of the Quit India Movement). Second, he was of the view that the Cripps proposals provided a definite path towards freedom as well as towards a framework for discussion with various parties on how to keep India united.[11]

Some Congress leaders did share Sri Aurobindo's views. C. Rajagopalachari even managed to pass a resolution in the Madras legislature that broadly supported the Cripps approach. However, Gandhi and INC President Abul Kalam expressed their disapproval, and Rajagopalachari was forced to resign. In a broadcast on the All India Radio on 11 April 1942, Stafford Cripps publicly withdrew the proposals.

With the failure of the Cripps Mission, the stage was set for Gandhi to launch a new round of civil disobedience. On 12 July, the Congress Working Committee passed a resolution that is commonly referred to as the 'Quit India' proclamation. It demanded that British rule in India end with immediate effect. The political establishment in London was not pleased to hear this. British communist leader Rajni Palme-Dutt sent a desperate message to Jawaharlal Nehru, asking him to avert the launch of a new movement, but the die had been cast.[12] Faced with an impending foreign invasion, the British were in no mood to compromise. Within weeks, Gandhi and most INC leaders were arrested and the party's headquarters in Allahabad sealed.

Despite the lack of any senior leadership, the Quit India Movement spread quickly across the country. Large protests spontaneously took place, there were many industrial strikes, and widespread arson caused damage to public property. In many campuses, such as Banaras Hindu University, the students created 'liberated zones', where they took over the administration and issued their own entry passes. The government responded with full-scale repression. The military machinery was already mobilized in anticipation of a Japanese invasion, and its fury was directed at the civilian population. Some 60,000 people were arrested and thousands were shot dead. No one knows for sure how many protesters were killed, but the number was likely higher than 10,000 and perhaps as high as 25,000. Leaderless and faced with such vicious repression, the Quit India Movement was crushed by early 1943.

THE INDIAN INDEPENDENCE LEAGUE

Rashbehari Bose had arrived in Japan in 1915 and lived in the country thereafter (indeed, he had become a Japanese citizen). He had not been able to visit India in all these years as he was still considered dangerous and would have been immediately arrested. Nonetheless, he had remained committed to the struggle for Independence and had closely followed events. He continued to write prolifically, a lot of it in Japanese. He was a well-respected member of the expatriate Indian community in Tokyo and regularly hosted prominent Indian visitors.

He also kept up correspondence with many Indian leaders, including those of the INC. His writings suggest that, like most revolutionaries, he had mixed feelings about Gandhi. He appreciated Gandhi's ability to mobilize large numbers, but repeatedly felt let down. In 1931, he wrote an article titled 'Concessions by Gandhi and India's Independence Movement', where he severely criticized Gandhi.[13] In contrast, he had high regard for Vinayak Savarkar and established contact after his release from prison. When Savarkar took over the leadership of the Hindu Mahasabha, Rashbehari even set up a branch of the organization in Japan.

At the same time, he also advised leaders from other colonized Asian countries on their freedom struggles. For instance, when Indonesian leader Mohammed Hatta visited Japan in 1932, they together established the Japan-Indonesia Association with the objective of ending Dutch colonial rule.[14] In the age of stormy ideological battles, Rashbehari remained committed to an earlier era of nationalism, to Pan-Asianism, and to the Hindu ideals of Dharma. He did not approve of either Marxism or Fascism and wrote strongly against them. With support from the Japanese establishment, Rashbehari edited and published a dual language Pan-Asianist journal named *The New Asia – Shin Ajia*, which was soon banned in British India but found a widespread underground circulation in South East Asia.[15]

Growing militarism in Japan, however, became increasingly problematic. When Rashbehari had arrived in the country, the Japanese supported all Asian countries in their struggles; even Chinese republicans such as Sun Yat-sen received enthusiastic support. By 1930, attitudes towards the Chinese, in particular, changed. Rashbehari initially spoke out against some of Japan's excesses, but as a foreign refugee, he was in a difficult position. He even endured the resultant cold shoulder of some of his erstwhile supporters in the establishment. In the end, he took the pragmatic view that Japanese paranoia about Western powers was a useful tool against his primary concern—the British occupation of India.

In the late 1930s, Rashbehari was able to re-establish contact with his old comrade, Sachindra Nath Sanyal, who had returned after a decade in the Cellular Jail—his second stint. Their letters suggest that they retained their friendship and mutual respect, despite the decades of separation.[16] As he had done after his first stint in Port Blair, Sanyal immediately went back to re-establishing the revolutionary network across India. Similarly, we know that Subhas was in touch with the older Bose in the late 1930s. The latter wrote admiringly about Subhas in Japanese publications.

Rashbehari, meanwhile, was also in touch with other Indian nationalists based in east Asia. There was a particularly active group in Bangkok led by Giani Pritam Singh and Swami Satyananda Puri. Together they formed the Indian Independence League (IIL). Their efforts got a boost from Japanese gains in

South East Asia during the early phase of the war. In March 1942, Rashbehari organized a conference in Tokyo for this group. It was here that a resolution was passed to form the Indian National Army (INA), or the Azad Hind Fauj, using recruits from Indian expatriates and surrendered soldiers of British Indian forces. Unfortunately, Pritam Singh and Satyananda Puri died in a plane crash on their way to Tokyo, and Rashbehari was suddenly deprived of two trusted comrades.

A second conference was held in June, with delegates from Malaya, Hong Kong, Singapore, Indonesia, Thailand, Indo-China and so on. The tricolour was flown and a formal constitution was drawn up, stating that the IIL's objective was the complete independence of India. It is important to note that the IIL was explicitly signalling that it was not aiming to replace a British colony with a Japanese vassal state. The resolution read: 'The Indian National Army which would be commanded entirely by Indian officers and would only fight for the liberation of India.'[17]

The question arose of finding a suitable commander for the INA. None of the revolutionary leaders had any formal military training. Pritam Singh and Iwaichi Fujiwara, a Japanese officer, had earlier decided on Captain Mohan Singh, of the 1/14 Punjab Regiment, who had surrendered to the Japanese during the early phase of the invasion of north Malaya in December 1941. The Bangkok conference in June 1942 elected Rashbehari Bose as the president. He was to be assisted by a four-member council. Mohan Singh was made a member of the council in his capacity as commander-in-chief.

Bose made an appeal over radio broadcasts for volunteers to join an army of liberation. After the fall of Singapore, the Indian prisoners of war were separated from the others and brought to Farrer Park. Here, Japanese officials, translated by Colonel N.S. Gill, gave them the choice of joining the INA. By the end of August 1942, around 40,000 prisoners of war had signed up for the new army. They were joined by many expatriate Indians, mostly Tamil, living in Singapore and Malaya. It must be added that a section of the Indian prisoners of war remained loyal to the Allied cause and refused to sign up. They faced harsh treatment from the Japanese.

With the support of the Japanese, arrangements were made for the housing and the training of INA soldiers. However, after the initial momentum, internal divisions arose. Some of the newly inducted military officers, such as Colonel Gill, were unhappy that a relatively junior officer such as Mohan Singh had been made the commander-in-chief. Mohan Singh, in turn, did not help the situation by taking on an increasingly haughty attitude towards the leadership of the IIL. Matters reached boiling point when he made a speech where he demanded that the INA swear loyalty to him rather than to the IIL. With his behaviour becoming increasingly erratic, Mohan Singh was eventually dismissed.

Unfortunately, at this critical juncture, Rashbehari's health deteriorated sharply. His diabetes became worse and he contracted pulmonary tuberculosis. Sitting in sultry Singapore, without Pritam Singh, Satyananda Puri or other close confidants, he must have felt alone. He was ageing, suffering from poor health and yet so close to achieving what he had attempted all his life. One finds the following line written on many of his personal notes from this time, as if he was willing himself on: 'I was a fighter. One more fight, the last and the best.'[18]

CHALO DILLI

Subhas Bose arrived in Berlin as Orlando Mazzotta on 2 April 1941, and was given a quasi-diplomatic status. He immediately put together a detailed plan on how the Germans could undermine the British by fomenting a revolution in India and the Middle East. Importantly, he argued that this needed a clear statement from the Germans on Indian Independence.

Subhas had hoped for two things when had arrived in Berlin. First, an early meeting with Hitler to pitch his ideas directly to the top German leadership. Second, a clear declaration of support for the Indian freedom movement. He would be disappointed on both accounts. Eventually, he was allowed to meet the foreign minister Joachim von Ribbentrop at the Imperial Hotel in Vienna on 29 April. Ribbentrop seems to have been evasive, and Bose decided to head for Rome. It was here that he heard on 22 June that Germany had invaded the Soviet Union. This came as a shock to him. In his characteristically frank style, he made it clear to the Germans that he thought this was a terrible mistake. He even sent a letter to Ribbentrop that, in the light of Operation Barbarossa, the Indians would see German expansionism as hostile unless there was a clear statement on Indian Independence.[19]

The German attack on the Soviet Union also compromised Subhas's direct communications link with his supporters in India. Bhagat Ram Talwar, who had helped Subhas reach Kabul, now switched sides. Instead of carrying Bose's messages to the intended recipients, Talwar now reported them to British intelligence and to his communist handlers. In turn, they wrote misleading replies that were passed back to Bose through the Axis embassies in Kabul.[20]

Nonetheless, when Subhas returned to Berlin in the third week of July, he was pleasantly surprised to find that the German Foreign Office had made arrangements for a well-furnished office for the 'Special India Division' at Wilhelmstrasse 75, run by the cosmopolitan Rhodes Scholar Adam von Trott (note he was strongly anti-Nazi and would be executed in 1944 for taking part in a failed attempt to assassinate Hitler). By October, he was able to establish the office of the Free India Centre at Liechtenstein Alle 2A-1, a prestigious location opposite the Spanish embassy.[21] He was also given a spacious villa on Sophensein Strasse, which had earlier been the home of the United States military attaché in Berlin. This provided the privacy to invite Emily to spend time with him.

The Free India Centre soon attracted a number of Indian activists such as Abid Hasan, N.G. Swami and A.C.N. Nambiar. It was also at the centre that the Azad Hind Radio was established to transmit in short wave. A powerful transmitter in Holland beamed it to India, where these broadcasts were clandestinely heard by thousands. So when a rumour spread in March 1942 that Subhas had been killed in an air crash in east Asia, Subhas himself came on the radio and thundered, 'This is Subhas Chandra Bose, who is still alive, speaking to you over Azad Hind Radio ...'[22]

An effort was also made to recruit Indian soldiers held as prisoners of war into an 'Indian Legion'. This proceeded slowly, as most of the prisoners of war from north Africa were held in Italy and many of them feared the consequences for their families back in British India. Only about 4,000 signed up. The legion wore a German-style uniform with a tricolour emblem and a springing royal Bengal tiger stitched to the left sleeve.

Although the legion and the Free India Centre would have little impact on the course of the war, they had a lasting impact on Independent India. It was here that Subhas decided on Tagore's *Jana Gana Mana* as the national anthem. It was also here that the common Indian greeting 'Jai Hind!' was coined, and where Subhas came to be known as 'Netaji'.

For all these little successes, Subhas had still neither been able to meet Hitler nor had he received a clear statement on Indian Independence. He made another trip to Rome, where Mussolini assured him support. He was also heartened when Japanese premier Hideki Tojo promised 'India for Indians' in a radio broadcast. The Japanese also sent a strongly worded draft resolution for the Axis powers on India's freedom. The German Foreign Office toned it down before forwarding it to Hitler, but he still waivered. He even turned down Mussolini's personal request to issue a declaration. It is unclear why Hitler was so unwilling to sign off on the resolution, but it is possible that he still dreamt of a compromise with the British Empire that would allow the Germanic race, which included the English, to divide up the world between them.

Subhas Bose was already thinking about how he could make his way to Japanese-held Asia when he finally got to meet Hitler on 24 May 1942. The meeting did not go well. Hitler lectured the Indian leader on the global war situation but did not commit to a declaration about Indian Independence. Bose then asked Hitler to withdraw racist references to Indians in *Mein Kampf*.[23] He most likely would not have known about Nazi death camps, but Bose was under no illusion that Hitler was anything but an unpredictable dictator. Therefore, this was a brave thing to bring up, even if it was hardly likely that the Führer was going to relent. The meeting came to an end after this.

Back in Asia, as Rashbehari's health deteriorated, he pressed for Subhas to take over the IIL. The Japanese began to negotiate with the Germans on how to safely get him to east Asia. They initially debated flying him non-stop from Italy to Singapore, but decided it was too dangerous. Eventually it was decided that he would make his way to the Indian Ocean by submarine. The departure date was set for 8 February 1943. He decided to take along a young engineering student, Abid Hasan, as his personal secretary. All the arrangements were kept secret, and even Hasan did not know where they were headed.

At dawn on the designated date, Commander Werner Musenberg received them at Kiel harbour on the Baltic and led them to the submarine U-180. The underwater craft made its way through the enemy-controlled waters of the North Atlantic and then around the southern tip of Africa. Meanwhile, the Japanese submarine I-29 surreptitiously made its way out of Penang harbour and headed for Madagascar. The two submarines made their rendezvous 400 nautical miles south-west of Madagascar on 26 April.

The problem was that the sea was too rough for the transfer. Things had still not improved by the next afternoon. Two audacious Germans now swam across to the Japanese submarine and rowed back with a lifeboat tied to a strong rope. The next morning, with the sea still rough, it was decided to attempt the transfer. Subhas and his young assistant climbed into the boat, and the Japanese reeled them in with the rope. Drenched, the two climbed into the Japanese vessel. They were given a warm welcome. The Japanese flotilla commander vacated his cabin for Subhas. The Indians were dropped off at Sabang, Sumatra, on 6 May. Yet again, Subhas Bose had pulled off an amazing getaway. A few days later, he was on a Japanese military aircraft bound for Tokyo.

Many of Subhas Bose's critics to this day question his willingness to ally with the Axis powers. This is unfair, as he was merely looking for ways to end the brutal colonial occupation of his motherland. No one accuses President Roosevelt of being a communist sympathizer for allying with a murderous despot such as Stalin or being a colonial sympathizer for helping an imperialist such as Churchill. It is assumed that these were alliances of convenience and not ideological preferences. Why, then, should Subhas Bose not be judged by the same standard? Indeed, he would go out of his way to make the distinction in his radio broadcasts, where he explicitly stated that his mission to free India required difficult choices: 'In this fateful hour in Indian history, it would be a grievous mistake to be carried away by ideological considerations alone. The internal politics of Germany or Italy or Japan do not concern us—they are the concern of the people of those countries.'[24]

After arriving in Tokyo, Subhas Bose spent several weeks getting to know key individuals in the Japanese political and military establishment. He then had multiple meetings with the Japanese premier Tojo and seems to have quickly built up a rapport with him. Unlike Hitler, Tojo was willing to publicly commit support for Indian Independence. On 16 June, Subhas addressed the Diet as a special guest and was again assured by Tojo of the fullest support for Indian Independence.

Subhas left from Singapore, along with Rashbehari, at the end of June. They received a rapturous welcome at Singapore's Kallang Airport when they landed on 2 July (the airport was shifted to Changi in 1955 and part of its area is now the National Stadium and Sports Hub). The INA presented a guard of honour while Indian civilians cheered loudly.

Two days later, members of the IIL assembled at the Cathay Theatre for a solemn ceremony, where Rashbehari Bose formally handed over the leadership to the younger Bose. It was a very emotional moment for everyone present. Rashbehari was not merely handing over the leadership of the IIL and the INA, but the baton of the cumulative efforts of the revolutionary movement over half a century: 'In your presence today, I resign my office and appoint *Deshsevak* Subhas Chandra Bose as President of the Indian Independence League in East Asia. From now on, Subhas Chandra Bose is your President and your leader in your fight for India's Independence ...'[25] Cathay Theatre, the scene of this historic event, no longer exists, and the site is now a shopping mall, but the facade has been preserved.

The next morning, Bose inspected the INA troops on the Padang field in the middle of Singapore. Dressed in military uniform, he took the salute from the steps of the Town Hall, as 12,000 INA soldiers marched past. In his address, he gave them the battle cry '*Dilli Chalo* (Onward to Delhi)', evoking a vision of doing their victory parade at the Red Fort. A day later, Tojo also reviewed the Indian troops at the same location.

The open field of Padang and the Town Hall are still there. Despite being overpowered by the towering skyscrapers of the Central Business District next door, it is still possible to recognize the place from old photographs of the events described above. Among those who witnessed these momentous events was a young Tamil boy named S.R. Nathan, who would go on to become the President of Singapore.

Subhas now embarked on a whirlwind of activity—making arrangements for the INA, meeting delegations of various civilian groups, negotiating with the Japanese and so on. He occupied a spacious bungalow on Meyer Road, along the island's east coast. The bungalow no longer exists and the location is now occupied by a residential condominium. By some quirk of fate, the neighbourhood is today very popular with expatriate Indians, although most of them would be unaware of the historical link.

THE BENGAL FAMINE

The politics of Bengal went through a convulsion in the late 1930s. As already discussed, the communally separated electorate generated a fractured mandate, which left no party with a majority. The Congress was the largest bloc as it swept the Hindu seats, but internally divided between the Bose faction on the one extreme and the Gandhi faction on the other extreme, and the Jugantar nationalists somewhere in between. The Muslim seats were divided between the Muslim League and the Krishak Praja Party. The latter party was led by a moderate Muslim named Fazlul Huq and mostly represented rural peasantry. Huq was in favour of forming a coalition with the Congress. The Bose faction was in favour of this, but the national leadership adamantly refused. This was followed by a complicated sequence of events that are described below in a simplified way.

Fazlul Huq became the chief minister of Bengal with support from the Muslim League, independents and the European/Anglo-Indian members. His Cabinet had five Hindus and five Muslims, but was not trusted by the Bengal governor John Herbert, who kept undermining him. A major cause of friction was the release of political prisoners. Huq soon discovered that colonial officials were encouraging the Muslim League and rivals from within his party to undermine him. With the emergence of the Hindu Mahasabha as a political force, Huq tried to shore up support by inducting Dr Syamaprasad Mookerjee into the Cabinet as the finance minister. However, the governor continued to interfere in the running of the provincial government. Eventually, Dr Mookerjee resigned in disgust in November 1942.[26] The Huq government survived for some more months and even defeated hostile motions on the floor of the assembly. On 28 March, the governor called for Huq and gave him a typed letter of resignation. The chief minister was then threatened and cajoled into resigning.[27] A few weeks later, a Loyalist Muslim League chief minister, Sir Khwaja Nazimuddin, was sworn in with support from the overrepresented European lobby in the assembly and backroom manoeuvrings by the civil service.[28] Both the viceroy and the provincial governor now had full effective control.

The above events must be seen in the context of Japanese advances into Burma in 1942 and the chaotic retreat of the British forces. The British responded to the Quit India Movement and the feared Japanese invasion by unleashing an unprecedented regime of repression. It is shocking to read how casually disproportionate violence was unleashed on the population. For instance, when a group of protesters in Bihar lynched two Canadian pilots, air force fighter planes were used to strafe civilians. Hundreds were killed.[29]

As the repression grew, so did the resistance. In Tamluk, in Bengal's Midnapur district, a group of activists decided to cut off all communication in August 1942 by blocking the roads and cutting the telegraph lines. The colonial administration sent in the police, who opened fire on the protesters and killed a few of them. On seeing this, a local prostitute, Sabitri Dasi, ran into her hut and emerged with a *'bonti'*—a long, curved knife attached to a wooden board that is commonly used in Bengal for cutting fish or tough vegetables. Some fisherwomen from a local market joined her with their bloodstained bontis. The symbolism of an angry Goddess Kali was not lost on anyone, and the crowd of protesters surged forward. The police was forced to retreat.

The colonial administration, however, soon retaliated with extreme brutality. Whole hamlets were burnt down, and bands of criminals, with support from the police and the army, looted the Tamluk area. There were many instances of mass rape. Twenty-one-year-old Sindhubala Maity was raped repeatedly by uniformed men and died of internal injuries.[30] She was just one of several dozen. It should never be forgotten that most of those who ordered and carried out this brutality were themselves Indian. Many of these collaborators would continue to work in the government after Independence and some would enjoy senior positions.

By the time Syamaprasad Mookerjee heard of these excesses, he had already resigned from the Cabinet. Nonetheless, he wrote to Chief Minister Huq, who, in turn, promised a senior-level inquiry. Governor Herbert was furious when he heard that an inquiry would be instituted, and vetoed it. This added to his dislike of Huq.

As if things were not bad enough, Bengal was hit by a cyclone on 16 October 1942. The storm and the accompanying tidal wave and floods devastated the fields, killed livestock, destroyed homes, washed away fish ponds and damaged food stock in southern Bengal, including in Midnapur. The district administration deliberately denied flood relief in those areas that were deemed 'disloyal'.

It was against this backdrop that the British decided to implement a 'Denial Policy'—a euphemism for a scorched-earth strategy aimed at denying food and other supplies to the advancing Japanese. Rice stocks in south and east Bengal were removed at a time when normal imports from Burma had been disrupted. Some of this was diverted towards feeding the amassing troops. However, as scholar Madhusree Mukerjee has documented, the authorities simply destroyed tonnes of rice that could not be removed. In three river ports in east Bengal, large quantities of rice were just thrown into the water. At the same time, the Ispahani Company, owned by a key financier of the Muslim League, became the government's principal buying agent, with the unrestrained power to commandeer foodgrains if the owners refused to sell.[31]

The scorched-earth policy was not restricted to foodgrains. Anything that could be useful to the Japanese was just commandeered or destroyed—boats, automobiles, cycles, radio sets and so on. Of the 66,700 boats in coastal Bengal, two-thirds were rendered inoperable or taken away. Most of the larger boats were taken away. The remaining operable vessels were pressed into government service for transporting supplies needed for the war effort. Thus, as the famine took root, the poor peasants were not even able to catch fish, a very important part of the local diet. Combined with the rice-denial policy and the cyclone, the conditions were in place for a catastrophe.

By the end of 1942, Calcutta and other urban centres witnessed a sharp increase in famished peasants wandering around begging for food. Many were widows with small children living on the pavements, their husbands having killed themselves for failing to find food for the family. There were reports from the villages that mothers were killing their infants, unable to watch their children starve slowly to death. Alarm bells were rung by Nalinaksha Sanyal, now the official chief whip of the INC in the Bengal provincial assembly. However, the tottering Huq government was too consumed with its own survival to pay attention. Nonetheless, when Sanyal and Mookerjee kept up the pressure, Huq did write to Governor John Herbert, but the latter was dismissive.

The government bureaucracy was so focused on maintaining the scorched-earth policy that it went out of its way to withhold help, including that which would have been triggered by its own Famine Code of 1883. In a caustic speech, Dr Nalinaksha Sanyal pointed out that even when government rules required food stocks to be released, the bureaucrats made sure that there were no bullock carts and workers to help move them.[32] This is why it is more than fair to state that the Bengal Famine of 1943 was deliberate and man-made.

By April 1943, the news of a famine in Bengal had reached both Delhi and London, but the new provincial government continued to dither, despite spiralling food prices. Civil Supplies Minister Suhrawardy continued to claim that there was no major shortage of foodgrains in Bengal and that it was a minor localized problem caused by 'hoarding' by traders (it helped his politics that many of the traders were Marwari Hindus). As a telling reflection of racial bias, the Indians were accused of hoarding, while European-owned establishments were officially told to 'stockpile' food.

Even when it was obvious by mid-1943 that millions of people were starving, colonial authorities continued to minimize the issue. Secretary of State for India L.S. Amery told the House of Commons that 'there is no overall shortage of foodgrains ... There is, however, grave maldistribution for which the responsibility is shared by all parties from the cultivator upward.' In other words, he spread the responsibility to everyone, including the poor peasants, who had evidently brought it upon themselves due to 'widespread tendency of the cultivators to withhold foodgrain from the market'.³³ At least Prime Minister Churchill was more direct about what he thought of Indians in general and Hindus in particular: 'I hate Indians. They are a beastly people with a beastly religion.'³⁴

One of the least discussed aspects of the Allied war effort was the officially sanctioned brothels in the rapidly proliferating army camps in eastern India. The colonial establishment used the easy availability of starving girls to cheaply stock these brothels. A survey of 30,000 women serving in military camps in Chittagong in 1944, supposedly to dig trenches and build runways, found that 90 per cent suffered from venereal diseases.³⁵ Much has been written about 'comfort women' used by the Japanese army during this period, but almost none about how Allied forces did the same thing in India.

Despite wartime censorship, Subhas Bose learnt of the famine raging in his home province in mid-1943. He immediately conferred with Japanese officials and Burmese leaders, and offered to send a large shipment of rice from Burma. The British rejected the offer, possibly because it would have further increased Bose's popularity. Nevertheless, it should be noted that when a similar famine situation had arisen in occupied Greece in 1941, the Germans had permitted humanitarian agencies to bring in food consignments. It is remembered as an example of Allied–Axis cooperation during the war. In contrast, the War Cabinet even turned down offers of help from Australia on the grounds that it would divert critical shipping.

The reason for the callous behaviour of the British was not just preoccupation with the war or even Churchill's personal prejudices. It must be recognized that racist views had deep roots in the British colonial establishment. If one reads the views of

Churchill's key scientific adviser Professor Lindemann (later Lord Cherwell), it is difficult to distinguish them from those of the Nazis. He not only believed in human eugenics, but was a strong advocate of curating the education of the lower races such that it would remove the ability of slaves to see themselves as slaves.[36] It should also not be assumed that it was only the Conservative aristocrats who harboured such views. Enthusiasm for eugenics was shared by many leading intellectuals of the Left, including John Maynard Keynes, Harold Laski, Sidney and Beatrice Webb, and Marie Stopes.[37] Seen from the Indian perspective, therefore, the Second World War was not one between good and evil, as is often portrayed, but one between two sets of evil empires that both had blood on their hands.

The food-supply situation began to improve by November 1943, as the new harvest came and the government machinery finally started mobilizing some relief supplies. By then, it is estimated that 3 million people had died in the famine. One of the biggest political beneficiaries of the famine were the communists. As allies of the government during the war, they stayed out of jail, blamed the hoarders as class enemies and helped distribute whatever little relief was available. If the CPI was a minor force in Bengal in 1942, by 1944 it had a significant footprint.

THE FLAG IN MOIRANG

By the time Subhas Bose landed in Singapore, the tide of the war had already turned. The Germans had been pushed back from Stalingrad and the Japanese navy had been decimated at Midway. Even as he inspected the INA troops, therefore, he would have known that the chances of an outright military victory were eroding. However, the old revolutionary objective of triggering a full-fledged revolt in the Indian armed forces was still very much possible. The idea was to create an unstoppable vortex that would trigger a revolution in the British Indian Army as well as the general population.

In mid-October 1943, Subhas threw himself into writing a 'Proclamation of Independence'. We know that he was working non-stop at this time at his Meyer Road residence to build up the INA and create the architecture of a provisional government. The only time he spent away from work was to meditate at the Ramakrishna Mission, an organization set up by his childhood inspiration Swami Vivekananda. The Ramakrishna Mission in Singapore still exists.

S.A. Ayer would later recall that when Bose had finished writing the draft proclamation, he turned to his aides and asked them if they knew what had happened to the signatories of the Irish proclamation of independence—they had all been shot dead. With a laugh, he added that the same might happen to the signatories of this one.[38]

On 21 October 1943, a large IIL meeting was called at the Cathay Theatre, where Subhas Bose announced the formation of the Provisional Government of Free India (*Arzi Hukumat-e-Azad Hind*). Subhas Chandra Bose was sworn in as the head of state and premier; Rashbehari was given the title of supreme adviser. None of the witnesses would have been in any doubt that this was a historic moment. Within days, the provisional government was recognized by Japan, Germany, Italy, Croatia, Thailand, Burma, the Philippines and Manchukuo. President Eamon de Valera of the Irish Free State also sent a personal note of congratulations to Subhas. Before the end of the month, the Japanese government had handed over the Andaman and Nicobar Islands to the provisional government. Given that the Andamans were where generations of revolutionaries had been imprisoned and tortured, this was emotionally charged symbolism. Thus, the Provisional Government of Free India now had international recognition, an army and de jure control over territory. It would later issue its own currency. Unlike the provisional government set up in Kabul in the previous war, this one had acquired all the attributes of a legitimate state. As we shall see, this was an important argument put forward at the post-war trials.

Subhas was keen that the INA be deployed soon in Burma as part of an invasion of the Indian mainland. The Japanese, however, dithered as they were distracted by developments in the Pacific. Moreover, they were unsure of the fighting preparedness of the INA, including that of a newly recruited women's unit called the Rani of Jhansi Regiment. Even as he waited for the Japanese to make a decision, Subhas visited the Cellular Jail in Port Blair in December. At a press conference, he explained the significance of his visit: 'Like the Bastille in Paris, which was liberated first during the French Revolution, setting free political prisoners, the Andamans, where our patriots suffered much, is the first to be liberated in India's fight for Independence.'[39]

In anticipation of the main thrust into India's North-East, a small covert operations group was sent by submarine to the Kathiawar coast. They were equipped with sophisticated wireless sets so that they could communicate with the INA. Their mission was to connect with the remaining revolutionary groups, such as the Bengal Volunteers, and instigate them to carry out guerrilla attacks across British India. The group was successful in connecting with several people, including members of the

Bose family, but they seem to have been too trusting of contacts with communist links. Bhagat Ram Talwar, for instance, passed on all information to his party leadership, who, in turn, gave it to British intelligence. As a result, the members of the covert operations were arrested over the course of 1944. Meanwhile, the Communist Party of India ran an aggressive propaganda campaign against Subhas Bose, calling him names such as 'the running dog' of Tojo.

In an ironic twist, the nationalist-turned-communist Subodh Roy returned to the Chittagong hills as a guerrilla fighting for the British cause. He had been the youngest member of Surya Sen's team at the time of the armoury raid in 1930. In his memoirs, he describes the situation along the borderlands. The Allies were arming the Bengali-speaking Muslims, while the Japanese were arming the Burmese Buddhists called 'Maghs'.[40] Extreme brutalities were carried out by both sides (this is the origin of the Rohingya problem that festers to this date). It was in these troubled borderlands that Roy first heard rumours that INA soldiers were going to join the Japanese invasion.

In January 1944, the INA finally moved north to Burma and established a new headquarters in Rangoon. One unit of the INA finally saw action in the Arakan sector in February. This was the first time that the INA soldiers had participated in a live operation. Although they were not able to capitalize on some initial successes, the Indians had performed well on the field and the Japanese were now more confident of their capabilities. So when the Japanese Imperial Army commenced their offensive against Imphal and Kohima in the second week of March, the INA regiments were deployed along with them. Around 84,000 Japanese troops, plus 12,000 INA soldiers, faced 155,000 British, British Indian, West African and American troops.[41]

The Japanese–INA forces entered Manipur on 18 March 1944 and initially made rapid progress. They were travelling light as their tactics depended on speed and hoped to capture enough supplies from the Allies to sustain their momentum. They were accompanied by a group of nationalist Meitei Manipuris led by L. Guno Singh, who had joined the INA in Rangoon. This group quickly established contact with local organizations such as the Nikhil Manipuri Mahasabha and Praja Sammelani. Similarly, contact was established with Kuki tribal chiefs to elicit their support. At a large gathering of chiefs, the Kukis solemnly bit a tiger tooth and vowed to help the Indo-Japanese forces.[42]

A few days later, the Praja Sammelani smuggled handbills into Imphal, appealing to the Manipuri to rise up against the British. Many young Meiteis, including P. Tomal Singh, L. Irabot Singh, O. Keinya Devi and M. Randhoni Devi responded to the appeal. They quietly sneaked out of Imphal and headed towards the small town of Moirang, which lay in the path of the approaching Indo-Japanese forces.

The Allies, meanwhile, were forced to retreat. As part of the scorched-earth 'Denial Policy', they burnt down food stocks and even houses along the path of retreat. On the morning of 14 April, when Manipuris were celebrating their New Year festival, the activists in Moirang heard that Indo-Japanese troops had reached a village just 5 km away. They immediately went there to welcome them. At 5 p.m. that evening, an INA column led by Colonel Shaukat Ali Malik and Japanese troops led by Captain Ito entered Moirang. They were welcomed by M. Koireng Singh (who later became the chief minister of Manipur). They next proceeded to Moirang Kangla, a sacred citadel where local kings were traditionally crowned. It was here that Malik raised the INA flag—a tricolour with a springing tiger. This was the first time that the Provisional Government of Free India had taken control of territory on the Indian mainland. He then gave a rousing speech (translated into Manipuri by Koireng Singh): 'Our commitment is to march to Delhi and unfurl the tricolor flag at Red Fort. Many have died on the way to reach here, and many will die on our way to Delhi.'[43]

During their retreat, the British commanders had burnt down many of the houses in Moirang. Two of the surviving houses were converted into field hospitals. A house belonging to Hemam Nilamani Singh was converted into the local INA headquarters. The activists then organized food supplies for the Indo-Japanese forces. This was not easy, as the Allies had destroyed whatever they could find, but surrounding villages generously sent in enough provisions for some 10,000 troops for three months. The British were aware that the locals were helping the Indo-Japanese forces. Moirang was declared an 'enemy zone' and 'shoot at sight' orders were issued against known activists.

There is a small museum today at the spot where Colonel Malik had raised the flag. The house that served as the INA headquarters is nearby and has also survived. It is a modest single-storey affair with a tin roof. When I visited the site in October 2021, the state government was making arrangements to preserve it by building a giant canopy over it.

Through April and May, battles raged in many places in Manipur. In a major battle at Lokpaching (Red Hill) during 25–30 May, both sides suffered heavy casualties in fierce hand-to-hand combat. The British, nonetheless, were able to stall the advance towards Imphal. There is a sombre memorial built recently by the Japanese at Red Hill. Several of the British casualties are interred at the well-maintained war cemetery in Imphal.

The advance towards Kohima was similarly quick in the initial phase. Subhas Bose would even stay for a few days at Ruzazho village (in Phek district, Nagaland) while visiting the front. He must have made quite an impression on the local tribes, as they sing folk songs in his honour to this day. Bose would appoint Poswuyi Swuro as area administrator. Incredibly, Swuro is still alive at the time of writing (at the age of 103)![44]

Unfortunately, here, too, the momentum stalled, with heavy casualties on both sides. The Allied garrison in Kohima had received advance warning and hastily dug into defensive positions along a mile-long ridge. The assistant district commissioner's bungalow fell along the ridge, and the attached garden and tennis court exchanged hands several times in the course of an eyeball-to-eyeball confrontation. Known as the Battle of the Tennis Court, it marks the turning point in the campaign. The Japanese lost the tennis court and were then forced back from Kohima by mid-May. The Allies were exhausted but had held on to Kohima and Imphal.

The Indo-Japanese forces had lost their momentum. At this stage, they were still a potent force, but the monsoon arrived early that year. India's North-East is among the wettest places on Earth, and the Indo-Japanese strategy of travelling light backfired. The supply routes through the jungles of Burma quickly became mired in impassable mud. Short on food, medicine and ammunition, both the INA and the Japanese soldiers were trapped in their waterlogged trenches. Diseases took a heavy toll on the exhausted troops. In the middle of the deteriorating situation, a senior commander, Major B.J.S. Garewal, defected to the British and took crucial details of INA positions with him (he would be assassinated by the revolutionaries in Lahore just after the war).[45]

Even before Subhas Bose met his commanders in Mandalay in September, he would have realized that the situation was difficult.

It was made worse by the fact that the Japanese were waging a desperate defence in the Pacific and were in no position to spare their military aircraft. This left the skies open to the Allies for strafing and bombing Indo-Japanese positions with impunity. The tin roof of the INA headquarters in Moirang still has the bullet holes from aerial strafing. Hundreds of Manipuri civilians were also killed in Allied bombing in Moirang and surrounding villages. Many of the Manipuri activists joined the INA as it retreated into Burma.

Bose had hoped to be able to hold a line along the Irrawaddy river. By February 1945, however, the INA soldiers were fighting a war that they knew could not be won. The Axis powers were now facing a rout everywhere across the world, supplies were running short and the Allies were on the offensive. And yet, despite occasional desertions, the INA held together as a fighting unit and retained the ability to punch back even as it withdrew. The Indians fought courageously at Mount Popa in early April against overwhelming odds before being forced to abandon the position. By mid-May, however, the Allies had captured three key field commanders—Prem Kumar Sahgal, Shah Nawaz Khan and Gurbaksh Singh Dhillon.

Meanwhile, Rashbehari Bose passed away from a cerebral haemorrhage in Tokyo on 21 January 1945. He was fifty-eight and died before seeing his beloved motherland liberated. His son Masahide was with him in his last moments, but returned to the front shortly afterwards. He was killed in Okinawa on 15 June.

Atom bombs were dropped on Hiroshima and Nagasaki on 6 and 9 August 1945. The Japanese surrendered on 15 August. Subhas Bose was in Singapore at that time. His chief concern was to make sure that the INA soldiers were paid and that the

500 women of the Rani of Jhansi Regiment were sent back to their families. On the morning of 15 August, Bose ordered the erection of a memorial to the INA martyrs. It was built along the sea face but would be destroyed on the orders of the British commander-in-chief Lord Mountbatten as soon as he landed (there is now a second memorial at the site, built by the Singaporean government in 1995).

Bose now had rapidly diminishing options, and he discussed them with his Cabinet on the verandah of his Meyer Road bungalow. It was almost certain that the British would arrest him and treat him as a war criminal. Leaving behind Major General M.Z. Kiani in charge of the remnants of the INA, he flew to Bangkok, where Mahoyang, the priest of the royal family, agreed to keep him hidden in a Buddhist monastery until other arrangements were made. Instead, Bose flew to Saigon (now Ho Chi Minh City) and Da Nang before landing in Taipei on 18 August.

What happened next is a matter of controversy. The official narrative is that his plane crashed while taking off for Tokyo and that Subhas Bose died of severe burns. Right from the beginning this was disputed by those who believed (or hoped) that he had staged yet another escape. Debating the evidence against various theories is beyond the scope of this book. It is enough for our purposes that he was not seen in public after 18 August 1945, although his long shadow would fall on subsequent events.

THE INA TRIALS

With the Japanese defeated and their leader missing, the remaining INA units were forced to surrender. In purely military terms, it had not been a success. The British decided to make an example of the 'traitors' through a series of high-profile trials at the Red Fort in Delhi, followed by exemplary punishments. The thinking was presumably driven by the idea that the Indian population could yet again be frightened into submission, as had happened after the Revolt of 1857–58 and again after the First World War. The Red Fort was specifically chosen as the venue to rub it in. This time, however, they miscalculated. Due to wartime censorship, the general public had only dimly known of the INA and had not been aware of the scale of its operations, the bold adventures of its leader and the fact that an army of liberation had actually managed to enter India. By making these facts known widely through high-profile trials, the British inadvertently stirred up passions across the country.

The INA veterans were accused of 'waging war against the King-Emperor', which was punishable by death or transportation for life, and a hefty fine (usually confiscation of all property). One can judge the importance of the case in the eyes of the colonial authorities from the fact that Sir Noshirwan Engineer, the advocate general of India, himself appeared as the counsel for the prosecution.[46] That he was an Indian was also expected to make a point.

The first three officers chosen to be tried in November 1945 were Shah Nawaz Khan, Prem Kumar Sehgal and Gurbaksh Singh Dhillon. At a time when the spectre of Partition was looming, the symbolism of their religious affiliations would not have been lost on anyone. The Congress organized a strong defence team led by the renowned lawyers Tej Bahadur Sapru and Bhulabhai Desai. Interestingly, Jawaharlal Nehru donned his barrister's gown after thirty years to join the team, although he did not play an active role in the proceedings. His critics argue to this day that this was just a cynical move to appropriate his rival's legacy after having been adamant during the war that he 'would not hesitate to resist' an army of liberation led by Subhas Bose.[47] Readers are free to make what they wish of it.

The line of defence was an interesting one. Against the accusations of disloyalty and treachery, the defence argued that the Provisional Government of Free India was a recognized and legitimate government and that the INA was its regular army. The Allies had themselves recognized several governments in exile, such as that of Poland and France. Therefore, the INA veterans should be treated as prisoners of war and could not be considered traitors.

Many of the undertrials were housed in Salimgarh Fort, a smaller military fortress adjoining Red Fort. This fort was long used by the Mughals as a high-security prison for royals and high nobility. It is said that Emperor Aurangzeb held his brothers Murad and Dara in this fort before having them killed. Following the Revolt of 1857, several high-profile prisoners, including Bahadur Shah Zafar, were held here. The use of this fort as a prison for the INA veterans, therefore, was filled with symbolism for both sides. The trio of Khan, Dhillon and Sehgal, however, were kept separately in a room built into a medieval *baoli* (stepwell) within the Red Fort. The baoli is still in good condition, although few tourists know its significance and almost no one visits it.

Even as the judgment was awaited for the first set of undertrials, a new batch was put on trial. With one exception, they were again defended using similar arguments. The exception was Abdul Rashid, who swore that he had remained loyal to the King-Emperor and had only joined the INA to protect Muslim soldiers from being victimized by Hindu officers. Rashid's defence was organized by the Muslim League, but fell flat when several Muslim INA veterans spoke up against him.[48]

The Red Fort trials were followed in minute detail in the press, and the first three accused officers became instant heroes. There were demonstrations held across the country in solidarity with their cause. The mood did not merely impact the civilian population but also those serving in the British Indian armed forces—the same men who had fought against the INA just months earlier!

It should be remembered that the British Indian Army held large swathes of Asia in late 1945, including Burma, Indonesia, Malaya, Singapore and even southern Vietnam. Indian troops were also stationed in the Middle East. As troops from the other Allied countries were systematically sent home, the Indians were left holding the territory (as well as guarding Japanese prisoners of war). They soon realized that they were being used to control the locals in each country until their respective European colonizers could come back. For instance, British Indian troops were used to fight Indonesian freedom fighters in pitched battles in Surabaya in November 1945, even as the Dutch prepared to reoccupy the islands. Thousands of Indonesians were killed, but a couple of hundred British Indian troops were also killed. Resentment was so high that the British commanders feared that some of the Indian units would switch sides. Thus, the change in mood in the British Indian armed forces was no small matter on the international stage. By the end of 1945, the senior echelons of the British establishment were becoming aware of the precarious position. It is not surprising, therefore, that when Sehgal, Dhillon and Khan were given life sentences, Commander-in-Chief

Claude Auchinleck was forced to commute the sentences and release them.

THE NAVAL MUTINY[49]

The Royal Indian Navy had its origins in the Bombay Marine, which was set up as a local auxiliary to support the Royal Navy against the Maratha navy in the eighteenth century. It was formalized into the Royal Indian Marine in 1892 and participated in the First World War, mostly for the transportation of Indian troops to the Middle East and for coastal patrols. In 1934, it was upgraded to the Royal Indian Navy (RIN) but remained a modest force until the eve of the Second World War in 1939, with two sloops, one survey ship, four escort patrol vessels and thirty-three auxiliary boats. By the end of the Second World War in 1945, however, it had dramatically expanded to 132 ships, including gunboats and frigates.

The staff strength of the navy similarly expanded. In 1939, the RIN had merely 212 officers—and most of them were British. By 1945, the number had gone up to 2,852 and included 949 Indians. Similarly, the number of ratings (sailors) jumped from 1,475 to around 28,000 during this period.

Interestingly, the communal mix of the RIN changed dramatically during the Second World War. Given its origins as an auxiliary for fighting the Marathas, the ratings had always been overwhelmingly Muslim until the eve of the war (Hindu caste rules on crossing the seas may also have played a role). In 1939, Muslims accounted for 75 per cent of the sailors, while Hindus accounted for less than 10 per cent (the rest were Christian). This was one of the factors that had stoked Savarkar's anxieties about the relative military strengths of the two communities in a post-Independence scenario. However, by 1945, Hindus accounted for 43 per cent of the ratings, compared to 35 per cent for Muslims. Thus, the events of February 1946 were a genuine reflection of a popular mood that cut across communities.[50]

In late 1945, a large number of these sailors were being demobilized and were sent to camps in Mumbai for the process. However, with the war over, the British authorities had lost interest in them, and the camps were severely overcrowded. There were inadequate arrangements for food and housing. Two-thirds of the ratings did not even have cots to sleep on and were forced to sleep cheek-by-jowl on the floor. There were frequent complaints about the food: gravel in the rotis and rice, undercooked vegetables, diluted dal and so on. What made it worse was the attitude of the British officers, who met all complaints by hurling racist slurs at them.

Huddled in these crowded camps, therefore, the RIN sailors followed the INA trials with a growing sense of disillusionment. These were fertile grounds for spreading revolutionary ideas. A small group of relatively educated ratings, including Madan Singh, Mohammad Shuaib Khan, Rishi Dev Puri and Balai Chandra Dutt, began to meet regularly to discuss the situation. They called themselves the 'Azad Hindi', a direct reference to the INA and Subhas Bose's provisional government. They decided to carry out an act of revolt during the Navy Day celebrations on 1 December 1945. In addition to senior military and government officials, several prominent citizens had been invited. The event was to be held at HMIS Talwar, a shore establishment in Bombay's Colaba area, that was used by the navy's signals corps for training and operations.

The midnight-to-4 a.m. slot for sentry duty was not popular, so the Azad Hindis easily managed to get one of their own on duty. Thus, it was not difficult for a small group led by Dutt and Puri to gain entry into Talwar. As a senior telegraphist in the RIN, Dutt was already familiar with the facility and could have conjured up a good reason for being there. The buildings had been spruced up for the Navy Day event, but by 4 a.m., the group had prominently painted the walls with slogans such as 'Quit India', 'Revolt Now', 'Down with the Imperialists' and 'Kill the British'. When these were discovered the next day, the RIN became the laughing stock of the city.[51]

The British were unable to identify the culprits, so they responded by putting Commander Arthur Frederick King, a foul-mouthed racist with a reputation for toughness, in charge of Talwar. They also dismissed and sent away Puri, whom they suspected despite a lack of any direct evidence.

The commander-in-chief of British forces in India, Field Marshal Claude Auchinleck, was expected to visit Bombay in early February 1946. King managed to convince the higher authorities that holding an event in Talwar would be a good way to showcase the re-imposition of order. Thus, it was decided that Auchinleck would deliver a speech at the facility on 2 February. A stage was erected and the buildings repainted.

Not surprisingly, the security was very tight this time. However, Dutt had a legitimate reason to be there, as he was from the signals unit. He stayed back overnight and painted 'JAI HIND' on the stage built for the commander-in-chief. Then, he pasted a large number of revolutionary posters all over the yard. As can be imagined, there was pandemonium when these were discovered at first light, just hours before the speech.

Dutt may have escaped a second time for lack of evidence, but he had been seen taking a bottle of gum from the wireless room. His locker was checked, and it yielded copies of a revolutionary pamphlet and several books. He was immediately thrown into solitary confinement. The contents of the pamphlet make for interesting reading today, as they throw light on the dilemma faced in 1946 by Indians with a revolutionary bent. They felt let down by all political parties, especially by the INC. However, with the senior revolutionary leadership either dead or missing, they also did not know where to turn for direction.

Extracts from the pamphlet in Dutt's locker read as follows:

> For 25 years now we have been actively trying to get rid of our British rulers but failed. Large sections among the Congress as also in the country (mostly vested interests) feel that we are not strong enough to fight the British and must therefore, try to win independence through peaceful and constitutional methods. At Shimla, the Congress showed how anxious it was to come to a compromise with the Government at practically any cost ...
>
> ... The result is that in spite of 25 years of struggle and bitterness, the Englishmen and their Indian servants are the most comfortable people in the country.[52]

Since the pamphlet repeatedly mentions twenty-five years, it is clear that it is a reference to the Gandhian approach dating back to the Non-Cooperation Movement of 1920–21 (the freedom movement was obviously much older). There is also bitterness that the class of Indian collaborators continued to prosper. Ironically, this point would continue to rankle even decades after Independence. Nonetheless, the same pamphlet ends by stating that no one should try to undermine the Congress at a delicate time and that the Azad Hindis were explicitly apolitical: 'They will not oppose or discredit the Congress or any national organization nor set up rival organizations.'

The arrest of Dutt did not end small acts of rebellion at Talwar. A few days later, King found 'Quit India' written on his official car and his tyres deflated. The tinderbox just needed a spark, and it came in the form of a complaint about the quality of food. King responded with a barrage of racist expletives, which enraged the ratings.

The site of HMIS Talwar is still with the Indian Navy and is used today as a transport depot. It is just past the railways housing colony of Badhwar Park in Colaba and diagonally across from the well-known designer shirt shop of Charagh Din. There is nothing there to remind visitors of the momentous events that unfolded there in February. I lived in the neighbourhood in the late 1990s and can confirm that almost no one knew the significance of what is now just a repair and parking lot for navy trucks.

When the bugles were sounded for assembly at 8.45 a.m. on 18 February 1946, none of the ratings at Talwar showed up. They had earlier refused to eat breakfast as they deemed the food unfit for consumption. When King arrived at the facility, nationalist slogans were raised. Moreover, since these were signals men, they telegraphed their strike to the ships and other shore establishments. By evening, a mutiny was rapidly spreading across the RIN.

Next morning, the British realized that they had a full-fledged revolt on their hands. Ten thousand naval ratings left their barracks and demobilization camps and marched to the harbour. This was an organized group that had fought together. Within hours they had taken over two more shore establishments,

Castle Barracks and Fort Barracks. Next, they took over, one by one, the RIN ships in the harbour: *Berar, Moti, Neelum, Jumna* and so on. Officers, both Indian and British, were confined to their cabins even as the sailors took control. They pulled down the Union Jack and unfurled the Congress and Muslim League flags. The CPI flag was added shortly thereafter. The ratings did not want to be seen as politically aligned with any specific party.

A large group of ratings gathered at the Talwar by noon. A central strike committee was formed with leading signalman M.S. Khan as president and telegraphist Madan Singh as vice president. They also renamed RIN the Indian National Navy— again, an obvious reference to the INA. All of these developments were quickly transmitted to the ships and shore establishments controlled by the ratings. The committee also presented its demands, which included an immediate release of all political prisoners and INA veterans, an independent inquiry into the large number of deaths from police/military firing in the previous few years, and an immediate withdrawal of Indian troops from South East Asia and the Middle East.

The above events were reported across India and the world. It is interesting to read how different papers reported the same set of events. On the one hand, there were papers such as the *Free Press Journal*, which were sympathetic to the striking sailors, while, on the other hand, there were pro-British publications like the *Times of India* and the *Statesman*, which presented them as lumpen elements. The *Times of India*, for example, called it: 'REIGN OF TERROR BY RATINGS ON "STRIKE".'

With the situation spiralling out of control, Rear Admiral Rattray called for army troops to re-establish control. Troops from the Mahratta regiment were sent to Castle Barracks. Known today as INS Angre, it is a fortified complex built originally by the Portuguese in the sixteenth century and then further enhanced by the East India Company in the subsequent centuries. The Mahrattas took up positions and set up machine-gun posts outside Castle Barracks by mid-afternoon. The ratings responded by arming themselves from the naval armoury and setting up defences. They also started to prime the big guns on the ships. The sailors, after all, were recent veterans of the war and no pushovers.

By the morning of 21 February, the mutiny included 20,000 ratings, 78 ships and 21 shore establishments. Moreover, the revolt had spread beyond Bombay. In Karachi, for instance, the sailors took over two ships, HMIS *Hindustan* and *Travancore*, and the shore establishment HMIS Himalaya. Calcutta also witnessed a strike.

Back at Castle Barracks in Bombay, the Mahratta brigade was ordered to open fire. The sailors retaliated. An officer who had climbed on top of the Reserve Bank of India building was shot down. This led to an exchange of fire until the British commanders realized that the Mahrattas were deliberately making sure that they were not hitting targets. Recognizing the changing mood, Indian troops were quickly replaced by those of the Leicestershire Regiment. The British next ordered the Royal Indian Air Force (RIAF) to get ready to bomb the ships. The airmen flatly refused and themselves went on strike. An RIAF squadron told to proceed immediately to Bombay was grounded in Jodhpur when all the planes mysteriously developed engine problems.

With European troops now surrounding the naval establishments, the attack began in earnest, with armoured vehicles and machine guns. A squadron of Royal Air Force Mosquitoes flew over the harbour to intimidate the rebels.

The sailors fought back. HMIS *Punjab* fired 120 rounds from its twelve-pounder at government forces on the shore, followed by firing from its anti-aircraft guns.

Karachi also witnessed similar developments when the Gurkha and Baloch soldiers refused to fire on the sailors and had to be replaced by European troops. A generation earlier, the same regiments had unquestioningly opened fire at Jallianwala Bagh; something had clearly changed. It is a pity that revolutionary leaders such as Sachindra Nath Sanyal and Rashbehari Bose did not live to see the revolt, as this was exactly what they had repeatedly attempted to trigger over the decades.

As their authority over the Indian armed forces crumbled, it was obvious to the British authorities that they were no longer in a position to sustain their colonial occupation of the country. Thus, even as battles raged on the streets of Bombay, British Prime Minister Clement Attlee announced the visit of a three-member Cabinet Mission to start the process for an 'early realization of full self-government in India'.[53] The moment had finally arrived!

By the time news of Attlee's announcement arrived, the whole city of Bombay was in full revolt. A large number of students, factory workers and other common citizens had gathered in support of the RIN ratings. They quickly established a system of supplying food to the sailors holed up in different parts of the city. The British responded by ordering the troops to fire on the protesters. The number of casualties is estimated to be between 400 and 700 dead, and 1,500 wounded. Yet again, it should be remembered that many of the atrocities were ordered and/or carried out by Indian officers of the Indian Imperial Police service. The crackdown did not deter large gatherings of protesters in

Madras, Visakhapatnam, Calcutta, Ahmedabad, Karachi and other cities across the subcontinent; many died in police firings.

The Naval Revolt had triggered what seemed like an unstoppable wave, but the RIN ratings knew that they could not sustain this for too long. Not only were they surrounded, but they were also not in a position to use their big guns on the city without risking large-scale civilian casualties. A political solution was needed. Unfortunately, the rebels lacked a leader of national stature. If leaders such as Subhas Bose, Tilak or Lajpat Rai had been around, it would have been a different matter, but the rebels were forced to appeal to the Congress and the Muslim League leaders, who their own pamphlets had accused of letting them down in the past. Gandhi came out publicly against the rebels: 'In resorting to mutiny they are badly advised ... if they mutinied for freedom of India, they are doubly wrong.' This was followed by Vallabhbhai Patel, who dismissed the rebellion as 'hooliganism'. When representatives of the sailors met Jinnah, he refused to help and replied ominously: 'I would want uniform and discipline in the Pakistan Navy.'[54]

The only party that expressed any support for the naval ratings was the CPI. Although they did little more than issue statements and send some of their trade unions to the protests, the communists did not dismiss the rebels. A handful of other leaders such as Minoo Masani and Aruna Asaf Ali also expressed support. Nonetheless, it was clear that the bulk of the political establishment was not going to support the revolt. The rebels were disappointed when they realized they were being advised to surrender unconditionally. Arriving in Bombay, Nehru and Patel assured M.S. Khan that the ratings would not be victimized if they laid down arms.

Although he was not entirely convinced by the assurances, he placed the proposal to the committee. Some such as Madan Singh were in favour of fighting to the bitter end, but the ratings eventually surrendered on 24 February. Despite the assurances of the Congress leaders, hundreds of ratings were arrested and imprisoned. One of the places they were imprisoned was the dungeons of Castle Barracks. Now named INS Angre, the facility still exists and is well preserved. I stood in the dark dungeons even as Commodore Odakkal Johnson described how his father Muhammad Odakkal, one of the rebels, was dragged into the prison along with dozens of others.

Just like the Revolt of 1857, this one, too, had been crushed, but it was obvious that the game had changed. The INA and the Naval Revolt had irrevocably broken the Indian soldier's loyalty to the British crown. As already mentioned, this had major consequences for the empire. A glance at the newspapers from that time shows that British troops were fighting independence movements across the world. At the same time that they were fighting with mutineers in Bombay, firing on 'Quit Egypt' demonstrators in Cairo killed ten Egyptians.[55]

The chain of events triggered by Attlee's announcement of a Cabinet Mission led India to become independent on 15 August 1947, just eighteen months after the Naval Mutiny. It is not the purpose of this book to make the case that the non-violent movement led by Gandhi was irrelevant to the freedom movement. Rather, the goal is to show how the armed resistance of the revolutionary movement was also an important part of the story. The central role of the revolutionaries in the freedom struggle is attested by many credible eyewitnesses, including Dr B.R. Ambedkar, among others. He is on record in a BBC interview, stating that the undermining of the loyalty of the Indian soldier was the critical factor. Indeed, there is evidence that Attlee himself believed that the INA and the RIN revolt were critical to his decision to give India Independence. Phani Bhushan Chakravartti, Chief Justice of Calcutta High Court, wrote in his autobiography that Attlee had himself told him in 1956 that his decision was driven by the INA and the RIN mutiny.[56]

Unfortunately, the revolutionary leadership had been decimated by the time India became free, and the movement had splintered across the political spectrum. The only two major leaders to have survived were, ironically, the ones who had started it—Aurobindo Ghosh and Vinayak Savarkar—but both of them had drifted away from the movement decades earlier. Therefore, revolutionaries as a group did not play a major political role in post-Independence India (although a few individuals and derivative groups did remain prominent). The Nehruvian branch of the INC, having captured power, systematically emphasized its own role in the official narrative of the freedom movement and downplayed the role of the armed struggle. This partial narrative was also echoed in the international sphere by British historians, as it conveniently edited out inconvenient facts, such as the atrocities of the Cellular Jail and the millions who died in the Bengal famine of 1943.

Sachindra Nath Sanyal, in the preface to *Bandi Jeevan*, expressed his fear that future generations would not be told the truth about what the revolutionaries had done. He was proved right, as many major events and characters were systematically scrubbed out of public memory. This was not just a case of passive, wilful memory loss, but an active effort backed by the State over decades. In 1965, the Congress Chief Minister of West Bengal P.C. Sen made every effort to disallow a Bengali play by Utpal Dutt named *Kallol* about the Naval Mutiny. The playwright even ended up in jail for a few months. It is extraordinary that the history of a major event such as the Naval Mutiny was scrubbed out so effectively that I would be unaware of it until my late twenties, when I accidentally came across a small memorial while walking around Colaba. As I researched this book, I found that this was systematically done to many other parts of the story.

EPILOGUE

After centuries of foreign occupation, India finally became free on 15 August 1947. This should have been a moment of unalloyed joy for the revolutionaries and their families, who had sacrificed so much for this moment. But this was not to be. Independence also meant the Partition of India, and specifically that of Punjab and Bengal, the two provinces that had provided a disproportionate share of revolutionaries. Places such as Lahore and Dhaka, which had been important hubs of India's freedom struggle, were no longer part of the country. In one stroke, millions of Indians became foreigners in their own land. Hundreds of thousands faced death, rape and a loss of all their possessions. The revolutionaries had repeatedly felt let down by the political leadership, but this was arguably the greatest betrayal of all.

Yet, amid the confusion and violence, a few individuals worked desperately to prevent a bad situation from becoming worse. In the months leading up to Partition, a new proposal was put forward by Sarat Chandra Bose, Subhas's elder brother, and Hussain Shaheed Suhrawardy, the Muslim League premier of Bengal, for the creation of a united, independent Bengal. The argument was that this would avoid the partition of the province. The idea of an independent Bengal had never been in serious discussion, but, in April–May 1947, it suddenly took the shape of a concrete proposal that had the support of Jinnah and a section of the British officialdom (and possibly even Gandhi until Patel dissuaded him). That Subhas Bose's brother, of all people, would sacrifice India to the altar of Bengali regionalism is inexplicable. His willingness to go along with Suhrawardy is particularly baffling, given the latter's recent role in the savage riots of August 1946 (known as the Great Calcutta Killings).

Syamaprasad Mookerjee immediately realized that the proposal would leave Bengal's Hindu minority permanently at the mercy of the Muslim majority, and the possibility that Suhrawardy would subsequently opt for Pakistan anyway. The problem was that his party, the Hindu Mahasabha, did not have the strength to sway the course of events. Therefore, he reached out to prominent leaders of the Bengali Hindu community for help. One of those who responded was Dr Nalinaksha Sanyal, with whom he had worked closely during the famine of 1943. Together they systematically swayed enough Congress legislators to vote for the Partition of Bengal. It was a sad moment for the revolutionaries—their movement had been born opposing the Partition of Bengal in 1905 and it ended with many of them with no option but to support it.

Sanyal next threw himself into trying to salvage as much of Bengal as possible for India. As the country's leading transportation economist at that time, he made the case that the main railway lines and the river system feeding Calcutta port had to be retained in India on the grounds of economic viability. The Radcliffe Commission accepted the arguments. This is why Murshidabad, Maldah and most of Nadia district stayed with India. Unfortunately, the new boundary left his newly married daughter on the wrong side of the border, in Kushtia. She and her husband became refugees, along with millions of others. This is how the new state of West Bengal was born. Sarat Bose eventually reconciled to it, but he never forgave Nalinaksha Sanyal.[1]

Sanyal led an active life after Independence as a technocrat, a politician and a businessman. However, one of his important concerns was the infiltration of the network of akhadas in West Bengal by the communists. These religious gymnasiums had existed across India since the early medieval period and had played an important role in sustaining indigenous resistance to foreign invaders. In Bengal, they mostly belonged to the Shakta stream of Hinduism (dedicated to various forms of Goddess Shakti, such as Durga and Kali). As readers will recall, the Anushilan Samiti and the Jugantar networks had been built on the back of these akhadas, and the British had systematically tried to weaken them. In the 1960s, however, Nalinaksha Sanyal was concerned that the communists were gradually infiltrating and 'secularizing' them into 'youth clubs'. He tried to counteract this by encouraging the more traditional akhadas. He also supported the Bratachari Movement set up by his friend Gurusaday Dutt to encourage traditional martial arts. His efforts were mostly unsuccessful and, by the 1980s, the akhadas had become youth clubs affiliated with different communist factions. Later they were taken over by the Trinamool Congress, the regional party that rules West Bengal today. Nonetheless, they have continued to organize the annual Durga Puja festival in each neighbourhood—an echo of their origins.

If Partition was devastating for the revolutionaries of Bengal and Punjab, Independence did not prove to be kind to the other community that had provided so many revolutionaries—the Maharashtrian Brahmins. A member of the community, Nathuram Godse assassinated Gandhi in Delhi on 30 January 1948. This unleashed a wave of mob violence against the Brahmin community across Maharashtra. Estimates vary, but thousands of homes and businesses were burnt down, and hundreds were killed.[2] In some ways, this had been building up for a while because the British, ever fearful of a revival in the Maratha empire, had invested in anti-Brahminism since the nineteenth century to create cleavages in Maharashtrian society. What made it worse was that the government of Independent India deliberately suppressed information about the 1948 pogrom—it is spoken of in whispers to this day. This was unfortunate, as no lessons were learnt, and the sequence of events was repeated during the anti-Sikh riots that followed the assassination of Indira Gandhi in 1984. Let it be clear that the assassination of both the Gandhis was wrong, but so was the mob violence against whole communities that followed.

The mobs particularly targeted the Savarkar brothers, as they were not just Brahmins but suspected of being directly involved in the assassination plot. A large mob of Congress party workers turned up at the home of Narayanrao Savarkar and dragged him out on to the street. Then they beat and stoned him mercilessly before leaving him in a pool of blood. Narayan suffered severe head injuries from which he never recovered and, after more than a year on a hospital bed, died from brain haemorrhage.[3] He had been a prominent freedom fighter in his own right and was ultimately killed by the very people to whose freedom he had dedicated his life.

The mob then went to look for Vinayak Savarkar at his house in Dadar, where he was staying with his wife Yamuna and son Vishwas on the first floor. As the mob stormed into the ground floor, they were delayed long enough by a couple of supporters to allow the police to arrive. This likely saved the family from meeting the same fate as Narayanrao. Nonetheless, Vinayak was arrested on suspicion of being part of the Gandhi-assassination plot. This led to yet another historic trial at Red Fort in 1948, where he was tried along with Nathuram Godse and several others. Godse had always admitted to killing Gandhi and was hanged in November 1949. The case against Savarkar was weak, and he was acquitted. Although he returned to his social work, he was, by now, suffering from poor health and was a shadow of the firebrand of India House.

Having suffered years of torture in prison and then Partition, many former revolutionaries suffered from what we today call post-traumatic stress disorder (PTSD). Several found it difficult to hold regular jobs and drifted into a life of extreme poverty. When researching the post-Independence lives of some of these freedom fighters, I really felt sad about how they had just been abandoned.

Ullaskar Dutt had been a key member of Barin Ghosh's original Anushilan Samiti. Before he was arrested in 1908, Ullaskar was engaged to be married to his college sweetheart Lila, the daughter of the nationalist leader Bipin Chandra Pal. Readers will recall that he was so severely tortured in the Cellular Jail that he almost lost his mind. One of the things that allowed him to survive the repeated electrocutions was the thought of Lila. He was subsequently sent to a mental asylum in Madras for a long and painful recovery. It is said that through it all, he would see a floating image of Lila that kept him going.

During all these years, however, Lila had no idea what had happened to him. According to scholar Bibek Debroy, when Ullaskar finally went looking for her, he discovered that Lila, after waiting for a long time, had married someone else. Disappointed, Ullaskar returned to the revolutionary life and was jailed again in the early 1930s. By the time India gained Independence, he is said to have become a recluse in a village in East Bengal. However, when he heard that Lila was a widow and paralysed from the waist down, he located her in Bombay and took her with him to live in Silchar, Assam (many Hindu refugees from East Bengal had settled there). Here he finally married Lila and looked after her in her last years. It is a real love story that is more heart-wrenching than any novel.

Bina Das had been sentenced to nine years in prison for shooting at Bengal Governor Stanley Jackson in 1932. After her early release in 1939, she continued to participate in the freedom movement. She became a teacher and married a fellow revolutionary. After Independence, she also served for a term in the West Bengal legislative assembly. However, after the death of her husband in the mid-1980s, she became a recluse and shifted to Varanasi to engage in spiritual pursuits. She lived alone for some months in a modest guest house near the Ganga ghats. She initially kept in touch with her family and friends through regular letters. According to Jay Bhattacharjee, her nephew, the family became concerned when the letters suddenly stopped. Another nephew went to the city looking for her, but the owner of the guest house said that she had suddenly packed her bags and left. He was unsure where she had gone, but felt that it could be Haridwar or Rishikesh to further pursue her spiritual journey. At the end of 1986, the same nephew went to Rishikesh looking for her. Initially he made no headway but then he heard that the emaciated body of an old lady had been recently found abandoned by the roadside. He identified the body in the morgue as that of Bina Das.

Raja Mahendra Pratap had led the Kabul Mission in the First World War and set up the first Provisional Government of India. The mission failed and his German sponsors were defeated. Like many Ghadarites, he was left in the lurch, as he could not return to British India. Thus, he spent the next three decades wandering around the world as a nomad. He even briefly spent time with M.N. Roy at his school for communist indoctrination in Tashkent. He eventually returned to India on the eve of Independence. In 1957, he successfully fought the country's second general election from the Mathura Lok Sabha seat as an independent candidate. One of the rival candidates was a young Atal Bihari Vajpayee, who came a distant fourth on a Jana Sangh ticket.[4]

Some of the other revolutionaries also have interesting afterlives. After participating in Ghadarite activities in Japan and North America, and then fighting the British in Persia during the First World War, Pandurang Khankhoje knew he could not return to India, where the colonial authorities were waiting to arrest him. Therefore, he headed to Mexico, where he became a famous agricultural expert. Indeed, his innovations in farm technology, initially in wheat and maize cultivation, transformed the sector worldwide. For instance, he developed 'rust-resistant', frost-resistant and drought-resistant varieties of wheat that greatly benefited global food production. These innovations eventually found their way to India in the form of the 'Green Revolution' in the late 1960s and 1970s. This alone would have been enough to give him a place in history, but Khankhoje next dabbled in the indigenous plants of Central America and collected local knowledge about them. This led to the discovery of plant-derived steroids and hormones. The hormones that are used in birth-control pills, for instance, were made possible by these discoveries. Similarly, his collaborations with Vicks Chemical Company led to innovations in mint-oil extraction that are still used.⁵

Although Khankhoje did not patent these discoveries, he did become a reasonably wealthy man by the time the Second World War started. Along the way, he had married Jeanne, a Belgian lady much younger than him, and had two daughters, Savitri and Maya. By the time the war ended, Khankhoje had sunk much of his capital into mining. His luck did not hold this time, and he lost most of his wealth in the venture.

Through all these years, however, he yearned to return to India, a country he had left in 1906. Therefore, when India became Independent, he decided to go back. His exploits during the Ghadar Movement were remembered by many supporters and the chief minister of the Central Provinces even sent him a personal invitation. The bureaucratic paperwork took two years before Khankhoje could fly back in April 1949. He was carrying with him the first formal letter from the Mexican President to initiate direct diplomatic links between the two countries. Nonetheless, his name was still on the proscribed list, which had not been updated. The immigration officials in Bombay detained him at the airport and subjected him to interrogation before matters were clarified. The old revolutionary was deeply hurt by this. He was even more dismayed by the fact that, despite his international stature, Indian officials would simply not take his suggestions on agricultural modernization seriously just because he was not white. The colonial-era inferiority complex was deeply entrenched—Khankhoje referred to elite Indians as 'black Englishmen'. Irritated by this attitude, he decided to go back to Mexico, but his heart remained in India.[6]

The Indian government finally woke up to Khankhoje's work in the mid-1950s, and he was invited back to advise various institutions. He moved to Nagpur with his family in 1955. Khankhoje spent the rest of his life in India. Over the course of his extraordinary life, he had learnt many languages—English, Marathi, Hindi, Persian, Japanese and Spanish. In his seventies, he learnt Vedic Sanskrit to be able to read the original Rig Veda and understand the philosophical origins of Hinduism. He passed away in Nagpur in January 1987. What a life!

The international legacy of the early revolutionaries has begun to attract the attention of expatriate Indian communities in recent years after being ignored for almost a century. However, the unfortunate consequence of the British response to their activities also lives on. As readers will recall, British intelligence had invested heavily in infiltrating Sikh gurudwaras in Canada and Britain to counter the Ghadarites. Their effort focused on separating Sikh identity from the Hindus and creating a wedge with Indian nationalists. This is why the Khalistani separatist movement remains concentrated in Canada to this day. In June 1985, Canadian Khalistani terrorists blew up Air India's Montreal-to-London flight, killing 329 passengers and crew. As one can see, it is important to understand the long history of the Ghadarite revolutionaries and the British counter-offensive to understand why British Columbia in Canada, of all places, is the hub of Khalistani separatism. In a similar vein, today's Rohingya conflict along the Bangladesh–Myanmar border has its origins in the militarization of the local Muslim–Buddhist rivalry during the Second World War.

One of the ironies of history is that Independent India refused to rehabilitate the INA veterans and RIN rebels. Not only were they not taken back into the armed forces, they were not even given recognition as freedom fighters until the 1970s. The justification given was that it would impact 'discipline' in the armed forces. The more likely reason is that many colonial-era officials, both British and Indian, continued to occupy positions of power in newly Independent India. Not surprisingly, they were not sympathetic to the revolutionaries in general and the INA/RIN veterans in particular. Many readers will be shocked to learn that the first four admirals to head the Indian Navy after 1947 were all British. It was only in 1958 that the first Indian, Admiral Ram Das Khatri, headed the Indian Navy. Even Commander Arthur King, whose racist behaviour had triggered the RIN revolt, was offered a senior role by the government of free India, although he preferred to return to the United Kingdom.[7]

Although the government of Pakistan did not re-absorb the RIN rebels either, Jinnah enthusiastically welcomed Muslim INA veterans into the army. Some senior commanders of the INA, such as Mohammad Zaman Kiani and Habibur Rahman, fought for the Pakistani cause in the first Indo-Pak War of 1947–48 over Jammu and Kashmir. Thus, the irony is that the only veterans of Subhas Bose's INA to participate in war after Independence ended up fighting against Azad Hind (Free India).

The better-educated RIN ratings managed to make a life for themselves after their dismissal. B.C. Dutt tried his hand at journalism at the *Free Press Journal*, where he shared a cabin with a young cartoonist named Balasaheb Thackeray. However, after three years, he switched to advertising and spent two decades working for the well-known firm Lintas. M.S. Khan, who had served as the president of the RIN strike committee, is known to have gone to Gujranwala, now in Pakistan. However, nothing is known of what happened to him after Partition. Recent efforts by writer Pramod Kapoor to trace him did not provide any leads. His deputy Madan Singh helped Biju Patnaik, the famous Odiya politician-activist, set up Kalinga Airlines in 1948. When the airline was nationalized in 1952 as part of Prime Minister Nehru's socialist policies, he ended up in London, working for British Overseas Airlines Corporation (now British Airways).[8]

The INA veterans and RIN rebels who came from more modest backgrounds did not fare well. Deprived of pensions and recognition, many drifted into penury. Nonetheless, a handful did end up leading interesting lives. After returning briefly to his village in Kerala, Muhammad Odakkal got involved in the movement to liberate Goa from Portuguese rule. He was arrested in 1955 by the Portuguese and spent time in prison. Ever restless, he then cycled across India, living off the generosity of common folk. In the 1960s he became a tour guide in Agra, where he met and married a nurse named Mariamma. Their son, Commodore Odakkal Johnson, accompanied me to various sites across Mumbai as I tried to work out the events of the 1946 revolt.

But what happened to all the people who had actively helped the British perpetuate their occupation of India? Just to clarify, it would be unfair to paint everyone who had dealings with the British as collaborators. Obviously, most Indians had no choice but to deal with the colonial government if they wanted to get a job, run a business and so on. However, as the reader would have seen in this book, there were many Indians who went out of their way to undermine the freedom movement for personal gain—informers, approvers, certain government officials and contractors. They had prospered under the British and continued to do so in Independent India. In the interest of continuity, there was no effort to purge them. So, when spaces opened up in the country's power structure due to the departure of the British, members of the old collaborator class and their descendants were often in the best position to occupy them as they were already insiders. Thus, yet another irony of history is that many of the top officials, journalists and intellectuals of Independent India were drawn from the collaborator class.

Hans Raj Vohra was one of the HSRA members who turned approver and provided evidence against Sukhdev, Rajguru and Bhagat Singh. After the trial, the British arranged for his education at London University. He was then given a job at the *Civil and Military Gazette* in Lahore and later worked at the *Statesman*, a British-owned daily. However, he always had a nagging feeling that people saw him as a traitor. After Independence, therefore, he left the country as the Washington DC correspondent of the *Times of India*. He never returned to live in India again. It is said that he lived his last few years as a recluse, evidently haunted by the memories of the Lahore trials.[9]

Most collaborators, however, brazened it out. Yashpal, the police informer who likely supplied the information that led to the death of Chandrashekhar Azad, became one of the most celebrated authors in Hindi after Independence. He received some of the country's most coveted awards, such as the Sahitya Akademi Award and the Padma Bhushan. The revolutionaries had always suspected him, long before Dharmendra Gaur chanced upon hard evidence of his collaboration in the police intelligence records. Their suspicion was strengthened when he was given special treatment in prison. At a time when revolutionaries were routinely subjected to extreme torture, he was even allowed to get married in jail! Therefore, it irked many of them that Yashpal's post-Independence success as a writer was based largely on books in which he milked his own role as a revolutionary![10]

Since almost none of their top leaders survived till Independence, the revolutionary movement did not hold together as a united force, and its political legacy got scattered across the political spectrum. Nonetheless, a few individuals did have successful political careers. Arguably the most successful survivor of the armed struggle was Shah Nawaz Khan, part of the trio from the INA trials. Although most of his family shifted to Pakistan, he stayed back in India and represented the Meerut constituency four times in the Lok Sabha as a member of the INC; he even became a minister.[11] His best-remembered contribution is serving as the chairman of a commission to investigate the death or disappearance of Subhas Bose. His findings are hotly debated to this day.

Mairembam Koireng Singh, who had welcomed the INA into Moirang, became the first chief minister of Manipur. Hemam Nilamani Singh, whose house was used by the INA as the forward headquarters, became the deputy education minister of the state. Thus, in this tiny corner of India, the memory of the INA continued to be celebrated, despite a prolonged period of political instability.

As mentioned earlier in the book, the revolutionary movement had many offshoots and spin-offs. Two important offshoots, at opposite ends of the ideological spectrum, were the

Revolutionary Socialist Party and the Rashtriya Swayamsevak Sangh. The RSP had been formed by Jogesh Chandra Chatterjee and Tridib Chaudhuri in 1940 as a platform for the Anushilan Marxists. Despite imbibing Marxist ideas, they remained wary of the Communist Party of India because of the suspicion of foreign influences. Although the RSP had networks across India, its core base was among the Hindus of East Bengal (the old base of the Dhaka Anushilan Samiti). This support base was uprooted and scattered after Partition. Nonetheless, unlike in West Pakistan, a significant Hindu population continued to live in East Pakistan. Thus, part of the RSP network, already used to functioning underground, continued to exist in East Bengal.

In 1970–71, the Pakistan government unleashed a genocide in East Pakistan. An estimated 3 million Bengalis, particularly Hindus, were killed and another 10 million ended up in India as refugees. This resulted in the Indo-Pak War of 1971 and the formation of Bangladesh. Despite the end of hostilities, a large number of Hindu refugees refused to return to East Bengal and had to be rehabilitated in India. Many of them were relocated by the central government to places such as Dandakaranya—the forests of the Eastern Ghats and the Chotanagpur Plateau. This was unfamiliar land for the Bengali refugees and most of them yearned to be rehabilitated in West Bengal. They reached out to the RSP as the natural party to represent them.

Meanwhile, the CPI had split in 1964 into pro-Soviet and pro-Chinese factions (the former was still called CPI, while the latter was called the Communist Party of India [Marxist], or the CPI[M]). The RSP continued to be wary of both factions—after all, the split itself demonstrated the impact of foreign allegiances. They also disliked the CPI/CPI(M)'s attempts from the 1960s to appropriate the legacy of the revolutionary movement, despite having actively opposed the INA and Subhas Bose during the Second World War. In spite of these reservations, the RSP joined the Left Front alliance led by the CPI(M) for the West Bengal state elections of 1977. When the alliance won, the RSP found itself in government for the first time.

The Left Front government, partly at the urging of the RSP, promised to resettle Bengali refugees from Dandakaranya to West Bengal. As a result, large numbers began to move to the state, but on arrival found that no concrete arrangements had been made for their rehabilitation. One large group of more than a lakh ended up on an island called Marichjhapi on the edges of the Sunderbans mangrove forest (roughly 100 km south-east of Calcutta). They just lived in the open or set up temporary camps, but soon set up their own dispensary, school and a boat-making unit. Jyoti Basu, the CPI(M) chief minister of West Bengal, suddenly realized that this would change the demographics of the area in favour of the RSP. Even if the party was an ally, it could not be allowed to create a power base in what was a CPI(M) bastion. Thus, the government issued orders to evict the refugees from Marichjhapi. The refugees refused to budge. They had fled their homes in East Bengal a few years earlier and then moved here on the basis of government promises. Desperately poor and at their wits' end, these East Bengal Hindus had nowhere to go.

What followed is one of the most shameful incidents in the history of Independent India. In early 1979, Jyoti Basu sent a large force of armed policemen to surround Marichjhapi and prevent food and other supplies from getting in. The blockade was steadily tightened. By April–May, the police moved into the island, burning huts, poisoning wells and destroying boats. Men, women and children were herded off the island at gunpoint. Many of those who refused were shot; even more died from hunger and thirst. The death toll is not known for sure but is likely to be in the range of 4,000 to 6,000. According to journalist Deep Halder, one of the few people to have researched and written about the incident, the death toll could be as high as 10,000.[12] To have done this to desperate, brutalized refugees is unforgivable. Yet, the Marichjhapi massacre was systematically covered up for decades in both media and academia. Growing up in Calcutta in the 1980s, I was barely aware that such a major event had taken place. The RSP could have stood up for the refugees, but decided that it was politically expedient to remain quiet. For an organization that derived its legitimacy from its revolutionary origins, the suspicion of cowardice proved fatal. The party slowly drifted into oblivion.

The RSS had been very active at the time of Partition and played an important role in providing support and rehabilitation for Hindu refugees pouring into the country from Pakistan. This allowed it to significantly expand its network. However, this growth was disrupted when it was briefly banned after Gandhi's assassination, and thousands of RSS members were jailed. After the ban was lifted, many supporters wanted the organization to directly participate in politics. However, the old reluctance to join the political system remained. Instead, the RSS decided to help Syamaprasad Mookerjee, now a Cabinet minister, set up a new party after he left the Hindu Mahasabha due to his differences with traditionalists within the party. A new party named Bharatiya Jana Sangh (BJS) was formed in 1951. The party did moderately well in the next few decades, but never enough to threaten the hegemony of the Congress.

The RSS itself, meanwhile, turned its attention to the enclaves still controlled by the Portuguese on the west coast of India—Daman, Diu, Goa, Dadra and Nagar Haveli. In 1954, it formed an alliance with two parties operating in Portuguese India—the National Movement Liberation Organization and the Azad Gomantak Dal. On 2 August 1954, a small group of just a hundred volunteers stormed Dadra and Nagar Haveli and took over the enclaves. The Portuguese officials and the contingent of 175 soldiers were so completely taken by surprise by this audacity that they surrendered without a fight. For a short while, Dadra and Nagar Haveli were independent countries in the eyes of international law, until they were absorbed into the Republic of India.[13]

The freedom movement in the remaining Portuguese-held enclaves was ramped up. The Portuguese responded by reinforcing their position. On 15 August 1955, large protests were organized by the alliance. The Portuguese police opened fire and killed thirty protesters (several from the RSS). Hundreds were arrested and put in prison. An armed resistance began to take shape. The escalating situation finally forced a reluctant Nehru to order a military takeover of Goa, Daman and Diu in December 1961.

The RSS and the Bharatiya Jana Sangh remained a significant presence in India's sociopolitical landscape in the 1960s and 1970s. When Prime Minister Indira Gandhi suspended democracy and declared the Emergency in 1975, tens of thousands of RSS volunteers and members of affiliated entities were thrown into jail. The organization's origins in the revolutionary movement, however, allowed it to continue functioning underground and keep up a resistance to the regime. The friendships built in jail and clandestine political activity welded together a network that would eventually flower in the 1990s. Future Prime Minister Narendra Modi and Finance Minister Arun Jaitley were products of this period. Inadvertently, Indira Gandhi had turned this offshoot of the revolutionary movement into a potent political force.

In 1977, the BJS would merge into the Janata Party—a rainbow alliance that ousted Indira Gandhi. The new government did not last as it lacked a coherent ideology and leadership, and Indira Gandhi returned to power in 1980. With the Janata Party disintegrating, the remnants of the BJS were reconvened as the Bharatiya Janata Party (BJP). After a shaky start, the party gathered steam and anchored coalition governments under Prime Minister Atal Bihari Vajpayee between 1998 and 2004. It then returned in 2014 with a full majority under Prime Minister Narendra Modi, and then again in 2019. Thus, after many twists and turns, this particular derivative of the revolutionary movement became the dominant political force in India in the twenty-first century.

The RSS has grown to become one of the world's largest organizations, with shakhas across India and even abroad. Along with its affiliates, it runs disaster relief programmes, schools, hospitals and other social services. While itself remaining apolitical, it continues to have a strong relationship with the BJP. However, anyone familiar with the movement will see the influence of the revolutionaries everywhere. Bharat Mata (Mother India) is venerated in the form of Goddess Durga at all its facilities. A large idol of Durga–Bharati presides over the main hall at the RSS headquarters in Nagpur—a direct link to the Shakti worship that inspired the Anushilan Samiti. In the same vein, the idea of the shakha is derived from the ancient network of the quasi-religious akhadas, while the core leadership is run by bachelor '*pracharak*s (monk missionaries)', who are not dissimilar to what Aurobindo Ghosh had described in his pamphlet *Bhawani Mandir* in 1905.[14]

As one can see, the revolutionary movement continued to impact Independent India, even though it did not survive as a unified movement or organization. In December 1958, the surviving revolutionaries organized a large conference in Delhi under the chairmanship of Bhupendra Nath Dutta, the younger brother of Swami Vivekananda. Around 400 delegates attended the event and included representatives from every generation of the movement: Barin Ghosh, Sohan Singh Bhakna, Jogesh Chatterjee and so on. Prime Minister Nehru even invited them for tea at his official residence.

The attendees recalled many of the great freedom fighters who had not survived; a special cheer went up for Rashbehari Bose who had been involved for almost the entire duration of the movement. One of the topics that was discussed at the conference was the fact that, even by the 1950s, the official narrative about the freedom movement had systematically edited out the contributions of the armed resistance. The attendees experienced first-hand how this was done. At the event it was proposed that part of the Central Jail in Delhi, where many revolutionaries had been incarcerated and even hanged, be converted into a memorial to this movement. Nehru wrote back that this was not possible as the location was being converted to the Maulana Azad National Medical College. As a compromise, the Prime Minister proposed that the spot of the gallows could be preserved and a plaque put up. Reluctantly the revolutionaries agreed. Jogesh Chatterjee tells us in his autobiography that when the proposal was sent to the home ministry, it was flatly refused.[15]

The revolutionaries, however, were never fully forgotten by Indians despite official antipathy. The events were too recent and their activities still vividly remembered in collective memory. The memories of individual revolutionaries were kept alive by friends, family and their native towns/villages. However, they were systematically reduced to no more than a passing reference in school textbooks and national events, even as the contributions of one branch of the INC were provided exclusive coverage. Thus, generations of Indians were sold a narrative where the contributions of the revolutionaries were shown to have been no more than random acts without coherent objectives, and, consequently, as having no impact on the course of events. As we have seen, this is clearly not true. The story of the revolutionaries is essential to understanding the INC itself. Indeed, as Subhas Bose demonstrated, they were capable of winning an open election for the Congress President even against Gandhi's explicit opposition.

The good news is that in recent years, there has been renewed interest in the history of the armed resistance. Long-forgotten revolutionaries have started popping up in social media and popular culture. In 2019, four of the last remaining INA veterans were driven down Raj Path as part of the Republic Day Parade. The Indian Navy celebrated the RIN revolt as a float at the annual event in 2022. It had taken the institution three-quarters of a century to get itself to do this. In January 2022, Prime Minister Narendra Modi announced that a statue of Subhas Bose would be erected under the canopy on Raj Path (now renamed Kartavya

Path). Anyone familiar with the place will realize the symbolic importance of this. Netaji, 'the Leader', will permanently stand, taking the salute to not just the National War Memorial but to all future Republic Day parades. He had said 'Dilli Chalo' in 1943, and has finally arrived at the heart of the Republic.

Jai Hind! Vande Mataram!

NOTES

1. THE AGE OF REVOLUTION

1. Uma Mukherjee, *Two Great Indian Revolutionaries*, Dey's Publishing, 2004.
2. *ibid*.
3. Sachindra Nath Sanyal, *Bandi Jeevan*, reprinted in Hindi by Sakshi Prakashan, 2015. Section translated by the author.
4. Vikram Sampath, *Savarkar: Echoes from a Forgotten Past, 1883–1924*, Penguin Viking, 2019.
5. *Subhas: A Political Biography*, Sitanshu Das, Rupa Publications 2006.
6. First verse of Rabindranath Tagore's *Shivaji Utsav* (A Celebration of Shivaji). Translated by the author.
7. Bhupendra Nath Sanyal, *Facets of Indian Politics* (Allahabad: Mahabir Prasad, 1945).
8. Peter Heehs, *The Lives of Sri Aurobindo*, Columbia University Press, 2008.
9. Author's translation.
10. *Speeches: On Politics and National Education*, Sri Aurobindo, 1922, reprinted in 2018 by Sri Aurobindo Ashram, Pondicherry.

11. *British Paramountcy and the Indian Renaissance, Vol. II*, edited by R.C. Majumdar, Bharatiya Vidya Bhawan, 1965 (reprinted 2018).
12. *Ibid.*
13. Vikram Sampath, *Savarkar: Echoes from a Forgotten Past 1883-1924*, Penguin Viking, 2019.
14. *British Paramountcy and the Indian Renaissance, Vol. II*, edited by R.C. Majumdar, Bharatiya Vidya Bhawan, 1965 (reprinted 2018).
15. Sugata Bose, *His Majesty's Opponent: Subhas Chandra Bose and India's Struggle against Empire*, Penguin India, 2011.
16. Chandrakant Lahariya, 'A Brief History of Vaccines and Vaccination in India', *Indian Journal of Medical Research*, April 2014.

2. BHAWANI MANDIR

1. Peter Heehs, *The Lives of Sri Aurobindo*, Columbia University Press, 2008.
2. Alastair Lawson, 'Indian maharajah's daring act of anti-colonial dissent', BBC News, 10 December 2011, https://www.bbc.com/news/world-asia-16051168
3. Sunil Raman and Rohit Agarwal, *Delhi Durbar 1911: The Complete Story*, Lotus, 2011.
4. *Ibid.*
5. Peter Heehs, *The Lives of Sri Aurobindo*, Columbia University Press, 2008.
6. *Ibid.*
7. Aurobindo Ghosh, 'Bhawani Mandir', 1905. For an online digital copy, see http://wiki.auroville.org.in/w/images/b/b7/Bhawani_Mandir.pdf
8. *Struggle for Freedom*, edited by R.C. Majumdar, Bharatiya Vidya Bhavan, 1969 (reprinted in 1979).
9. Note that these terms were used by Aurobindo Ghosh, although he saw it as a three-way division: nationalists (Lal–Bal–Pal and himself),

moderates (Dadabhai Naoroji and Surendranath Bannerjea) and Loyalists (G.K. Gokhale and Pherozeshah Mehta). The distinction between Loyalists and moderates became irrelevant after the latter sided with the former in 1907.
10. *Khudiram Bose vs Emperor*, Bench: Bell Ryves, Calcutta High Court, 13July 1908.
11. Sri Aurobindo, *Tales of Prison Life*, Sri Aurobindo Ashram, 1922 (reprinted in 2014).
12. Sri Aurobindo, *Speeches: On Indian Politics and National Education*, Sri Aurobindo Ashram Pondicherry, 1922 (reprinted in 2018).

3. INDIA HOUSE

1. Vikram Sampath, *Savarkar: Echoes from a Forgotten Past*, Penguin India, 2019.
2. Ibid.
3. Vaibhav Purandare, *Savarkar: The True Story of the Father of Hindutva*, Juggernaut Books, 2019.
4. Vikram Sampath, *Savarkar: Echoes from a Forgotten Past*, Penguin India, 2019.
5. Vinayak Savarkar, *The Indian War of Independence 1857*, 1909 (online digital copy from Columbia University Library).
6. Ibid.
7. Vikram Sampath, *Savarkar: Echoes from a Forgotten Past*, Penguin India, 2019.
8. As quoted in Vikram Sampath, *Savarkar: Echoes from a Forgotten Past*, Penguin India, 2019.
9. Ibid.
10. Ibid.
11. 'Vile Attack on Lord & Lady Minto', Press Association report, Calcutta, 15 November 1909(National Library of New Zealand,

online digital library, https://paperspast.natlib.govt.nz/newspapers/ESD19091116.2.49).

12. Prithwindra Mukherjee, *The Intellectual Roots of India's Freedom Struggle (1893-1918)*, Routledge, 2017.

13. Vikram Sampath, *Savarkar: Echoes from a Forgotten Past*, Penguin India, 2019.

4. THE GHADAR

1. As quoted in Vikram Sampath, *Savarkar: Echoes from a Forgotten Past*, Penguin India, 2019.
2. Uma Mukherjee, *Two Great Revolutionaries*, Dey's Publishing, 1966 (reprinted 2004).
3. Takeshi Nakajima, *Bose of Nakamuraya: An Indian Revolutionary in Japan*, translated from Japanese by Prem Motwani, Promilla & Co, 2005.
4. *Struggle for Freedom*, edited by R.C. Majumdar, Bharatiya Vidya Bhavan, 1969 (reprinted in 1979).
5. Uma Mukherjee, *Two Great Revolutionaries*, Dey's Publishing, 1966 (reprinted in 2004).
6. Dr Ashok Kumar Chatterjee, *Purana Purusha: Yogiraj Sri Shama Churn Lahiree: A Complete Biography*, Yogiraj Publications, 1981 (reprinted in 2014).
7. 'Reminiscences of Shri J.N. Mukherjee, J.N. Sanyal and Others', Commemorative brochure for the 90th year of Sachindra Nath Sanyal, 1983.
8. Harish K. Puri, *Ghadar Movement: A Short History*, National Book Trust, 2011.
9. *Ibid.*
10. As translated in Harish K. Puri, *Ghadar Movement: A Short History*, National Book Trust, 2011.

11. Harish K. Puri, *Ghadar Movement: A Short History*, National Book Trust, 2011.
12. Sachindra Nath Sanyal, *Bandi Jeevan*, reprinted in Hindi by Sakshi Prakashan, 2015.
13. Uma Mukherjee, *Two Great Revolutionaries*, Dey's Publishing, 1966 (reprinted in 2004).
14. M.M. Juneja, *Biography of Bhagat Singh*, Modern Publishers, 2016.
15. As quoted in Takeshi Nakajima, *Bose of Nakamuraya: An Indian Revolutionary in Japan*, translated from Japanese by Prem Motwani, Promilla & Co, 2005.
16. Harish K. Puri, *Ghadar Movement: A Short History*, National Book Trust, 2011.
17. Peter Hopkirk, *On Secret Service East of Constantinople: The Plot to Bring Down the British Empire*, John Murray, 1994.
18. Uma Mukherjee, *Two Great Revolutionaries*, Dey's Publishing, 1966 (reprinted in 2004).
19. Peter Hopkirk, *On Secret Service East of Constantinople: The Plot to Bring Down the British Empire*, John Murray, 1994.
20. Prithwindra Mukherjee, *Bagha Jatin: The Revolutionary Legacy*, Indus Source Books, 2015.
21. Richard James Popplewell, *Intelligence and Imperial Defence: British Intelligence and the Defence of the Indian Empire 1904-1924*, Routledge, 2018.
22. Peter Hopkirk, *On Secret Service East of Constantinople: The Plot to Bring Down the British Empire*, John Murray, 1994.
23. Savitri Sawhney, *I Shall Never Ask for Pardon: A Memoir of Pandurang Khankhoje*, Penguin India, 2004.
24. *Ibid*.
25. *Ibid*.
26. As quoted in Kishwar Desai, *Jallianwala Bagh, 1919: The Real Story*, Westland Books, 2018.

27. *The Congress Punjab Inquiry 1919-20*, Volume II, first published in 1920, reprinted by National Book Trust in 1996.

5: KALA PAANI

1. Barindra Kumar Ghosh, *The Tale of My Exile*, Sri Aurobindo Ashram, 1922 (reprinted in 2014).
2. Ibid.
3. Vikram Sampath, *Savarkar: Echoes from a Forgotten Past 1883-1924*, Penguin India, 2019.
4. Ibid.
5. As quoted in *Struggle for Freedom*, edited by R.C. Majumdar, Bharatiya Vidya Bhavan, 1969 (reprinted in 1979). This is part of *The History and Culture of the Indian People* series, Volume XI.
6. Kishwar Desai, *Jallianwala Bagh, 1919: The Real Story*, Westland Books, 2018.
7. Ibid.
8. Ibid.
9. *Struggle for Freedom*, edited by R.C. Majumdar, Bharatiya Vidya Bhavan, 1969 (reprinted in 1979). This is part of *The History and Culture of the Indian People* series, Volume XI.
10. *The Congress Punjab Inquiry 1919-1920*, Volume II, 1920 (reprinted by the National Book Trust in 1996).
11. *Struggle for Freedom*, edited by R.C. Majumdar, Bharatiya Vidya Bhavan, 1969 (reprinted in 1979). This is part of *The History and Culture of the Indian People* series, Volume XI.
12. Kishwar Desai, *Jallianwala Bagh 1919*, Westland Books, 2018. Also, Divya Goyal, 'Judging the Erstwhile Royals: An Unkind Cut or a Bitter Truth?', *The Indian Express*, 13 April 2019, https://indianexpress.com/article/india/jallianwala-bagh-judging-the-erstwhile-royals-an-unkind-cut-or-a-bitter-truth5673646/

13. *The Edinburgh Gazette, January 6, 1920*, https://www.thegazette.co.uk/Edinburgh/issue/13547/page/28/data.pdf
14. Sachindra Nath Sanyal, *Bandi Jeevan*, reprinted in Hindi by Sakshi Prakashan, 2015.
15. Peter Heehs, *The Lives of Sri Aurobindo*, Columbia University Press, 2008.
16. C. Gopalan Nair, *The Moplah Rebellion: 1921*, Norman Printing Bureau, 1923.
17. *Ibid.*
18. *Ibid.*
19. Sugata Bose, *His Majesty's Opponent*, Penguin India, 2011.
20. Subhas Chandra Bose, *The Indian Struggle (1920-1934)*, Abhishek Publications (reprinted in 2019).
21. *Ibid.*
22. *Ibid.*
23. *Ibid.*
24. *Ibid.*
25. Birth Centenary Brochure of Dr Nalinaksha Sanyal, published 1998.
26. Nalinaksha Sanyal, *Development of Indian Railways*, Calcutta University Press, 1930 (reprinted by National Railway Museum in 2007).
27. Takeshi Nakajima, *Bose of Nakamuraya: An Indian Revolutionary in Japan*, translated from Japanese by Prem Motwani, Promilla & Co, 2005.
28. *Ibid.*
29. *Ibid.*

6: THE HINDUSTAN REPUBLICAN ASSOCIATION

1. Sachindra Nath Sanyal, *Bandi Jeevan*, reprinted in Hindi by Sakshi Prakashan, 2015.

2. Jogesh Chandra Chatterjee, *In Search of Freedom*, published by Paresh Chandra Chatterjee, 1958 (printed by B.K. Majumdar, Calcutta).
3. Sachindra Nath Sanyal, *Bandi Jeevan*, reprinted in Hindi by Sakshi Prakashan, 2015.
4. Jogesh Chandra Chatterjee, *In Search of Freedom*, published by Paresh Chandra Chatterjee, 1958 (printed by B.K. Majumdar, Calcutta).
5. Sachindra Nath Sanyal, *Bandi Jeevan*, reprinted in Hindi by Sakshi Prakashan, 2015. Translation by the author.
6. Compiled from various sources, including K.V. Kurmanath, 'Alluri Seetha Rama Raju: A Folk Hero of Rampa Rebellion', Heroes of Freedom Struggle-2 series, Press Information Bureau, Government of India, 9 August 2016, https://pib.gov.in/newsite/printrelease.aspx?relid=148563
7. Sumit Bhattacharjee, 'Andhra Pradesh: Alluri Sitharama Raju was first to unite tribal muttas against British, say historians', *The Hindu*, 12 July 2022, https://www.thehindu.com/news/cities/Visakhapatnam/andhra-pradesh-alluri-sitharama-raju-was-first-to-unite-tribal-muttas-against-british-say-historians/article65626873.ece
8. Jogesh Chandra Chatterjee, *In Search of Freedom*, published by Paresh Chandra Chatterjee, 1958 (printed by B.K. Majumdar, Calcutta).
9. *Ibid.*
10. Dr C.P. Sharma, *The Builder of Modern India: Bhagat Singh*, Avishkar Prakashan, 2017.
11. Subhas Chandra Bose, *The Indian Struggle*, 1935 (reprinted by Abhishek Publications in 2019).
12. Nimaichand Pramanik, *Gandhi & the Revolutionaries*, University of Calcutta, 1982.
13. Dr C.P. Sharma, *The Builder of Modern India: Bhagat Singh*, Avishkar Prakashan, 2017.
14. As reproduced in Dr C.P. Sharma, *The Builder of Modern India: Bhagat Singh*, Avishkar Prakashan, 2017.

15. Ram Prasad Bismil, *The Revolutionary*, translated and edited by Saket Suryesh, Notion Press, 2020.
16. *Ibid.*
17. *Ibid.*
18. Dharmendra Gaur, *Krantivir Chandrashekhar Azad Aur Unke Do Gaddar Sathi*, reprinted by Bhagat Singh Vichar Manch, Sakshi Prakashan, 2016 (in Hindi).
19. *Ibid.*
20. *Ibid.*
21. Ram Prasad Bismil, *The Revolutionary*, translated and edited by Saket Suryesh, Notion Press, 2020.
22. Rabindranath Sanyal, *Reminiscences of Rabindra Nath Sanyal: Essays written in memory of Shahid Sachindra Nath Sanyal*, 1983.
23. Jogesh Chandra Chatterjee, *In Search of Freedom*, published by Paresh Chandra Chatterjee, 1958 (printed by B.K. Majumdar, Calcutta).
24. Ram Prasad Bismil, *The Revolutionary*, translated and edited by Saket Suryesh, Notion Press, 2020.
25. *Struggle for Freedom*, edited by R.C. Majumdar, Bharatiya Vidya Bhavan, 1969 (reprinted in 1979).
26. Dharmendra Gaur, *Krantivir Chandrashekhar Azad Aur Unke Do Gaddar Sathi*, reprinted by Bhagat Singh Vichar Manch, Sakshi Prakashan, 2016 (in Hindi).
27. *Ibid.*
28. Jitendra Nath Sanyal, *Bhagat Singh: A Biography*, reprinted by Hope India Publications, 2014.
29. Sachindra Nath Sanyal, *Vichar Vinimay*, edited by Sudhir Vidyarthi, reprinted by National Book Trust in 2019 (in Hindi).
30. Subhas Chandra Bose, *The Indian Struggle*, 1935 (reprinted by Abhishek Publications in 2019).
31. *Struggle for Freedom*, edited by R.C. Majumdar, Bharatiya Vidya Bhavan, 1969 (reprinted in 1979).

32. Multiple sources, including Kuldip Nayar, *Without Fear: The Life and Trial of Bhagat Singh*, HarperCollins Publishers India, 2012; Dharmendra Gaur, *Krantivir Chandrashekhar Azad Aur Unke Do Gaddar Sathi*, reprinted by Bhagat Singh Vichar Manch, Sakshi Prakashan, 2016 (in Hindi); and Jitendra Nath Sanyal, *Bhagat Singh: A Biography*, reprinted by Hope India Publications, 2014.

33. Kuldip Nayar, *Without Fear: The Life and Trial of Bhagat Singh*, HarperCollins Publishers India, 2012.

34. Kama Maclean, *A Revolutionary History of Interwar India*, Penguin India, 2015.

35. *Ibid*.

36. Jitendra Nath Sanyal, *Bhagat Singh: A Biography*, reprinted by Hope India Publications, 2014.

37. Kuldip Nayar, *Without Fear: The Life and Trial of Bhagat Singh*, HarperCollins Publishers India, 2012.

38. As reproduced in Dr C.P. Sharma, *The Builder of Modern India: Bhagat Singh*, Avishkar Prakashan, 2017.

39. Multiple sources, including Kuldip Nayar, *Without Fear: The Life and Trial of Bhagat Singh*, HarperCollins Publishers India, 2012; and Jitendra Nath Sanyal, *Bhagat Singh: A Biography*, reprinted by Hope India Publications, 2014.

40. Subhas Chandra Bose, *The Indian Struggle*, 1935 (reprinted by Abhishek Publications in 2019).

41. Anirudh Gupta, 'Nationalism's forgotten corner', *The Tribune*, 14 August 2018, https://www.tribuneindia.com/news/archive/punjab/nationalism-s-forgotten-corner-637570

42. Kama Maclean, *A Revolutionary History of Interwar India*, Penguin India, 2015.

43. As an aside, the niece's son, Shyamal Dev Goswamy, would be awarded the Mahavir Chakra for bravery during the Indo-China War of 1962.

44. Multiple sources, including Dharmendra Gaur, *Krantivir Chandrashekhar Azad Aur Unke Do Gaddar Sathi*, reprinted by Bhagat Singh Vichar Manch, Sakshi Prakashan, 2016 (in Hindi); Kama Maclean, *A Revolutionary History of Interwar India*, Penguin India, 2015; and Sanyal family oral history related to the author.
45. Dharmendra Gaur, *Krantivir Chandrashekhar Azad Aur Unke Do Gaddar Sathi*, reprinted by Bhagat Singh Vichar Manch, Sakshi Prakashan, 2016 (in Hindi).
46. Dharmendra Gaur, *Krantivir Chandrashekhar Azad Aur Unke Do Gaddar Sathi*, reprinted by Bhagat Singh Vichar Manch, Sakshi Prakashan, 2016 (in Hindi). Also, 'She fought for Independence at the tender age of 17', *Hindustan Times* (Lucknow), 4 February 2014, https://www.pressreader.com/india/hindustan-times-lucknow/20140204/281616713252343

7: CHITTAGONG

1. Multiple sources, including Uma Mukherjee, *Two Great Revolutionaries*, Dey's Publishing, 2004; Subodh Roy, *Chittagong Armory Raid: A Memoir*, LeftWord, 2015; Jalad Baran Das, *Hijli Detention Camp to IIT: An Untold Saga*, Nehru Museum of Science & Technology, 2009.
2. Subodh Roy, *Chittagong Armory Raid: A Memoir*, LeftWord, 2015.
3. *Ibid*.
4. Sugata Bose, *His Majesty's Opponent*, Penguin India, 2013.
5. Jalad Baran Das, *Hijli Detention Camp to IIT: An Untold Saga*, Nehru Museum of Science & Technology, 2009.
6. *Ibid*.
7. Dr. Nalinaksha Sanyal, birth centenary brochure, 1998.
8. *Selected Works of M.N. Roy Volume I: 1917-1922*, edited by Sibnarayan Ray, Oxford University Press, 1987.

9. Peter Hopkirk, *Setting the East Ablaze: Lenin's Dream of an Empire in Asia*, John Murray, 1984.
10. *Ibid.*
11. *Selected Works of M.N. Roy Volume I: 1917-1922*, edited by Sibnarayan Ray, Oxford University Press, 1987.
12. Subodh Roy, *Chittagong Armory Raid: A Memoir*, LeftWord, 2015.
13. *Ibid.*
14. *Selected Works of M.N. Roy Volume I: 1917-1922*, edited by Sibnarayan Ray, Oxford University Press, 1987.
15. Nilanjan Mukhopadhyay, *The RSS: Icons of the Indian Right*, Tranquebar, 2019.
16. *Ibid.*
17. Chandrachur Ghose, *Bose: The Untold Story of an Inconvenient Nationalist*, Penguin Random House India, 2022.
18. *Ibid.*
19. Subhas Chandra Bose, *The Indian Struggle, 1935* (reprinted by Abhishek Publications in 2019).
20. *Ibid.*
21. *Ibid.*
22. As quoted in Sitanshu Das, *Subhas: A Political Biography*, Rupa Publications India, 2001.
23. Sugata Bose, *His Majesty's Opponent*, Penguin India, 2013.
24. Chandrachur Ghose, *Bose: The Untold Story of an Inconvenient Nationalist*, Penguin Random House India, 2022.
25. *Ibid.*
26. *Ibid.*
27. *Ibid.*
28. Nimaichand Pramanik, *Gandhi and the Revolutionaries*, University of Calcutta, 1982.

29. Sitanshu Das, *Subhas: A Political Biography*, Rupa Publications India, 2001.
30. *Ibid.*
31. Nimaichand Pramanik, *Gandhi and the Revolutionaries*, University of Calcutta, 1982.
32. *Ibid.*
33. Jogesh Chandra Chatterjee, *In Search of Freedom*, published by Paresh Chandra Chatterjee, 1958 (printed by B.K. Majumdar, Calcutta).
34. As quoted in Nimaichand Pramanik, *Gandhi and the Revolutionaries*, University of Calcutta, 1982.
35. Chandrachur Ghose, *Bose: The Untold Story of an Inconvenient Nationalist*, Penguin Random House India, 2022.
36. Sikandar Singh, *Udham Singh: A Saga of the Freedom Movement and Jallianwala Bagh*, B. Chattar Singh Jiwan Singh, Amritsar, 2017 edition.
37. *Ibid.*
38. *Ibid.*

8: 'ONE MORE FIGHT. THE LAST AND THE BEST'

1. *Struggle for Freedom*, edited by R.C. Majumdar, Bharatiya Vidya Bhavan, 1969 (reprinted in 1979).
2. *Ibid.*
3. *Ibid.*
4. Jogesh Chandra Chatterjee, *In Search of Freedom*, published by Paresh Chandra Chatterjee, 1958 (printed by B.K. Majumdar, Calcutta).
5. *Ibid.*
6. 'Reminiscences of Shri J.N. Mukherjee, J.N. Sanyal and Others', Commemorative brochure for the 90th year of Sachindra Nath Sanyal, 1983.

7. Sugata Bose, *His Majesty's Opponent*, Penguin India, 2013.
8. Ibid.
9. Ibid.
10. As quoted in *Struggle for Freedom*, edited by R.C. Majumdar, Bharatiya Vidya Bhavan, 1969 (reprinted in 1979).
11. *Sri Aurobindo and the Cripps Mission*, edited by Sunayana Panda, Sri Aurobindo Ashram Press, 2012.
12. Sitanshu Das, *Subhas: A Political Biography*, Rupa Publications India, 2001.
13. Takeshi Nakajima, *Bose of Nakamuraya: An Indian Revolutionary in Japan*, translated from Japanese by Prem Motwani, Promilla & Co., 2005.
14. Ibid.
15. Cemil Aydin, 'Japan's Pan-Asianism and the Legitimacy of Imperial World Order, 1931-1945', *The Asia-Pacific Journal*, Vol. 6, Issue 3, 3 March 2008.
16. The Sanyal family has loaned most of the letters to the Biplobi Bharat Museum at Victoria Memorial, Kolkata, and to the Nehru Memorial Library, Delhi.
17. As quoted in *Struggle for Freedom*, edited by R.C. Majumdar, Bharatiya Vidya Bhavan, 1969 (reprinted in 1978).
18. Takeshi Nakajima, *Bose of Nakamuraya: An Indian Revolutionary in Japan*, translated from Japanese by Prem Motwani, Promilla & Co., 2005.
19. Sugata Bose, *His Majesty's Opponent*, Penguin India, 2013.
20. Sitanshu Das, *Subhas: A Political Biography*, Rupa Publications India, 2001.
21. John Jacob and Harindra Srivastava, *Netaji Subhas: The Tallest of Titans (But Betrayed and Belittled)*, Ess Ess Publications, 2000.
22. Ibid.
23. Ibid.

24. As quoted in Sugata Bose, *His Majesty's Opponent*, Penguin India, 2013.
25. John Jacob and Harindra Srivastava, *Netaji Subhas: The Tallest of Titans (But Betrayed and Belittled)*, Ess Ess Publications, 2000.
26. Dr Syamaprasad Mookerjee, *Eminent Parliamentarians Monograph Series*, Lok Sabha Secretariat, 1990.
27. *Struggle for Freedom*, edited by R.C. Majumdar, Bharatiya Vidya Bhavan, 1969 (reprinted in 1978).
28. *The Indian Annual Register, July-December 1943, Vol II*, Annual Register Office, Calcutta.
29. Madhusree Mukerjee, *Churchill's Secret War: The British Empire and the Ravaging of India during World War II*, Penguin India, 2010.
30. Ibid.
31. Ibid.
32. Bikramjit De, 'Imperial Governance and the Challenges of War: Management of Food Supplies in Bengal, 1943-44', *Studies in History*, Sage Publications, 2006.
33. As quoted in *The Indian Annual Register, July-December 1943, Vol II*, Annual Register Office, Calcutta.
34. Madhusree Mukerjee, *Churchill's Secret War: The British Empire and the Ravaging of India during World War II*, Penguin India, 2010.
35. Ibid.
36. Ibid.
37. Jonathan Freedland, *Eugenics: The Skeleton That Rattles Loudest in the Left's Closet*, The Guardian, 18 February 2012, https://www.theguardian.com/commentisfree/2012/feb/17/eugenics-skeleton-rattles-loudest-closet-left
38. Sugata Bose, *His Majesty's Opponent*, Penguin India, 2013.
39. John Jacob and Harindra Srivastava, *Netaji Subhas: The Tallest of Titans (But Betrayed and Belittled)*, Ess Ess Publications, 2000.

40. Subodh Roy, *Chittagong Armory Raid: A Memoir*, LeftWord, 2015.
41. Sugata Bose, *His Majesty's Opponent*, Penguin India, 2013.
42. *INA and Manipur: An Unforgettable Battle for India's Independence*, edited by Shukhdeba Sharma Hanjabam and Aheibam Koireng Singh, Intellectual Forum of North-East, 2021.
43. *Ibid.*
44. Hemanta Kumar Nath, 'Ruzhazo: Nagaland Governor Ravi visits village that was the first to get "independence"', *India Today*, 10 September 2021, https://www.indiatoday.in/india/story/ruzhazo-nagaland-governor-ravi-visits-village-that-was-the-first-to-get-independence-1851496-2021-09-10
45. Sugata Bose, *His Majesty's Opponent*, Penguin India, 2013.
46. L.C. Green, *The Indian National Army Trials*, Modern Law Review, January 1948.
47. *Ibid.*
48. *Ibid.*
49. This section has relied on a number of sources, including Lt Cdr G.D. Sharma, *Untold Story: 1946 Naval Mutiny: Last War of Independence*, Vij Books, 2015; Pramod Kapoor, *1946: Last War of Independence*, Roli Books, 2022; and contemporary news reports.
50. Lt Cdr G.D. Sharma, *Untold Story: 1946 Naval Mutiny: Last War of Independence*, Vij Books, 2015.
51. Pramod Kapoor, *1946: Last War of Independence*, Roli Books, 2022.
52. As quoted in Lt Cdr G.D. Sharma *Untold Story: 1946 Naval Mutiny: Last War of Independence*, Vij Books, 2015.
53. Pramod Kapoor, *1946: Last War of Independence*, Roli Books, 2022.
54. *Ibid.*
55. 'British Troops Fire on Cairo Crowds', *Dawn*, Delhi edition, 22 February 1946.
56. Chandrachur Ghose, *Bose: The Untold Story of an Inconvenient Nationalist*, Penguin Random House India, 2022.

EPILOGUE

1. Birth Centenary Brochure of Nalinaksha Sanyal, October 1987.
2. Vikram Sampath, *Savarkar: A Contested Legacy, 1924-66*, Penguin Random House India, 2021.
3. *Ibid.*
4. *Statistical Report on General Elections 1957 to the Second Lok Sabha*, Election Commission of India.
5. Savitri Sawhney, *I Shall Never Ask for Pardon: A Memoir of Pandurang Khankhoje*, Penguin India, 2005.
6. *Ibid.*
7. Pramod Kapoor, *1946: Last War of Independence*, Roli Books, 2022.
8. *Ibid.*
9. Kuldip Nayar, *Without Fear: The Life and Trial of Bhagat Singh*, HarperCollins Publishers India, 2012.
10. Dharmendra Gaur, *Krantivir Chandrashekhar Azad Aur Unke Do Gaddar Sathi*, reprinted by Bhagat Singh Vichar Manch, Sakshi Prakashan, 2016 (in Hindi). Also, 'She Fought for Independence at the Tender Age of 17', *Hindustan Times,* Lucknow, 4 February 2014, https://www.pressreader.com/india/hindustan-times-lucknow/20140204/281616713252343
11. Fifth Lok Sabha, Members Bioprofile, Shri Shah Nawaz Khan, http://loksabhaph.nic.in/writereaddata/biodata_1_12/792.htm
12. Deep Halder, *Blood Island: An Oral History of the Marichjhapi Massacre*, HarperCollins Publishers India, 2019.
13. Ratan Sharda, *The Sangh & Swaraj: Role of RSS in Freedom Struggle*, Prabhat Paperbacks, 2020.
14. Aurobindo Ghosh, *Bhawani Mandir*, underground pamphlet published in 1905.
15. Jogesh Chandra Chatterjee, *In Search of Freedom*, published by Paresh Chandra Chatterjee, 1958 (printed by B.K. Majumdar, Calcutta).

INDEX

Abbas, Mirza, 64
Abhinav Bharat, 51–54, 57, 62–64, 68–69
Adi-Shakti, 16, 35
Afghanistan, 110–11, 213, 238, 246
Ahmedabad, 69, 131, 287
Aiyar, Varahaneri Venkatesa Subramaniam, 57–58, 60–62, 72
Alexandra Parsi Girls' School, 58
Alfred park, 200–203
Ali, Daud, 115
Ali, Mirza Muhammad, 115
Aligarh Movement, 15–16
Alipore
  Bomb Case, 104–5
  Bomb Trials, 45
  Central Jail, 45, 208
  trials of 1908-09, 146
Allahabad Students' Association, 202
Alliance Bank, 132
All India Congress Committee, 217
All India Radio, 249
All India Students Conference, 153
Almora Jail, 151
Ambedkar, B.R., 29, 288–89
Amin, Chaturbhuj, 64
Amritsar, 58, 68, 95, 131, 133–34, 136–37, 195, 235–36, 239
Ananda Math, 33
Anarchical and Revolutionary Crimes Act, 130
Andaman and Nicobar Islands, 123, 269. *See also* Kala Paani
'*Angrezi Raj ka Dushman* (Enemy of the British Rule),' 89
Annie Larsen (ship), 106

anti-British literature, 177–78
Anushilan Marxists, 230, 233, 242–43, 304
Anushilan Samiti, 32–41, 48, 54, 69, 96, 114, 161, 165, 167, 221, 234–35
    attacks on British officials, 46
    in Bengal, 161, 180, 205, 211–12
    branches, 35, 38–39, 81, 95
    Dacca, 85, 95–96
    leaderless, 104–5
    in Murshidabad, 152
    in Nagpur, 219
    network, 161–62
    Rashbehari activities, 75, 77
    set up, 34
Arya Samaj
    Devanagari script and, 76
    Hindu reform movement, 54–55
    movement, 85, 182
    rise, 15–16, 172
    Sikhs and, 76
    temple, 189–90
Assam Rifles, 166
Ataturk, Kemal, 145, 213
Attlee, Clement, 286
Auchinleck, Marshal Claude, 279, 281
Ayer, S.A., 268
Ayerst, Charles, 23

Azad, Chandrashekhar, 5, 175, 180, 187, 211
Azad, Maulana Abul Kalam, 228–29, 249
Azad Hind Fauj, 253
Azad Hindi, 280–81, 283
Azad Hind Radio, 256
Azad Park, 202–3

Babarao (Ganesh), 50, 52, 54, 56, 62, 64–65, 69
Badhwar Park in Colaba, 283
Bahadur, Banda, 12
Bailey, Frederick, 213
Baisakhi, 134, 137
Bajaj, Jamnalal, 229
Bakshi, Sachindra Nath, 168
Baliram, Keshav, 218
Balraj, 188
Bambatha Rebellion of 1906, 64
Banaras Hindu University (BHU), 140, 250
Bande Mataram, 39, 43, 46–47, 87, 194
Bandhav Samaj, 113
Bandi Jeevan, 6, 94, 139, 163, 183–84, 289
Banerji, Jatindranath, 33
Bannerjea, Surendranath, 20, 35, 40
Bapat, Pandurang, 42, 57, 64
Baptista, Joseph, 17
Barkatullah, Maulana, 111–12

Baroda, 30, 32, 34
Barrie, David, 125
Basu, Benoy, 208
Battle of Alfred park, 200–203
Behrampur Jail, 155, 177
Bengal/Bengali
   agitation, 38
   Anushilan Samiti in, 161, 180, 205, 211–12
   Aurobindo trip to, 33–34
   elite, 83
   Famine, 261–67
   Hindu community, 37, 227
   and Maharashtra revolutionaries, 69
   revolutionaries, 97–98, 184
   volunteers, 269–70
Bengali Tola Intercollege, 180
Benoy–Badal–Dinesh Bagh, 208
Bentham, Jeremy, 124
Berhampur, 168, 204
Berlin India Committee, 102–3, 110–11, 115, 118–19, 155
Besant, Annie, 142
Bey, Casim, 111
'bhadralok,' 42
Bhagawad Gita, 35, 100, 179, 244
Bhanumati, 55
Bharat Mata, 16, 53, 84, 308
Bhattacharya, Madhusudhan, 108
Bhattacharya, Narendra Nath, 2, 106, 211–12
Bhawani Bharati, 36

Bhawani Mandir, 25–49
   Anushilan Samiti, 32–41
   Aurobindo's discovery of India, 30–32
   garden house, 41–47
   saint of Pondicherry, 47–49
Birla, Ghanshyam Das, 3
Birmingham, London, 1
Birsa Munda, 5, 51
Bishop of Lahore, 138
Bismil, Ram Prasad, 167–69, 172, 176, 178–79, 196
Black Dragon Society, 12
'Black Waters,' 124
Bodh Gaya, 11–12
Boer Wars, 145
Bolshevik Revolution, 17–18, 118
Bombay, 9, 19, 22, 31, 54–56, 58, 64, 73, 90, 148, 181, 226, 279, 281, 285–88
Bombay Marine, 279
Bombay's Wilson College, 54
bomb-making, 42–43
Bonnerjee, Womesh Chander, 20
Borodin, Michael, 212
Bose, Ananda Mohan, 37
Bose, Janakinath, 146
Bose, Khudiram, 43
Bose, Mrinalini, 32
Bose, Rashbehari, 4–5, 12, 40, 63, 94–96, 114, 169, 228, 233, 243, 251–53, 268–69, 274, 286
Bose, Satish Chandra, 33

Bose, Satyen, 45
Bose, Subhas Chandra, 7, 97, 146, 163, 185, 196, 199, 209, 216, 227, 231, 234, 244, 246–47, 255, 257–59, 266–68, 270, 273–75, 277, 280, 287
Bose brothers, 232
'Bose of Nakamuraya,' 159
'bourgeois-led' freedom struggle, 217
Bradley, Benjamin, 215, 217
Brahmoism, 32
Brahmo Samaj, 14, 25
British- and missionary-controlled institutions, 39
British authorities, 18–19, 48, 90, 130, 177, 237, 242, 280, 286
British colonial establishment, 266–67
British colonial rule, 249
British Columbia, 84, 86, 91–92, 299–300
British Empire, 1, 6, 17, 34, 92, 103, 109, 112, 170, 179, 186, 219, 226, 257
British Expeditionary Force, 240
British hegemony, 41
British Indian Army, 61–62, 65, 85, 93–94, 111, 268
British intelligence, 18–19, 39, 62, 85, 93, 97–98, 104, 107, 234, 247, 270

British Labour Party, 59
Brixton prison, 71, 239
Burma, 76, 103, 262, 264, 266, 268–70, 273–74, 278
Burmese Buddhists, 270

Calcutta, 1, 9, 37, 43, 92, 105, 139, 146, 149, 264–65
Calcutta Chemicals, 38
Calcutta Municipal Corporation, 232
Calcutta University, 153, 210
Cama, Bhikaji, 17, 56–58, 63, 69, 72
Cambridge, 27–28, 31, 147–48, 217
Carlyle, Thomas, 8
Cellular Jail in Port Blair, 47, 65, 73, 100–103, 124–29, 141, 150–51, 215, 230, 289
Central Legislative Assembly, 191–92
Chaki, Prafulla, 43, 46
Chakraborty, Trailokyanath, 234–35
Chakravartti, Phani Bhushan, 289
Chakravarty, Chandra Kanta, 108
Chakravarty, Keshab, 175
Chalo Dilli, 255–61
Chand, Amir, 76–77, 79, 91
Chand, Mahasha Rattan, 131

Chand, Rattan, 131, 133
Chandernagore, 48, 75, 77, 80, 82, 96, 99, 105, 169
Chandni Chowk, 91
  1912, 75–82
  bombing, 82, 91, 94
Chandra, Ram, 106
Chapekar, Balakrishna Hari, 23
Chapekar, Damodar Hari, 23–24, 50, 52
Chapekar, Vasudev, 23
Chapekar brothers, 51–52
Charagh Din, 283
Charan, Bhagwati, 189, 192–93, 197–99
Chartered Bank, 132
Chatterjee, Amarendra Nath, 152
Chatterjee, Basanta, 108–9
Chatterjee, Jogesh Chandra, 161–62, 167, 169, 177–79, 230, 233–34, 242–43
Chatterjee, Sarat Chandra, 182
Chattopadhyay, Bankim Chandra, 16, 20, 33
Chattopadhyay, Virendranath, 57, 102–3, 226
Chauri Chaura incident, 164
Chinese revolutionaries, 114
Chiplunkar, Bhaurao, 52
Chittagong, 165, 204–39, 266, 270
  armoury raid, 205–11
  avenging Jallianwala, 235–39

  preparing for second Ghadar, 233–35
  rebel president, 222–32
  Roy, Manabendra Nath, 211–18
  RSS, founding, 218–22
Christianity, 83
Christian missionaries, 57–58
Chuchura, Bengal, 128
Chuharkana, 120
Churchill, Winston, 68, 71, 248, 266
Church Missionary Society's Girls Normal School, 132
civil disobedience, 223–24
Civil Disobedience Movement, 219–20
Clinique La Lignière, 223
Colonelgunj neighbourhood, 200
colonial administration, 73, 83
colonial-era narratives, 14
Communism, 17–18, 183, 224–25
Communist International, 216
Communist Party of Great Britain, 217
Communist Party of India (CPI), 211, 213, 215–16, 229–30, 242, 287
Communist Party of Mexico, 212
Complex Adaptive System, 8
Congress and Muslim League flags, 284

Congress Socialist Party (CSP), 229, 231
Congress Working Committee, 249–50
Cripps Mission, 249–50

Dacca Anushilan Samiti, 85, 95–96
Dacca-Barisal group, 161
Daily News, 67
Daily Telegraph, The, 59
Dakshineshwar Kali temple, 15, 80, 105, 168, 177–78
Dane, Luis, 238
Danish colony, 123
Darjeeling, 3, 26, 104–5
Das, Beni Madhab, 210
Das, Bina, 210
Das, Chittaranjan, 46, 142, 146, 148–49, 160, 163, 187
Das, C.R., 222, 229
Das, Hemchandra, 42, 64
Das, Jatindra Nath, 168, 190, 196, 244
Das, Lala Sundar, 135–36
Das, Ram Saran, 190–91
Das, Sitanshu, 226
Das, Taraknath, 85–86, 118
Dashashwamedha Ghat, 168
Dasi, Sabitri, 262–63
Davoy, John, 55
Dayanand Anglo Vedic (DAV) College, 187–88

death penalty, 124
Deccan College, 52–53
Defence of India Act, 130, 153
Delhi Durbar of 1911, 30
'Denial Policy,' 263–64, 271
Deoghar, 31
Deoli detention camp, 243
Deshpande, K.G., 31, 36
Devanagari script, 76
Devi, Basanti, 187
Devi, Durga, 187, 189, 192, 199
Devi, Ratan, 135
Dhanbad, 246
Dhar, Bhujang Bhushan, 3
Dhingra, Madanlal, 57–58, 65–68
Dhoradaha, 152
Dhun, Krishna, 26, 28
dialectic materialism, 184
Diamond Jubilee of Queen Victoria, 23
Diwan, Khalsa, 119, 235
Dongri Jail, 73
Don Quixote, 62
Dora, Ghantam, 166
Dora, Mallu, 166
Douglas Kingsford, 43
Doulatram, Jairamdas, 229
'Down with the Imperialists,' 281
Dreamland, 190
Drewett, Reverend William, 26
Durga, 16, 35, 151, 228, 293–94
Dutch colonial rule, 251–52
Dutch East Indies, 103–4

Dutt, Balai Chandra, 281–83
Dutt, Batukeshwar, 190–92, 198–99
Dutt, Kanailal, 45
Dutt, Rajni Palme, 250
Dutt, Ullaskar, 47, 125, 127–28
Dutt, Utpal, 290
Dutta, Bhupendra Nath, 39, 89
Dutta, Haridas, 2
Dutta, Pramath Nath, 110
Dutta, Ullaskar, 43
Dyer, Reginald, 112–13, 133, 136, 138, 237
Dyer Appreciation Fund, 138

East Bengal, 37
Easter Rebellion, 204–5
East India Company, 22, 28–29, 32–33, 83, 123, 285
East Persian Cordon, 111–13, 133
Eka Movement, 163
Emergency (Indira Gandhi's), 231
Emperor versus Aurobindo Ghosh & Others, 45
English Channel, 56
English-language newspapers, 138
English Theism, 32
Epidemic Diseases Act, 1897, 22–23
'extremists,' 39–40

Faiz, Faiz Ahmad, 188

Famine Code of 1883, 265
Fascism, 224, 241, 251–52
Fergusson College, 52–54, 56
Fern, W.J.C., 188
Ferozepore military camp, 98
Festival of Shivaji, 12–13
First World War, 64, 93–94, 115, 129–30, 211
Fraser, Andrew, 43
Free Hindustan, 85–86
Free India Centre, 256–57
Free Press Journal, 284
French Resistance, 171
French Revolution, 10, 269
Frontier Mail, 246
Fujiwara, Iwaichi, 253
Fukuyama, Francis, 224–25

Gaekwad, Sayaji, 28–29, 31, 36–37
Ganapati festival, 21
Gandhi, Mohandas Karamchand, 4, 38, 63, 122, 131, 219–20
Gandhi's non-violent approach, 161
Ganganath Bharatiya Vidyalaya, 36
Ganguly, Pratul Chandra, 152, 167–68
Garewal, B.J.S., 273
Garibaldi, Giuseppe, 10
Gerlick, J.J., 209
Gaur, Dharmendra, 203

George, David Lloyd, 68, 149
German-American associates, 118
Germany, 6, 62, 94, 110, 118, 175, 225, 240, 247, 255, 259, 269
Ghadar, The, 89–91
Ghadar/Ghadarite(s), 91, 97
    Chandni Chowk 1912, 75–82
    community, 211–12
    February plan, 94–101
    Hindu–German trials, 117–19
    Jatin, Tiger, 104–9
    and Jugantar revolutionaries, 165
    Kabul Mission, 109–13
    Komagata Maru incident, 91–94
    loyalists during war, 119–22
    Persian Campaign, 113–17
    revolt, 167
    Siam scheme and Christmas day plot, 101–4
    Sikhs in North America, 83–86
    Yugantar Ashram, 86–91
Ghadar Movement, 53, 114–15, 149
Ghadar Party, 91, 118
Ghosh, Aurobindo, 6–7, 16–17, 24–27, 29, 39–42, 54, 87, 95, 104, 143, 147–48, 169, 185, 211–12, 289
    Alipore trials of 1908-09, 146
    in Anushilan Samiti, 35
    in Cambridge, 27, 147–48
    India discovery, 30–32
    in jail, 45
    National College in Calcutta, 39
    revolutionaries generation, 10
    saint of Pondicherry, 47–49, 80
    as spiritual guru, 249
    trip to Bengal, 33–34
    Uttarpara speech of 1909, 17
    vice principal of Baroda College, 36–37
    writings in *Bande Mataram*, 46
Ghosh, Barin, 26, 35, 38–40, 42, 44, 47, 64, 69, 95, 103, 125, 139, 211–12
Ghosh, Ganesh, 206
Ghosh, Krishna Dhun, 25
Ghosh, Prafulla Chandra, 232
Ghosh, Rashbehari, 40–41, 98, 100–101, 105, 156–58
Ghosh, Sirish, 169
Gill, N.S., 254
Goddess
    Adi-Shakti, 35
    Bharat Mata, 16
    Bhawani, 24, 35–36
    Kali, 35–36, 244, 263
Gokhale, Gopal Krishna, 40, 66

Golden Temple, 134, 138, 236
Gomoh railway station, 246
Gopal, Jai, 188, 195, 203
Gopal, Nani, 128–29
Gorakhpur, 140, 145, 179, 243
Goswami, Narendranath, 45
Government of India Act of 1919, 185
Great Calcutta Killings, 292
Great Charter of the Proclamation of 1858, 20
Great Famine of 1877, 50
Great Revolt of 1857-58, 5
Gujaranwala, 120
Gupta, Badal, 208
Gupta, Dinesh, 209
Gupta, Heramba Lal, 155
Gupta, Jogendra, 108–9
Gurkha and Baloch soldiers, 286
Guru Gobind scholarships, 88
Guru Granth Sahib, 93

Habibullah, Amir, 111–12
Haider, Agha, 197
Hamilton, Lord George, 65
Haque, Mazharul, 130
Hardayal, Lala, 57, 63, 83, 86–87
Hardinge, Charles, 77–80, 112
Hasan, Abid, 258
Hatta, Mohammed, 251
Hedgewar, Keshav Baliram, 113–14, 218, 220, 234

Herbert, John, 261
Hijli Detention Camp, 208–9
Hijli incident, 222
Himmatsinka, Prabhu Dayal, 2
Hindu/Hinduism, 55, 57–58
    nationalism, 230
    reform movement, 25, 54–55
    revivalism, 183–84
    revolutionaries, 125
Hindu–German Conspiracy trials, 118
Hindu–German trials, 117–19
Hindu Mahasabha, 221, 230
Hindu–Muslim riot, 200
Hindu–Muslim unity, 14, 131
Hindu–Sikh imagination, 17
Hindustan Park (near Gariahat), 210
Hindustan Republican Army, 11, 167
Hindustan Republican Association (HRA), 11, 166, 167, 169–170, 174, 176–177, 180–183, 190, 205

Hindustan Socialist Republican Association (HSRA), 185, 188, 194–195, 197, 200, 203, 205, 230, 235, 302

Hindustan Times, 193–94
Hindu symbolism, 16

Hiroshima, 274–75
History of the Sikhs, 69–70
Hitler, Herr, 225–26, 259
Home Rule League, 122
Hong Kong, 91, 97, 99–100, 156
Hopkinson, William, 85–86
Howrah, 47, 196, 209
Huq, Fazlul, 227, 261
Hyderabad, 30, 51

Ideals of the East, 12
ideological drift, 217–18
Imperial Art Museum, 11–12
Imperial Institute, 63–68
Imperial Legislative Council, 130
Imperial War Fund, 120
India/Indian
   communism, 18
   community of London, 66
   freedom movement, 255
   industrialization of, 225
   and Irish revolutionaries, 11
   migrants, 84–85
   nationalism, 139
   revolutionaries, 12, 71, 171
   revolutionary movement, 9
   student community, 62
India Home Rule League in 1916, 122
India House
   1857 book, 61–63
   Abhinav Bharat, 51–54
   duels with Scotland Yard, 57–61
   Imperial Institute, 63–68
   Indian sociologist, 54–57
   London, 55–56, 58
   SS *Morea,* 68–73
Indian Civil Service (ICS), 19, 26–27, 147
Indian Committee for National Independence, 102
Indian Councils Act, 74
Indian Evidence Act, 130
Indian Imperial Police service, 286–87
Indian Independence League (IIL), 251–54
Indian Institute of Technology in Kharagpur, 208–9
'Indian Legion,' 256
Indian National Army (INA), 119, 253, 269–70, 275–79
Indian National Congress (INC), 4, 19–20, 54, 121
Indian Ocean, 123
Indian Republican Army, 205, 216
Indian Sociologist, 55
Indian Struggle, The, 148, 223
Indian Tea & Provisions, 38
Indian War of Independence of 1857, The, 13–14, 61
India Office Crime Branch in London, 57

Indic civilization, 47–48
Indo–Japanese forces, 272
Indu Prakash, 31
In Search of Freedom, 161–62
International Socialist Congress
  in Stuttgart, 59
Ireland/Irish, 34, 166–67
  independence, 204
  nationalism, 5, 183–84
  nationalists, 63, 86, 109
  proclamation of
    independence, 268
  revolutionaries, 71, 226
  War of Independence, 9
Irish Republican Army, 11, 167, 205
Irish Republican Party, 55
Islam, Kazi Nazrul, 155
Islamic conquest of India, 242
Ispahani Company, 264
Istanbul, 109–11, 115, 247
Iyer, Duraiswami, 249

Jackson, Arthur, 69
Jackson, Stanley, 151, 210
Jadavpur University, 39
Jallianwala Bagh, 68, 119, 129–37, 149, 239, 286
  in Amritsar, 195–96
  avenging, 235–39
Jamshedpur union, 160–61
Jana Gana Mana, 257

Japan/Japanese
  immigrant, 84–85
  imperialists, 17
  invasion, 250
Japanese Imperial Army, 270
Japanese Pan–Asianism, 183–84
Jatin, Bagha, 4–5, 96, 103–9, 211–12
Jatin, Tiger, 104–9
Jenner, Edward, 22
Jharkhand, 51
Jilani, Gholam, 133
Jinnah, Mohammad Ali, 130, 142, 192
Johnson, Odakkal, 288
Joshi, P.C., 232
Jugantar
  group, 96–97, 102–5, 204, 211–12
  leadership, 105
  nationalists, 230, 232, 261
  revolutionaries, 152, 165
Jugantar, 39, 43, 47, 89
Jumnabai, Maharani, 29

Kabul mission, 109–13, 213, 247
Kaiser Wilhelm II, 111
Kakori train robbery, 172–80
Kala Paani, 123–59, 190, 203
  Cellular Jail, 124–29
  Chittaranjan's recruits, 146–51

grinding oil mill, 126
Jallianwala Bagh, 129–37
Khilafat Movement, 144–45
Rashbehari's bride, 155–59
rebel scholar, 152–55
return from hell, 139–41
Kalighat, 38, 140
Kallol, 290
Kanhere, Anantrao Laxman, 69
Kanta, Anadi, 105, 152
Karachi, 200, 214, 222, 285–87
Karmayogi, 47
Kathiawar coast, 269
Katju, K.N., 215
Kennedy, Pringle, 43–44
Khalsa Diwan Society, 86, 92
Khan, Ashfaqullah, 17, 167–68, 174–75, 177–79
Khan, Khoyedad, 125
Khan, Mirza, 125
Khan, Muhammad, 115
Khan, Sikandar Hayat, 62, 64
Khanderao, Maharaja II, 28–29
Khankhoje, Pandurang, 110, 113
Khilafat Movement, 144–45, 219–21
Kiani, M.Z., 275
King, Arthur Frederick, 281
King–Emperor George V., 30
Kipling, Rudyard, 138
Kiritkar, 60–61
Kitchlew, Saifuddin, 131

Kohima, 273
Kokko, 157–58
Kolkata Police Museum, 46
Komagata Maru incident, 91–94
Koya community, 165
Kraft, Vincent, 104, 108
Kranti Dal (Revolutionary Party), 219
Kripalani, J.B., 229
Krishak Praja Party, 227, 261
Krishnath College in Behrampur, 155
Krupp Agency in New York, 106
Kuchchh, Gujarat, 54–55
Kuka Rebellion of 1872, 83–84
Kumbh Mela, 33

Lahiri, Rajendra, 168–69, 175, 177–79, 181
Lahiri, Shyama Charan, 180
LakdiPul, 53
Lakshmi Vilas Palace, 30
Lal, Banarasi, 177, 179
Lal, Chaman, 193
Lal, Heramba, 156
Lal–Bal–Pal trio, 21, 39
Lancet, The, 21
Laskar, Adhar Chandra, 114
Lawrence of Arabia, 109–10, 117–18
'Left-Right' dichotomy, 185
Lenin, Vladimir, 63, 118, 212–14

Lingayat community, 51
Lokpaching, 272
London, 1, 55–56, 58, 66, 70–71, 235
London School of Economics, 155
Luxmi Tea, 38

MacDonald, Ramsay, 59
Madari Pasi, 164
Madras, 9, 58, 73, 128, 222, 249, 287, 295–96
Madras Presidency, 57
'Maghs,' 270
Maharaja Sayajirao University, 31
Maharana Pratap of Mewar, 56
Maharashtra, 13, 15, 21, 38, 41, 50–51, 53, 64, 69, 84, 182, 221–22
Maharashtra Youth Conference, 222
Mahasabha, Nikhil Manipuri, 271
Mahashaya, Lahiri, 180
Mahratta regiment, 284–85
Majumdar, Dinesh, 207–8
Majumdar, R.C., 20
Malabar, 143–44, 166
Malaviya, Madan Mohan, 130, 140, 142, 192–93
Malhotra, Uttam Chand, 247
Malik, Shaukat Ali, 271
Mall, Bugga, 131, 133
Mall, Chaudhuri Bugga, 131

Malvi, Tribhuvan Das, 41
Mandalay, 84, 121–22
Maniktola, 42
Mapillas, 143
Maratha administration, 50
Maratha period, 15–16
Martanda Varma of Travancore, 11
Marwari Hindus, 265
Marxist/Marxism, 233, 251–52
 communist movement in India, 18
 ideology, 215
 indoctrination school for Indians, 212–13
 interpretation of history, 8
 -Islamist mix, 213–14
 organization, 211
 theory of dialectic materialism, 184
Masahide, 274
Masaryk, Tomáš, 108
mass inoculation, 22
mass mobilization movement, 164
mass rakhi-bandhan ceremonies, 37
Mathew, Emmanuel, 26
Mazzini, Giuseppe, 10
Mazzini–Garibaldi combination, 10
Meerut Conspiracy Case, 215

Mehta, Pherozeshah, 40
Meiji Restoration of 1868, 11
Mein Kampf, 226, 257
Mera Rang De Basanti Chola, 178
Mexican communism, 212
Mian Mir cantonment, Lahore, 98
Midnapur, 96, 263
Mitra, Indubhushan, 179
Mitra, Srish, 1–2
Mitra Mela in Deccan College, 52–53
Mohini Mills, 38
Moirang, flag in, 267–75
Monarch Mills, 88
Mookerjee, Ashutosh, 154
Mookerjee, Syamaprasad, 262–63
Moonje, B.S., 218
Moplah riots, 143, 145, 220
Morley–Minto Reforms, 74
Morning Post, The, 138
Mount Tamalpais Military Academy, 115
Mrinalini, 45
Mughal Emperor Akbar, 56
Mukerjee, Madhusree, 264
Mukherjee, Anukul, 2–3
Munda, Birsa, 5
Musenberg, Werner, 258
Muslim
 community, 15–16
 League, 261, 264
 regiments in Singapore, 98–99
 Sunni Muslims, 109
Muzaffarpur, Bihar, 43–44
Mymensingh, 38
Mysore, 30

Nadia district of Bengal, 152
Nadia–Murshidabad belt, 105, 152
Nagasaki, 274–75
Nagpur, 113
Nagpur Congress, 141
Nainital, 32
Nair, C. Gopalan, 143
Nakamuraya, 157
Nalanda Club, 88
Namdhari Sikhs, 83–84, 88
Nana Saheb, 52
Naoroji, Dadabhai, 20, 56, 58–59
Narayan, Jayaprakash, 231
Narayanrao, 69
Nashik, 52–53, 69, 73
Nath, Bhupendra, 177–78, 180
Nath, Jitendra, 195
Nath, Pramath, 115
Nath, Sachindra, 180
Nathan, S.R., 260
National Bank, 132
National Circus!, 113–14
National College, Lahore, 161, 236
National College in Calcutta, 39

National Indian Association, 65
nationalism, 5, 17, 21, 33, 38, 47, 49, 216
National Socialist German Workers' Party, 185
Naval Revolt, 279–90

Navy Day celebrations, 280
Nazimuddin, Khwaja, 262
Nazi/Nazism
   and Japanese imperialism, 243
   occupation, 171
   party, 185
Nehru, Jawaharlal, 39, 140, 200–201, 214, 224, 231–32, 250
Nehru, Kamala, 202
Nehru, Motilal, 30, 41, 146, 163, 182, 192
New Asia - Shin Ajia, The, 252
New Delhi, 105, 121, 192
'New Lamps for Old,' 31
Newtonian determinism, 8
New York, 55, 86, 106, 108
Non-Cooperation Movement, 122, 141–43, 145–46, 148–49, 160–61, 163, 174, 181, 183, 282
   collapse, 161
North America, 84, 88
Nott-Bower, John, 201–2
Nundy, Manindra Chandra, 155

Oaten, Edward, 147

October Revolution of 1917, 118
Odakkal, Muhammad, 288
Odiyas, 37
O'Dwyer, Michael, 99, 120, 131, 136, 138, 237–38
Okakura, Kakuzo, 11
Operation Barbarossa, 255
Ottoman Empire, 141–42

Pakistan, 200
Pal, Bipin Chandra, 38–39, 128, 141
Palme-Dutt, Rajani, 217
Pan–Asianism, 11–12, 102, 251–52
Pandya, Mohanlal, 69
pan–Islamic ideologies, 15–16, 109
pan–Islamists, 17
Paramahansa, Ramakrishna, 15
Paranjpe, Raghunath Purushottam, 53–54, 56
Parmanand, Bhai, 57, 70, 140, 183
Patel, Vallabhbhai, 149, 223, 287
Patel, Vithalbhai, 70, 146, 223, 227–28
Pearl Harbor, 248
Peddie, James, 208
Penang, 97, 99, 258
Persia, 6, 109–13, 297, 299
Persian Campaign, 113–17

Peshawari, Ram Chandra, 91
Phadke, Vasudev Balwant, 50–52, 124
'Pilikothi' Dharamshala in Kanpur, 169
Pillai, Champak, 102–3
Pillai, V.O. Chidambaram, 54
Pingle, Vishnu Ganesh, 53, 95
Poddar, Hanuman Prasad, 2
political activism, 162–63
political mobilization, 22–23
Pollitt, Harry, 231
Pondicherry (Puducherry), 47–49, 80, 143, 249
Port Blair, 124, 252. *See also* Kala Paani
Posthumous Papers of the Pickwick Club, The, 62
post-Independence India, 6, 289
post-revolution Russia, 18
'Potato King' Jwala Singh, 97
'Potato King' of California, 84, 88
Prabhakar, 56
Prabhavati, 146
Prafulla, 44
Prasad, Amba, 113, 115–16
Prasad, Rajendra, 229, 231–32
Prasad, Sufi Amba, 110
Pratap, Maharana, 5, 12
Pratap, Mahendra, 112, 213, 247
Pratap, Raja Mahendra, 172
Presidency College, 147, 153
pro-British lobby, 94
'Proclamation of Independence,' 268
proselytization, 57, 87
Provisional Government of Free India, 268
Public Safety Bill, 191
Punjabi community
 in British Columbia, 86
 in California, 88
 migrants, 88
 Sikhs, 84
Puri, Satyananda, 252–54

'Quit Egypt,' 288
Quit India Movement, 19, 248–50, 262, 281, 283

racism, 84–85
Rae Bareli, 177
Rai, Lala Lajpat, 12, 21, 40, 56, 70, 84, 140–41, 150, 155, 161, 183, 186–87, 236
Raj, Hans, 195, 203
Raj, Sukhdev, 201
Rajagopalachari, C., 249
Rajguru, Shivaram, 187, 199
Raju, Seetha Rama, 164–66
Ram, Bhagat, 246–47
Ram, Chajju, 189–90
Ram, Mangoo, 106
Ram, Pundit Kashi, 95
Ramakrishna Mission, 268

Rampa Rebellion, 164–66
Rana, S.R., 56–57, 59, 69–70
Rand, Walter, 22–23, 33, 51–52
Rani Laxmibai of Jhansi, 52
Rani of Jhansi Regiment, 269, 275
Rashmoni, 15
Rashtriya Swayamsevak Sangh (RSS), 113–14, 218–22
Ratnagiri Jail, 141
Rawalpindi, 98
RB Rodda & Company, 1
Red Sea, 56
Reserve Bank of India, 285
Revolt of 1857-58, 13, 123–24, 288
Revolutionary, The, 179
Revolutionary Socialist Party of India, 242–43
River Hugli, 48
Rodda & Co., 2–4
Rowlatt, Sydney, 130
Rowlatt Acts in 1919, 122, 130–31
Roy, Bidhan Chandra, 232
Roy, Indu Bhushan, 127, 129
Roy, Manabendra Nath, 18, 211–18, 230
Roy, Raja Ram Mohan, 14
Roy, Subodh, 216, 270
Royal Air Force Mosquitoes, 285–86
Royal Asiatic Society, 55
Royal Central Asian Society at Caxton Hall, 237–38
Royal College of Physicians in London, 22
Royal Indian Air Force (RIAF), 285
Royal Indian Navy (RIN), 279, 284, 286
Russian communists, 63
Russian military technology, 43
Russian Revolution of 1917, 9, 183

Sahni, J.N., 193
Sahri, Harnam Singh, 85
Sammelani, Praja, 271
Sanatana Dharma, 17, 47
San Francisco, 88–89, 114
Sangh, Rashtriya Swayamsevak, 211
Sanskrit *pathshala*, 181
Sanuti Maru, 100
Sanyal, Anadi Kanta, 109
Sanyal, Bhupendra Nath, 14, 179
Sanyal, Jitendra Nath, 167–68, 196–97
Sanyal, Nalinaksha, 105, 107, 146, 150, 152–55, 168, 186, 210, 230, 232, 264–65
Sanyal, Pratibha, 202
Sanyal, Rabindra Nath, 201
Sanyal, Sachindra Nath, 4, 6, 11, 18, 94–96, 125, 129, 139–40, 153, 168–69, 177–81, 183–85, 190, 195, 200, 223, 230, 233, 235, 243, 252, 286
Saraba, Kartar Singh, 89, 95, 98–99

Saraswati, Dayanand, 54–55
Sarojini, 45
satyagraha, 131
Saunders, John, 188, 191–92
Savarkar, Babarao, 54
Savarkar, Ganesh, 125, 234
Savarkar, Narayan, 141
Savarkar, Vinayak, 5–6, 10, 13–14, 50, 52–54, 56–57, 61, 63, 65, 68, 71–73, 103, 125, 128, 140–41, 182, 221, 237–38, 241–42, 251, 289
Sayajirao, Maharaja III, 29
Scotland Yard, 57–62
Scott, James, 186–87
Scottish Church College, 147
Sea Customs Act, 90
Second Anglo-Sikh War of 1848-49, 83
second Ghadar, preparing for, 233–35
Second Lahore Conspiracy Case, 196–200
Second World War, 19, 97, 216, 243, 279
Secretary of State John Wodehouse, 28
Sen, Anuj, 208
Sen, Keshub Chander, 25
Sen, P.C., 289–90
Sen, Surya, 164, 167, 178, 204–7
sentimentalism, 31
Shah, Akbar, 245

Shahjahanabad, 174
Shahjahanpur, 167–68, 172, 177
Shakta Hindus, 151
Shanghai, 91, 103–4, 156
Shankaracharya of Kanchi, 57–58
Shekhar, Chandra, 181
Schenkl, Emilie, 223
Shivaji, Chhatrapati, 5, 12, 50, 52–53, 56
Shivaji festival in Raigad, Pune, 21
Shivaji Utsav, 12–13
'shuddhi,' 172
Shyamji, 85
Sikhs
    of Canada and Britain, 94
    community, 92
    gurudwaras, 90, 216
    in North America, 83–86
    reform movement, 15–16
Simon, John, 192
Simpson, J.J., 208
Singapore, 156, 259
Singh, Ajit, 84–85, 150, 161, 182
Singh, Arjan, 85, 93
Singh, Arur, 138
Singh, Bela, 85, 93
Singh, Bhagat, 5, 18, 100, 168, 180, 182–83, 187–89, 191–93, 195, 198–99, 205, 218
Singh, Bhagwan, 101–2
Singh, Chanan, 188
Singh, Duleep, 83
Singh, Giani Pritam, 252–53

Singh, Gurdit, 92–93
Singh, Guru Gobind, 5, 12
Singh, Hemam Nilamani, 272
Singh, Jwala, 84, 88
Singh, Kirpal, 98
Singh, Kishan, 182–83, 196
Singh, L. Guno, 271
Singh, Madan, 288
Singh, Mahendra Pratap, 111
Singh, Mewa, 93
Singh, M. Koireng, 271–72
Singh, Mohan, 253–54
Singh, Mula, 97–98
Singh, Naik Indar, 235
Singh, Pritam, 253
Singh, Roshan, 179
Singh, Santokh, 118
Singh, Tara, 120
Singh, Thakur Roshan, 178–79
Singh, Tikendrajit, 5
Singh, Ude, 235–36
Singh, Udham, 237–39
Singh, Visheshwar, 201–2
Sister Nivedita, 33–34, 47–48
smallpox vaccination, 22
social/socialism, 18, 185
   conquest, 83
   reform, 32
Soma, Aizo, 157
Somdev, Swami, 172
Soviet Russia, 119
Soviet Union, 226

'Special India Division' at Wilhelmstrasse 75, 256
Spratt, Philip, 215
Sri Aurobindo. *See* Ghosh, Aurobindo
SS *Maverick*, 106
SS *Morea*, 68–73
SS *Persia*, 56
Stalin–Hitler pact in 1939, 242
Statesman, The, 284
Suez Canal to Marseilles, 56
Sufi, Muhammad Hasan, 110
Suhrawardy, Hussain Shaheed, 150
Sukhdev, 191
Sunderbans, 45
Sunni Muslims, 109
Sun Yat-sen, 12, 101–2, 114, 252
Supreme Court of British Columbia, 91
Surat, 40, 54
Surma Valley Light Horse, 206
Swadeshi movement, 38, 41, 53
Swadesh Sewak (Servant of the Motherland), 85
Swaraj Party, 146, 150

Tagore, P.N., 99–101
Tagore, Rabindranath, 13, 37, 70, 100, 202, 209, 228, 257
Tale of My Exile, The, 125
Talib, Niranjan Singh, 234–35
Talwar, Bhagat Ram, 270
Tandon, Purushottam Das, 182, 202

Tegart, Charles, 107, 207
Tenyo-Maru, 157
Thailand, 103
Thapar, Sukhdev, 187, 199
'The Revolutionary,' 170
Third Anglo-Afghan War of 1919, 213
Tilak, Bal Gangadhar, 12, 21–23, 35, 41, 53, 84, 150, 185, 222
Times of India, The, 284
Tiwari, Chandra Shekhar, 180–81
Tiwari, Veerbhadra, 201, 203
Tojo, Hideki, 257, 259–60, 270
Tokyo, 12
Tope, Tatya, 52, 113
Tottenham Court Road, 66
Toyama, Mitsuru, 12, 102
Trade Disputes Bill, 191
Tripuri Congress, 231
Turko–German alliance, 109, 111, 213

Uganda Railway Workshops, 236
United India League, 86, 92
United Provinces (UP), 75–76, 95, 97, 102, 105, 111, 161, 163, 168–69, 172, 230
University of California, 87–88
Uttarpara speech, 17, 47

Vancouver, 85, 91–92, 156
Vande Mataram, 16, 37, 53, 59, 68, 89, 179, 181, 218, 311

Varanasi, 11–12, 94, 96–97, 99, 140, 146–47, 161–62
Varma, Shyamji Krishna, 54–55
Vedantic monism, 14
Vedic rituals, 68
Verma, Gyanchand, 68
Vichar Vinimay, 184
Visakhapatnam, 164–65
Vivekananda, Swami, 11–12, 15, 33–34, 39, 89, 146, 268
Vohra, Bhagwati Charan, 187
Vohra, Hans Raj, 188
Voska, Emanuel Viktor, 108

Wahhabi Islamists, 124
Wassmuss, Wilhelm, 109–10
West Coast universities, 88
Westernization, 49
Western 'liberal' system, 224–25
Western-style education, 9
Williams, Monier, 55
Wyllie, William Curzon, 65–66, 68

Yamuna, 52, 54, 56, 73, 295
Yashpal, 197–98, 200–201, 203, 216, 302
Yokohama, 91–92, 97
Young India, 171, 198
Yugantar Ashram, 86–91, 95

Ziauddin, Mohammad, 245–46

ABOUT THE AUTHOR

Sanjeev Sanyal is a writer, economist and urbanist. He grew up in Kolkata and attended Delhi University before going on to Oxford University as a Rhodes Scholar. He then spent two decades in international financial markets, where he became the managing director and global strategist of Europe's largest bank. He was named a Young Global Leader by the World Economic Forum in 2010. While living in Singapore he also took up the study of cities and was awarded the Eisenhower Fellowship for his work on urban dynamics.

In 2017, he joined the Indian government as the principal economic adviser. He became a member of Prime Minister Narendra Modi's economic advisory council in 2022. He has represented India in many international forums, including as co-chair of the Framework Working Group of G20 for five years.

His bestselling books include *Land of the Seven Rivers: A Brief History of India's Geography*, *The Ocean of Churn: How the Indian Ocean Shaped Human History* and *Life over Two Beers*.

30 Years *of* HarperCollins *Publishers* India

At HarperCollins, we believe in telling the best stories and finding the widest possible readership for our books in every format possible. We started publishing 30 years ago; a great deal has changed since then, but what has remained constant is the passion with which our authors write their books, the love with which readers receive them, and the sheer joy and excitement that we as publishers feel in being a part of the publishing process.

Over the years, we've had the pleasure of publishing some of the finest writing from the subcontinent and around the world, and some of the biggest bestsellers in India's publishing history. Our books and authors have won a phenomenal range of awards, and we ourselves have been named Publisher of the Year the greatest number of times. But nothing has meant more to us than the fact that millions of people have read the books we published, and somewhere, a book of ours might have made a difference.

As we step into our fourth decade, we go back to that one word – a word which has been a driving force for us all these years.

Read.